11-23-99

An introduction to
neural networks

An introduction to
neural networks

Kevin Gurney
University of Sheffield

London and New York

First published in 1997 by UCL Press

Reprinted 1999

UCL Press Limited
11 New Fetter Lane
London EC4P 4EE

UCL Press Limited is an imprint of the Taylor & Francis Group

The name of University College London (UCL) is a registered trade mark used
by UCL Press with the consent of the owner.

British Library Cataloguing in Publication Data
A catalogue record for this book is available from the British Library.

ISBNs: 1-85728-673-1 HB
      1-85728-503-4 PB

Typeset in Palatino by Fiona Dix.
Printed and bound by T.J. International Ltd, Padstow, UK.

Contents

Preface

This book grew out of a set of course notes for a neural networks module given as part of a Masters degree in "Intelligent Systems". The people on this course came from a wide variety of intellectual backgrounds (from philosophy, through psychology to computer science and engineering) and I knew that I could not count on their being able to come to grips with the largely technical and mathematical approach which is often used (and in some ways easier to do). As a result I was forced to look carefully at the basic conceptual principles at work in the subject and try to recast these using ordinary language, drawing on the use of physical metaphors or analogies, and pictorial or graphical representations. I was pleasantly surprised to find that, as a result of this process, my own understanding was considerably deepened; I had now to unravel, as it were, condensed formal descriptions and say exactly *how* these were related to the "physical" world of artificial neurons, signals, computational processes, etc. However, I was acutely aware that, while a litany of equations does not constitute a full description of fundamental principles, without some mathematics, a purely descriptive account runs the risk of dealing only with approximations and cannot be sharpened up to give any formulaic prescriptions. Therefore, I introduced what I believed was just sufficient mathematics to bring the basic ideas into sharp focus.

To allay any residual fears that the reader might have about this, it is useful to distinguish two contexts in which the word "maths" might be used. The first refers to the use of symbols to stand for quantities and is, in this sense, merely a shorthand. For example, suppose we were to calculate the difference between a target neural output and its actual output and then multiply this difference by a constant learning rate (it is not important that the reader knows what these terms mean just now). If t stands for the target, y the actual output, and the learning rate is denoted by α (Greek "alpha") then the output-difference is just $(t - y)$ and the verbose description of the calculation may be reduced to $\alpha(t - y)$. In this example the symbols refer to numbers but it is quite possible they may refer to other mathematical quantities or objects. The two instances of this used here are *vectors* and *function gradients*. However, both these ideas are described at some length in the main body of the text and assume no prior knowledge in this respect. In each case, only enough is given for the purpose in hand; other related, technical material may have been useful but is not considered essential and it is not one of the aims of this book to double as a mathematics primer.

The other way in which we commonly understand the word "maths" goes one step further and deals with the rules by which the symbols are manipulated. The only rules used in this book are those of simple arithmetic (in the above example we have a subtraction and a multiplication). Further, any manipulations (and there aren't many of them) will be performed step by step. Much of the traditional "fear of maths" stems, I believe, from the apparent difficulty in inventing the right manipulations to go from one stage to another; the reader will not, in this book, be called on to do this for him- or herself.

One of the spin-offs from having become familiar with a certain amount of mathematical formalism is that it enables contact to be made with the rest of the neural network literature. Thus, in the above example, the use of the Greek letter α may seem gratuitous (why not use a, the reader asks) but it turns out that learning rates are often denoted by lower case Greek letters and α is not an uncommon choice. To help in this respect, Greek symbols will always be accompanied by their name on first use.

In deciding how to present the material I have started from the bottom up by describing the properties of artificial neurons (Ch. 2) which are motivated by looking at the nature of their real counterparts. This emphasis on the biology is intrinsically useful from a computational neuroscience perspective and helps people from all disciplines appreciate exactly how "neural" (or not) are the networks they intend to use. Chapter 3 moves to networks and introduces the geometric perspective on network function offered by the notion of linear separability in pattern space. There are other viewpoints that might have been deemed primary (function approximation is a favourite contender) but linear separability relates directly to the function of single threshold logic units (TLUs) and enables a discussion of one of the simplest learning rules (the perceptron rule) in Chapter 4. The geometric approach also provides a natural vehicle for the introduction of vectors. The inadequacies of the perceptron rule lead to a discussion of gradient descent and the delta rule (Ch. 5) culminating in a description of backpropagation (Ch. 6). This introduces multilayer nets in full and is the natural point at which to discuss networks as function approximators, feature detection and generalization.

This completes a large section on feedforward nets. Chapter 7 looks at Hopfield nets and introduces the idea of state-space attractors for associative memory and its accompanying energy metaphor. Chapter 8 is the first of two on self-organization and deals with simple competitive nets, Kohonen self-organizing feature maps, linear vector quantization and principal component analysis. Chapter 9 continues the theme of self-organization with a discussion of adaptive resonance theory (ART). This is a somewhat neglected topic (especially in more introductory texts) because it is often thought to contain rather difficult material. However, a novel perspective on ART which makes use of a hierarchy of analysis is aimed at helping the reader in understanding this worthwhile area. Chapter 10 comes full circle and looks again at alternatives to the artificial neurons introduced in Chapter 2. It also briefly reviews some other feedforward network types and training algorithms so that the reader does not come away with the impression that backpropagation has a monopoly here. The final chapter tries to make sense of the seemingly disparate collection of objects that populate the neural network universe by introducing a series of taxonomies for network architectures, neuron types and algorithms. It also places the study of nets in the general context of that of artificial intelligence and closes with a brief history of its research.

The usual provisos about the range of material covered and introductory texts apply; it is neither possible nor desirable to be exhaustive in a work of this nature. However, most of the major network types have been dealt with and, while there are a plethora of training algorithms that might have been included (but weren't) I believe that an understanding of those presented here should give the reader a firm foundation for understanding others they may encounter elsewhere.

Chapter One

Neural networks – an overview

The term "Neural networks" is a very evocative one. It suggests machines that are something like brains and is potentially laden with the science fiction connotations of the Frankenstein mythos. One of the main tasks of this book is to demystify neural networks and show how, while they indeed have something to do with brains, their study also makes contact with other branches of science, engineering and mathematics. The aim is to do this in as non-technical a way as possible, although some mathematical notation is essential for specifying certain rules, procedures and structures quantitatively. Nevertheless, all symbols and expressions will be explained as they arise so that, hopefully, these should not get in the way of the essentials: that is, concepts and ideas that may be described in words.

This chapter is intended for orientation. We attempt to give simple descriptions of what networks are and why we might study them. In this way, we have something in mind right from the start, although the whole of this book is, of course, devoted to answering these questions in full.

1.1 What are neural networks?

Let us commence with a provisional definition of what is meant by a "neural network" and follow with simple, working explanations of some of the key terms in the definition.

> A neural network is an interconnected assembly of simple processing elements, *units* or *nodes*, whose functionality is loosely based on the animal neuron. The processing ability of the network is stored in the interunit connection strengths, or *weights*, obtained by a process of adaptation to, or *learning* from, a set of training patterns.

To flesh this out a little we first take a quick look at some basic neurobiology. The human brain consists of an estimated 10^{11} (100 billion) nerve cells or *neurons*, a highly stylized example of which is shown in Figure 1.1. Neurons communicate via electrical signals that are short-lived impulses or "spikes" in the voltage of the cell wall or *membrane*. The interneuron connections are mediated by electrochemical junctions called *synapses*, which are located on branches of the cell referred to as *dendrites*. Each neuron typically receives many thousands of connections from

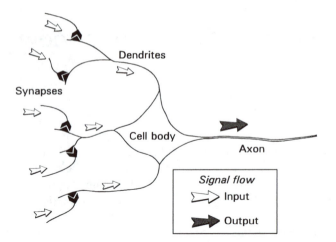

Figure 1.1 Essential components of a neuron shown in stylized form.

other neurons and is therefore constantly receiving a multitude of incoming signals, which eventually reach the cell body. Here, they are integrated or summed together in some way and, roughly speaking, if the resulting signal exceeds some threshold then the neuron will "fire" or generate a voltage impulse in response. This is then transmitted to other neurons via a branching fibre known as the *axon*.

In determining whether an impulse should be produced or not, some incoming signals produce an inhibitory effect and tend to prevent firing, while others are excitatory and promote impulse generation. The distinctive processing ability of each neuron is then supposed to reside in the type – excitatory or inhibitory – and strength of its synaptic connections with other neurons.

It is this architecture and style of processing that we hope to incorporate in neural networks and, because of the emphasis on the importance of the inter-neuron connections, this type of system is sometimes referred to as being *connectionist* and the study of this general approach as *connectionism*. This terminology is often the one encountered for neural networks in the context of psychologically inspired models of human cognitive function. However, we will use it quite generally to refer to neural networks without reference to any particular field of application.

The artificial equivalents of biological neurons are the nodes or units in our preliminary definition and a prototypical example is shown in Figure 1.2. Synapses are modelled by a single number or *weight* so that each input is multiplied by a weight before being sent to the equivalent of the cell body. Here, the weighted signals are summed together by simple arithmetic addition to supply a node *activation*. In the type of node shown in Figure 1.2 – the so-called *threshold logic unit* (TLU) – the activation is then compared with a threshold; if the activation exceeds the threshold, the unit produces a high-valued output (conventionally "1"), otherwise it outputs zero. In the figure, the size of signals is represented by

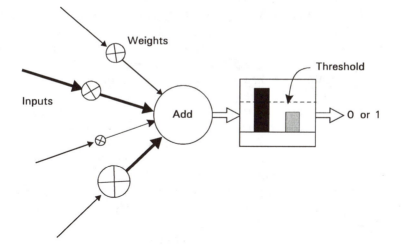

Figure 1.2 Simple artificial neuron.

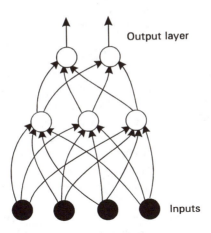

Figure 1.3 Simple example of neural network.

the width of their corresponding arrows, weights are shown by multiplication symbols in circles, and their values are supposed to be proportional to the symbol's size; only positive weights have been used. The TLU is the simplest (and historically the earliest (McCulloch & Pitts 1943)) model of an artificial neuron.

The term "network" will be used to refer to any system of artificial neurons. This may range from something as simple as a single node to a large collection of nodes in which each one is connected to every other node in the net. One type of network is shown in Figure 1.3. Each node is now shown by only a circle but weights are implicit on all connections. The nodes are arranged in a layered structure in which each signal emanates from an input and passes via two nodes before reaching an output beyond which it is no longer transformed. This *feedforward* structure is only one of several available and is typically used to place an input pattern into one of several classes according to the resulting pattern of outputs. For example, if the input consists of an encoding of the patterns of light and dark in an image of handwritten letters, the output layer (topmost in the figure) may contain 26 nodes – one for each letter of the alphabet – to flag which letter class the input character is from. This would be done by allocating one output node per class and requiring that only one such node fires whenever a pattern of the corresponding class is supplied at the input.

So much for the basic structural elements and their operation. Returning to our working definition, notice the emphasis on learning from experience. In real neurons the synaptic strengths may, under certain circumstances, be modified so that the behaviour of each neuron can change or adapt to its particular stimulus input. In artificial neurons the equivalent of this is the modification of the weight values. In terms of processing information, there are no computer programs here – the "knowledge" the network has is supposed to be stored in its weights, which evolve by a process of adaptation to stimulus from a set of pattern examples. In one training paradigm called *supervised learning*, used in conjunction with nets of the type shown in Figure 1.3, an input pattern is presented to the net and its response then compared with a target output. In terms of our previous letter recognition example, an "A", say, may be input and the network output compared with the classification code for A. The difference between the two patterns of output then determines how the weights are altered. Each particular recipe for change constitutes a *learning rule*, details of which form a substantial part of subsequent chapters. When the required weight updates have been made another pattern is presented, the output compared with the target, and new changes made. This sequence of events is repeated iteratively many times until (hopefully) the network's behaviour converges so that its response to each pattern is close to the corresponding target. The process as a whole, including any ordering of pattern presentation, criteria for terminating the process, etc., constitutes the *training algorithm*.

What happens if, after training, we present the network with a pattern it hasn't seen before? If the net has learned the underlying structure of the problem domain then it should classify the unseen pattern correctly and the net is said to *generalize* well. If the net does not have this property it is little more than a classification lookup table for the training set and is of little practical use. Good generalization is therefore one of the key properties of neural networks.

1.2 Why study neural networks?

This question is pertinent here because, depending on one's motive, the study of connectionism can take place from differing perspectives. It also helps to know what questions we are trying to answer in order to avoid the kind of religious wars that sometimes break out when the words "connectionism" or "neural network" are mentioned.

Neural networks are often used for statistical analysis and data modelling, in which their role is perceived as an alternative to standard nonlinear regression or cluster analysis techniques (Cheng & Titterington 1994). Thus, they are typically used in problems that may be couched in terms of classification, or forecasting. Some examples include image and speech recognition, textual character recognition, and domains of human expertise such as medical diagnosis, geological survey for oil, and financial market indicator prediction. This type of problem also falls within the domain of classical artificial intelligence (AI) so that engineers and computer scientists see neural nets as offering a style of *parallel distributed computing*, thereby providing an alternative to the conventional algorithmic techniques that have dominated in machine intelligence. This is a theme pursued further in the final chapter but, by way of a brief explanation of this term now, the parallelism refers to the fact that each node is conceived of as operating independently and concurrently (in parallel with) the others, and the "knowledge" in the network is distributed over the entire set of weights, rather than focused in a few memory locations as in a conventional computer. The practitioners in this area do not concern themselves with biological realism and are often motivated by the ease of implementing solutions in digital hardware or the efficiency and accuracy of particular techniques. Haykin (1994) gives a comprehensive survey of many neural network techniques from an engineering perspective.

Neuroscientists and psychologists are interested in nets as computational models of the animal brain developed by abstracting what are believed to be those properties of real nervous tissue that are essential for information processing. The artificial neurons that connectionist models use are often extremely simplified versions of their biological counterparts and many neuroscientists are sceptical about the ultimate power of these impoverished models, insisting that more detail is necessary to explain the brain's function. Only time will tell but, by drawing on knowledge about how real neurons are interconnected as local "circuits", substantial inroads have been made in modelling brain functionality. A good introduction to this programme of *computational neuroscience* is given by Churchland & Sejnowski (1992).

Finally, physicists and mathematicians are drawn to the study of networks from an interest in nonlinear dynamical systems, statistical mechanics and automata theory.[1] It is the job of applied mathematicians to discover and formalize the properties of new systems using tools previously employed in other areas of science. For example, there are strong links between a certain type of net (the Hopfield net – see Ch. 7) and magnetic systems known as spin glasses. The full mathematical apparatus for exploring these links is developed (alongside a series of concise summaries) by Amit (1989).

All these groups are asking different questions: neuroscientists want to know how animal brains work, engineers and computer scientists want to build intelligent machines and mathematicians want to understand the fundamental properties of networks as complex systems. Another (perhaps the largest) group of people are to be found in a variety of industrial and commercial areas and use neural networks to model and analyze large, poorly understood datasets that arise naturally in their workplace. It is therefore important to understand an author's perspective when reading the literature. Their common focal point is, however, neural networks and is potentially the basis for close collaboration. For example, biologists can usefully learn from computer scientists what computations are necessary to enable animals to solve particular problems, while engineers can make use of the solutions nature has devised so that they may be applied in an act of "reverse engineering".

In the next chapter we look more closely at real neurons and how they may be modelled by their artificial counterparts. This approach allows subsequent development to be viewed from both the biological and engineering-oriented viewpoints.

1.3 Summary

Artificial neural networks may be thought of as simplified models of the networks of neurons that occur naturally in the animal brain. From the biological viewpoint the essential requirement for a neural network is that it should attempt to capture what we believe are the essential information processing features of the corresponding "real" network. For an engineer, this correspondence is not so important and the network offers an alternative form of parallel computing that might be more appropriate for solving the task in hand.

The simplest artificial neuron is the threshold logic unit or TLU. Its basic operation is to perform a weighted sum of its inputs and then output a "1" if this sum exceeds a threshold, and a "0" otherwise. The TLU is supposed to model the basic "integrate-and-fire" mechanism of real neurons.

1.4 Notes

1. It is not important that the reader be familiar with these areas. It suffices to understand that neural networks can be placed in relation to other areas studied by workers in these fields.

Chapter Two

Real and artificial neurons

The building blocks of artificial neural nets are artificial neurons. In this chapter we introduce some simple models for these, motivated by an attempt to capture the essential information processing ability of real, biological neurons. A description of this is therefore our starting point and, although our excursion into neurophysiology will be limited, some of the next section may appear factually rather dense on first contact. The reader is encouraged to review it several times to become familiar with the biological "jargon" and may benefit by first re-reading the précis of neuron function that was given in the previous chapter. In addition, it will help to refer to Figure 2.1 and the glossary at the end of the next section.

2.1 Real neurons: a review

Neurons are not only enormously complex but also vary considerably in the details of their structure and function. We will therefore describe typical properties enjoyed by a majority of neurons and make the usual working assumption of connectionism that these provide for the bulk of their computational ability. Readers interested in finding out more may consult one of the many texts in neurophysiology; Thompson (1993) provides a good introductory text, while more comprehensive accounts are given by Kandel et al. (1991) and Kuffler et al. (1984).

A stereotypical neuron is shown in Figure 2.1, which should be compared with the simplified diagram in Figure 1.1. The cell body or *soma* contains the usual subcellular components or *organelles* to be found in most cells throughout the body (nucleus, mitochondria, Golgi body, etc.) but these are not shown in the diagram. Instead we focus on what differentiates neurons from other cells allowing the neuron to function as a signal processing device. This ability stems largely from the properties of the neuron's surface covering or membrane, which supports a wide variety of electrochemical processes. Morphologically the main difference lies in the set of fibres that emanate from the cell body. One of these fibres – the axon – is responsible for transmitting signals to other neurons and may therefore be considered the neuron output. All other fibres are dendrites, which carry signals from other neurons to the cell body, thereby acting as neural

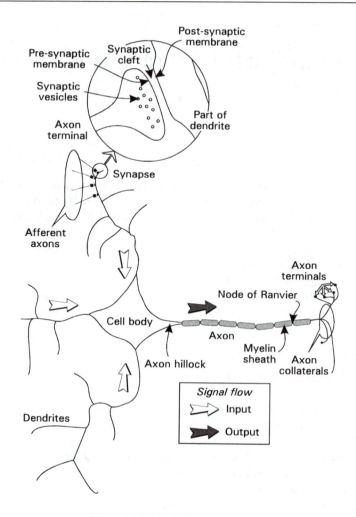

Figure 2.1 Biological neuron.

inputs. Each neuron has only one axon but can have many dendrites. The latter often appear to have a highly branched structure and so we talk of dendritic *arbors*. The axon may, however, branch into a set of *collaterals* allowing contact to be made with many other neurons. With respect to a particular neuron, other neurons that supply input are said to be *afferent*, while the given neuron's axonal output, regarded as a projection to other cells, is referred to as an *efferent*. Afferent axons are said to *innervate* a particular neuron and make contact with dendrites at the junctions called *synapses*. Here, the extremity of the axon, or *axon terminal*, comes into close proximity with a small part of the dendritic surface – the *postsynaptic* membrane. There is a gap, the *synaptic cleft*, between the *presynaptic* axon terminal membrane and its postsynaptic counterpart, which is of the order of 20 nanometres (2×10^{-8} m) wide. Only a few synapses are shown in Figure 2.1 for the sake of clarity but the reader should imagine a profusion of these located over all dendrites and also, possibly, the cell body. The detailed synaptic structure is shown in schematic form as an inset in the figure.

So much for neural structure; how does it support signal processing? At equilibrium, the neural membrane works to maintain an electrical imbalance of negatively and positively charged *ions*. These are atoms or molecules that have a surfeit or deficit of electrons, where each of the latter carries a single negative charge. The net result is that there is a *potential difference* across the membrane with the inside being negatively *polarized* by approximately 70 mV[1] with respect to the outside. Thus, if we could imagine applying a voltmeter to the membrane it would read 70 mV, with the inside being more negative than the outside. The main point here is that a neural membrane can support electrical signals if its state of polarization or *membrane potential* is dynamically changed. To see this, consider the case of signal propagation along an axon as shown in Figure 2.2. Signals that are propagated along axons, or *action potentials*, all have the same characteristic shape, resembling sharp pulse-like spikes. Each graph shows a snapshot of the membrane potential along a segment of axon that is currently transmitting a single action potential, and the lower panel shows the situation at some later time with respect to the upper one. The ionic mechanisms at work to produce this process were first worked out by Hodgkin & Huxley (1952). It relies

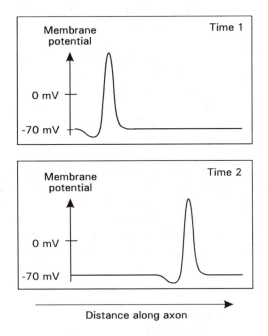

Figure 2.2 Action-potential propagation.

on the interplay between each of the ionic currents across the membrane and its mathematical description is complex. The details do not concern us here, but this example serves to illustrate the kind of simplification we will use when we model using artificial neurons; real axons are subject to complex, nonlinear dynamics but will be modelled as a passive output "wire". Many neurons have their axons sheathed in a fatty substance known as myelin, which serves to enable the more rapid conduction of action potentials. It is punctuated at approximately 1 mm intervals by small unmyelinated segments (nodes of Ranvier in Fig. 2.1), which act rather like "repeater stations" along a telephone cable.

We are now able to consider the passage of signals through a single neuron, starting with an action potential reaching an afferent axon terminal. These contain a chemical substance or *neurotransmitter* held within a large number of small *vesicles* (literally "little spheres"). On receipt of an action potential the vesicles migrate to the presynaptic membrane and release their neurotransmitter across the synaptic cleft. The transmitter then *binds* chemically with *receptor sites* at the postsynaptic membrane. This initiates an electrochemical process that changes the polarization state of the membrane local to the synapse. This *postsynaptic potential* (PSP) can serve either to *depolarize* the membrane from its negative resting state towards 0 volts, or to *hyperpolarize* the membrane to an even greater negative potential. As we shall see, neural signal production is encouraged by depolarization, so that PSPs which are positive are excitatory PSPs (EPSPs) while those which hyperpolarize the membrane are inhibitory (IPSPs). While action potentials all have the same characteristic signal profile and the same maximum value, PSPs can take on a continuous range of values depending on the efficiency of the synapse in utilizing the chemical transmitter to produce an electrical signal. The PSP spreads out from the synapse, travels along its associated dendrite towards the cell body and eventually reaches the *axon hillock* – the initial segment of the axon where it joins the soma. Concurrent with this are thousands of other synaptic events distributed over the neuron. These result in a plethora of PSPs, which are continually arriving at the axon hillock where they are summed together to produce a resultant membrane potential.

Each contributory PSP at the axon hillock exists for an extended time (order of milliseconds) before it eventually decays so that, if two PSPs arrive slightly out of synchrony, they may still interact in the summation process. On the other hand, suppose two synaptic events take place with one close to and another remote from the soma, by virtue of being at the end of a long dendritic branch. By the time the PSP from the distal (remote) synapse has reached the axon hillock, that originating close to the soma will have decayed. Thus, although the initiation of PSPs may take place in synchrony, they may not be effective in combining to generate action potentials. It is apparent, therefore, that a neuron sums or integrates its PSPs over both space *and* time. Substantial modelling effort – much of it pioneered by Rall (1957, 1959) – has gone into describing the conduction of PSPs along dendrites and their subsequent interaction although, as in the case of axons, connectionist models usually treat these as passive wires with no temporal characteristics.

The integrated PSP at the axon hillock will affect its membrane potential and, if this exceeds a certain threshold (typically about $-50\,\text{mV}$), an action potential is generated, which then propagates down the axon, along any collaterals, eventually reaching axon terminals resulting in a shower of synaptic events at neighbouring neurons "downstream" of our original cell. In reality the "threshold" is an emergent or meta-phenomenon resulting from the nonlinear nature of the Hodgkin–Huxley dynamics and, under certain conditions, it can be made to change. However, for many purposes it serves as a suitable high-level description of what actually occurs. After an action potential has been produced, the ionic metabolites used in its production have been depleted and there is a short *refractory period* during which, no matter what value the membrane potential takes, there can be no initiation of another action potential.

It is useful at this stage to summarize what we have learnt so far about the functionality of real neurons with an eye to the simplification required for modelling their artificial counterparts.

- Signals are transmitted between neurons by action potentials, which have a stereotypical profile and display an "all-or-nothing" character; there is no such thing as half an action potential.

- When an action potential impinges on a neuronal input (synapse) the effect is a PSP, which is variable or *graded* and depends on the physicochemical properties of the synapse.

- The PSPs may be excitatory or inhibitory.

- The PSPs are summed together at the axon hillock with the result expressed as its membrane potential.

- If this potential exceeds a threshold an action potential is initiated that proceeds along the axon.

Several things have been deliberately omitted here. First, the effect that synaptic structure can have on the value of the PSP. Factors that may play a role here include the type and availability of neurotransmitter, the postsynaptic receptors and synaptic geometry. Secondly, the spatio-temporal interdependencies of PSPs resulting from dendritic geometry whereby, for example, synapses that are remote from each other may not effectively combine. Finally, we have said nothing about the *dynamics* of action-potential generation and propagation. However, our summary will serve as a point of departure for defining the kind of artificial neurons described in this book. More biologically realistic models rely on solving Hodgkin–Huxley-type dynamics and modelling dendrites at the electrical circuit level; details of these methods can be found in the review compilation of Koch & Segev (1989).

2.1.1 Glossary of terms

Those terms in italics may be cross-referenced in this glossary.

action potential The stereotypical voltage spike that constitutes an active output from a neuron. They are propagated along the *axon* to other neurons.

afferent With respect to a particular neuron, an axon that impinges on (or *innervates*) that neuron.

arbor Usually used in the context of a dendritic arbor – the tree-like structure associated with dendritic branching.

axon The fibre that emanates from the neuron cell body or *soma* and that conducts *action potentials* to other neurons.

axon hillock The junction of the *axon* and cell body or *soma*. The place where *action potentials* are initiated if the *membrane potential* exceeds a threshold.

axon terminal An axon may branch into several *collaterals*, each terminating at an axon terminal, which constitutes the *presynaptic* component of a *synapse*.

chemical binding The process in which a *neurotransmitter* joins chemically with a *receptor site* thereby initiating a *PSP*.

collateral An axon may divide into many collateral branches allowing contact with many other neurons or many contacts with one neuron.

dendrite One of the branching fibres of a neuron, which convey input information via *PSPs*.

depolarization The *membrane potential* of the neuron has a negative resting or equilibrium value. Making this less negative leads to a depolarization. Sufficient depolarization at the *axon hillock* will give rise to an action potential.

efferent A neuron sends efferent axon *collaterals* to other neurons.

EPSP Excitatory Postsynaptic Potential. A *PSP* that acts to *depolarize* the neural membrane.

hyperpolarization The *membrane potential* of the neuron has a negative resting or equilibrium value. Making this more negative leads to a hyperpolarization and inhibits the action of *EPSPs*, which are trying to *depolarize* the membrane.

innervate Neuron A sending signals to neuron B is said to innervate neuron B.

IPSP Inhibitory Postsynaptic Potential. A *PSP* that acts to *hyperpolarize* the neural membrane.

membrane potential The voltage difference at any point across the neural membrane.

neurotransmitter The chemical substance that mediates synaptic activity by propagation across the *synaptic cleft*.

organelle Subcellular components that partake in metabolism, etc.

postsynaptic membrane That part of a *synapse* which is located on the *dendrite* and consists of the dendritic membrane together with *receptor sites*.

potential difference The voltage difference across the cell membrane.

presynaptic membrane That part of a *synapse* which is located on the *axon terminal*.

PSP Postsynaptic Potential. The change in *membrane potential* brought about by activity at a *synapse*.

receptor sites The sites on the *postsynaptic membrane* to which molecules of *neurotransmitter* bind. This binding initiates the generation of a *PSP*.

refractory period The shortest time interval between two *action potentials*.

soma The cell body.

synapse The site of physical and signal contact between neurons. On receipt of an *action potential* at the *axon terminal* of a *synapse*, *neurotransmitter* is released into the *synaptic cleft* and propagates to the *postsynaptic membrane*. There it undergoes *chemical binding* with *receptors*, which, in turn, initiates the production of a postsynaptic potential (*PSP*).

synaptic cleft The gap between the pre- and postsynaptic membranes across which chemical *neurotransmitter* is propagated during synaptic action.

vesicles The spherical containers in the *axon terminal* that contain *neurotransmitter*. On receipt of an action potential at the axon terminal, the vesicles release their neurotransmitter into the *synaptic cleft*.

2.2   Artificial neurons: the TLU

Our task is to try and model some of the ingredients in the list above. Our first attempt will result in the structure described informally in Section 1.1.

The "all-or-nothing" character of the action potential may be characterized by using a two-valued signal. Such signals are often referred to as *binary* or *Boolean*[2] and conventionally take the values "0" and "1". Thus, if we have a node receiving n input signals $x_1, x_2, \ldots, x_n$, then these may only take on the values "0" or "1".

In line with the remarks of the previous chapter, the modulatory effect of each synapse is encapsulated by simply multiplying the incoming signal with a weight value, where excitatory and inhibitory actions are modelled using positive and negative values respectively. We therefore have n weights w_1, w_2, ..., w_n and form the n products w_1x_1, w_2x_2, ..., w_nx_n. Each product is now the analogue of a PSP and may be negative or positive, depending on the sign of the weight. They should now be combined in a process which is supposed to emulate that taking place at the axon hillock. This will be done by simply adding them together to produce the activation a (corresponding to the axon-hillock membrane potential) so that

$$a = w_1x_1 + w_2x_2 + \cdots + w_nx_n \tag{2.1}$$

As an example, consider a five-input unit with weights (0.5, 1.0, −1.0, −0.5, 1.2), that is $w_1 = 0.5$, $w_2 = 1.0$, ..., $w_5 = 1.2$, and suppose this is presented with inputs (1, 1, 1, 0, 0) so that $x_1 = 1$, $x_2 = 1$, ..., $x_5 = 0$. Using (2.1) the activation is given by

$$\begin{aligned} a &= (0.5 \times 1) + (1.0 \times 1) + (-1.0 \times 1) + (-0.5 \times 0) + (1.2 \times 0) \\ &= 0.5 \end{aligned}$$

To emulate the generation of action potentials we need a threshold value θ (Greek theta) such that, if the activation exceeds (or is equal to) θ then the node outputs a "1" (action potential), and if it is less than θ then it emits a "0". This may be represented graphically as shown in Figure 2.3 where the output has been designated the symbol y. This relation is sometimes called a *step function* or *hard-limiter* for obvious reasons. In our example, suppose that $\theta = 0.2$; then, since $a > 0.2$ (recall $a = 0.5$) the node's output y is 1. The entire node structure is shown in Figure 2.4 where the weights have been depicted by encircled multiplication signs. Unlike Figure 1.1, however, no effort has been made to show the size of the weights or signals. This type of artificial neuron is known as a threshold logic unit (TLU) and was originally proposed by McCulloch and Pitts (McCulloch & Pitts 1943).

It is more convenient to represent the TLU functionality in a symbolic rather than a graphical form. We already have one form for the activation as supplied by (2.1). However, this may be written more compactly using a notation that makes use of the way we have written the weights and inputs. First, a word on

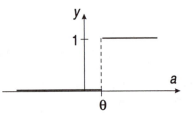

Figure 2.3 Activation–output threshold relation in graphical form.

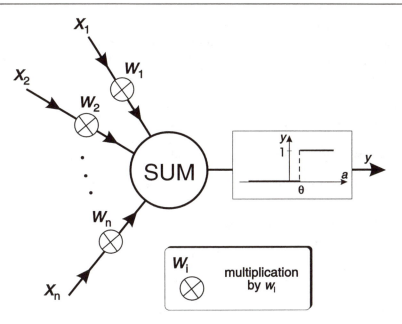

Figure 2.4 TLU.

the notation is relevant here. The small numbers used in denoting the inputs and weights are referred to as *subscripts*. If we had written the numbers near the top (e.g. x^1) they would have been *superscripts* and, quite generally, they are called *indices* irrespective of their position. By writing the index symbolically (rather than numerically) we can refer to quantities generically so that x_i, for example, denotes the generic or ith input where it is assumed that i can be any integer between 1 and n. Similar remarks apply to the weights w_i. Using these ideas it is possible to represent (2.1) in a more compact form

$$a = \sum_{i=1}^{n} w_i x_i \qquad (2.2)$$

where Σ (upper case Greek sigma) denotes summation. The expressions above and below Σ denote the upper and lower limits of the summation and tell us that the index i runs from 1 to n. Sometimes the limits are omitted because they have been defined elsewhere and we simply indicate the summation index (in this case i) by writing it below the Σ.

The threshold relation for obtaining the output y may be written

$$y = \begin{cases} 1 & \text{if} \quad a \geq \theta \\ 0 & \text{if} \quad a < \theta \end{cases} \qquad (2.3)$$

Notice that there is no mention of time in the TLU; the unit responds instantaneously to its input whereas real neurons integrate over time as well as space. The

15

dendrites are represented (if one can call it a representation) by the passive connecting links between the weights and the summing operation. Action-potential generation is simply represented by the threshold function.

2.3 Resilience to noise and hardware failure

Even with this simple neuron model we can illustrate two of the general properties of neural networks. Consider a two-input TLU with weights $(0, 1)$ and threshold 0.5. Its response to all four possible input sets is shown in Table 2.1.

Table 2.1 TLU with weights $(0, 1)$ and threshold 0.5.

x_1	x_2	Activation	Output
0	0	0	0
0	1	1	1
1	0	0	0
1	1	1	1

Now suppose that our hardware which implements the TLU is faulty so that the weights are not held at their true values and are encoded instead as $(0.2, 0.8)$. The revised TLU functionality is given in Table 2.2. Notice that, although the activation has changed, the output is the same as that for the original TLU. This is because changes in the activation, as long as they don't cross the threshold, produce no change in output. Thus, the threshold function doesn't care whether the activation is just below θ or is very much less than θ; it still outputs a 0. Similarly, it doesn't matter by how much the activation exceeds θ, the TLU always supplies a 1 as output.

Table 2.2 TLU with weights $(0.2, 0.8)$ and threshold 0.5.

x_1	x_2	Activation	Output
0	0	0	0
0	1	0.8	1
1	0	0.2	0
1	1	1	1

This behaviour is characteristic of *nonlinear* systems. In a linear system, the output is proportionally related to the input: small/large changes in the input always produce corresponding small/large changes in the output. On the other hand, nonlinear relations do not obey a proportionality restraint so the *magnitude* of the change in output does not necessarily reflect that of the input. Thus, in our TLU example, the activation can change from 0 to 0.2 (a difference of 0.2) and make no difference to the output. If, however, it were to change from 0.49 to 0.51 (a difference of 0.02) the output would suddenly alter from 0 to 1.

We conclude from all this that TLUs are robust in the presence of hardware failure; if our hardware breaks down "slightly" the TLU may still function perfectly well as a result of its nonlinear functionality.

Table 2.3 TLU with degraded signal input.

x_1	x_2	Activation	Output
0.2	0.2	0.2	0
0.2	0.8	0.8	1
0.8	0.2	0.2	0
0.8	0.8	0.8	1

Suppose now that, instead of the weights being altered, the input signals have become degraded in some way, due to noise or a partial power loss, for example, so that what was previously "1" is now denoted by 0.8, and "0" becomes 0.2. The resulting TLU function is shown in Table 2.3. Once again the resulting TLU function is the same and a similar reasoning applies that involves the nonlinearity implied by the threshold. The conclusion is that the TLU is robust in the presence of noisy or corrupted signal inputs. The reader is invited to examine the case where both weights and signals have been degraded in the way indicated here. Of course, if we increase the amount by which the weights or signals have been changed too much, the TLU will eventually respond incorrectly. In a large network, as the degree of hardware and/or signal degradation increases, the number of TLU units giving incorrect results will gradually increase too. This process is called "graceful degradation" and should be compared with what happens in conventional computers where alteration to one component or loss of signal strength along one circuit board track can result in complete failure of the machine.

2.4   Non-binary signal communication

The signals dealt with so far (for both real and artificial neurons) have taken on only two values. In the case of real neurons these are the action-potential spiking voltage and the axon-membrane resting potential. For the TLUs they were conveniently labelled "1" and "0" respectively. Real neurons, however, are believed to encode their signal values in the *patterns* of action-potential firing rather than simply by the presence or absence of a single such pulse. Many characteristic patterns are observed (Conners & Gutnick 1990) of which two common examples are shown in Figure 2.5.

Part (a) shows a continuous stream of action-potential spikes while (b) shows

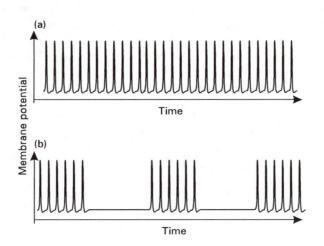

Figure 2.5 Neural firing patterns.

a pattern in which a series of pulses is followed by a quiescent period, with this sequence repeating itself indefinitely. A continuous stream as in (a) can be characterized by the frequency of occurrence of action potential in pulses per second and it is tempting to suppose that this is, in fact, the code being signalled by the neuron. This was convincingly demonstrated by Hartline (1934, 1940) for the optic neurons of the Horseshoe crab *Limulus* in which he showed that the rate of firing increased with the visual stimulus intensity. Although many neural codes are available (Bullock et al. 1977) the frequency code appears to be used in many instances.

If f is the frequency of neural firing then we know that f is bounded below by zero and above by some maximum value f_{max}, which is governed by the duration of the interspike refractory period. There are now two ways we can code for f in our artificial neurons. First, we may simply extend the signal representation to a continuous range and directly represent f as our unit output. Such signals can certainly be handled at the input of the TLU, as we remarked in examining the effects of signal degradation. However, the use of a step function at the output limits the signals to be binary so that, when TLUs are connected in networks (and they are working properly), there is no possibility of continuously graded signals occurring. This may be overcome by "softening" the step function to a continuous "squashing" function so that the output y depends smoothly on the activation a. One convenient form for this is the *logistic sigmoid* (or sometimes simply "sigmoid") shown in Figure 2.6.

As a tends to large positive values the sigmoid tends to 1 but never actually reaches this value. Similarly it approaches – but never quite reaches – 0 as a tends to large negative values. It is of no importance that the upper bound is not f_{max}, since we can simply multiply the sigmoid's value by f_{max} if we wish to interpret y as a real firing rate. The sigmoid is symmetric about the y-axis value of 0.5;

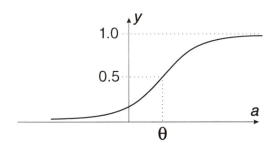

Figure 2.6 Example of squashing function – the sigmoid.

the corresponding value of the activation may be thought of as a reinterpretation of the threshold and is denoted by θ. The sigmoid function is conventionally designated by the Greek lower case sigma, σ, and finds mathematical expression according to the relation

$$y = \sigma(a) \equiv \frac{1}{1 + e^{-(a-\theta)/\rho}} \tag{2.4}$$

where $e \approx 2.7183$ is a mathematical constant[3], which, like π, has an infinite decimal expansion. The quantity ρ (Greek rho) determines the shape of the function, large values making the curve flatter while small values make the curve rise more steeply. In many texts, this parameter is omitted so that it is implicitly assigned the value 1. By making ρ progressively smaller we obtain functions that look ever closer to the hard-limiter used in the TLU so that the output function of the latter can be thought of as a special case. The reference to θ as a threshold then becomes more plausible as it takes on the role of the same parameter in the TLU.

Artificial neurons or units that use the sigmoidal output relation are referred to as being of the *semilinear* type. The activation is still given by Equation (2.2) but now the output is given by (2.4). They form the bedrock of much work in neural nets since the smooth output function facilitates their mathematical description. The term "semilinear" comes from the fact that we may approximate the sigmoid by a continuous, piecewise-linear function, as shown in Figure 2.7. Over a significant region of interest, at intermediate values of the activation, the output function is a linear relation with non-zero slope.

As an alternative to using continuous or *analogue* signal values, we may emulate the real neuron and encode a signal as the frequency of the occurrence of a "1" in a pulse stream as shown in Figure 2.8.

Time is divided into discrete "slots" and each slot is filled with either a 0 (no pulse) or a 1 (pulse). The unit output is formed in exactly the same way as before but, instead of sending the value of the sigmoid function directly, we interpret it as the probability of emitting a pulse or "1". Processes that are governed by probabilistic laws are referred to as *stochastic* so that these nodes might be dubbed *stochastic semilinear* units, and they produce signals quite close in general

19

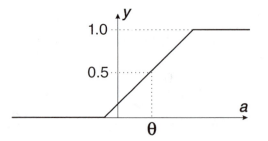

Figure 2.7 Piecewise-linear approximation of sigmoid.

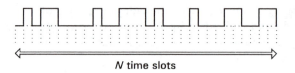

N time slots

Figure 2.8 Stream of output pulses from a stochastic node.

appearance to those of real neurons. How are units downstream that receive these signals supposed to interpret their inputs? They must now integrate over some number, N, of time slots. Thus, suppose that the afferent node is generating pulses with probability y. The expected value of the number of pulses over this time is yN but, in general, the number actually produced, N_1, will not necessarily be equal to this. The best estimate a node receiving these signals can make is the fraction, N_1/N, of 1s during its integration time. The situation is like that in a coin tossing experiment. The underlying probability of obtaining a "head" is 0.5, but in any particular sequence of tosses the number of heads N_h is not necessarily one-half of the total. As the number N of tosses increases, however, the fraction N_h/N will eventually approach 0.5.

2.5 Introducing time

Although time reared its head in the last section, it appeared by the back door, as it were, and was not intrinsic to the dynamics of the unit – we could choose *not* to integrate, or, equivalently, set $N = 1$. The way to model the temporal summation of PSPs at the axon hillock is to use the rate of change of the activation as the fundamental defining quantity, rather than the activation itself. A full treatment requires the use of a branch of mathematics known as the *calculus* but the resulting behaviour may be described in a reasonably straightforward way. We shall, however, adopt the calculus notation dx/dt, for the rate of change of a quantity x. It cannot be overemphasized that this is to be read as a single symbolic entity, "dx/dt", and not as dx divided by dt. To avoid confusion with the previous notation it is necessary to introduce another symbol for the weighted sum of inputs, so we define

$$s = \sum_{i=1}^{n} w_i x_i \tag{2.5}$$

The rate of change of the activation, da/dt, is then defined by

$$\frac{da}{dt} = -\alpha a + \beta s \tag{2.6}$$

where α (alpha) and β (beta) are positive constants. The first term gives rise to activation *decay*, while the second represents the input from the other units. As usual the output y is given by the sigmoid of the activation, $y = \sigma(a)$. A unit like this is sometimes known as a *leaky integrator* for reasons that will become apparent shortly.

There is an exact physical analogue for the leaky integrator with which we are all familiar. Consider a tank of water that has a narrow outlet near the base and that is also being fed by hose or tap as shown in Figure 2.9 (we might think of a bathtub, with a smaller drainage hole than is usual). Let the rate at which the water is flowing through the hose be s litres per minute and let the depth of water be a. If the outlet were plugged, the rate of change of water level would be proportional to s, or $da/dt = \beta s$ where β is a constant. Now suppose there is no inflow, but the outlet is working. The rate at which water leaves is directly proportional to the water pressure at the outlet, which is, in turn, proportional to the depth of water a in the tank. Thus, the rate of water emission may be written as αa litres per minute where α is some constant. The water level is now decreasing so that its rate of change is now negative and we have $da/dt = -\alpha a$. If both hose and outlet are functioning then da/dt is the sum of contributions from both, and its governing equation is just the same as that for the neural activation in (2.6). During the subsequent discussion it might be worth while referring back to this analogy if the reader has any doubts about what is taking place.

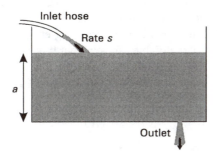

Figure 2.9 Water tank analogy for leaky integrators.

Returning to the neural model, the activation can be negative or positive (whereas the water level is always positive in the tank). Thus, on putting $s = 0$, so that the unit has no external input, there are two cases:

(a) $a > 0$. Then $da/dt < 0$. That is, the rate of change is negative, signifying a decrease of a with time.

(b) $a < 0$. Then $da/dt > 0$. That is, the rate of change is positive, signifying an increase of a with time.

These are illustrated in Figure 2.10, in which the left and right sides correspond to cases (a) and (b) respectively. In both instances the activity gradually approaches its resting value of zero. It is this decay process that leads to the "leaky" part of the unit's name. In a TLU or semilinear node, if we withdraw input, the activity immediately becomes zero. In the new model, however, the unit has a kind of short-term memory of its previous input before it was withdrawn. Thus, if this was negative, the activation remains negative for a while afterwards, with a corresponding condition holding for recently withdrawn positive input.

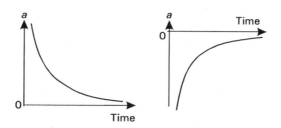

Figure 2.10 Activation decay in leaky integrator.

Suppose now that we start with activation zero and no input, and supply a constant input $s = 1$ for a time t before withdrawing it again. The activation resulting from this is shown in Figure 2.11. The activation starts to increase but does so rather sluggishly. After s is taken down to zero, a decays in the way described above. If s had been maintained long enough, then a would have eventually reached a constant value. To see what this is we put $da/dt = 0$, since this is a statement of there being no rate of change of a, and a is constant at some equilibrium value a_{eqm}. Putting $da/dt = 0$ in (2.6) gives

$$a_{eqm} = \left(\frac{\beta}{\alpha}\right) s \tag{2.7}$$

that is, a constant fraction of s. If $\alpha = \beta$ then $a_{eqm} = s$. The speed at which a can respond to an input change may be characterized by the time taken to reach some fraction of a_{eqm} ($0.75a_{eqm}$, say) and is called the *rise-time*.

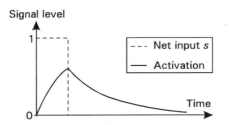

Figure 2.11 Input pulse to leaky integrator.

Suppose now that a further input pulse is presented soon after the first has been withdrawn. The new behaviour is shown in Figure 2.12. Now the activation starts to pick up again as the second input signal is delivered and, since a has not had time to decay to its resting value in the interim, the peak value obtained this time is larger than before. Thus the two signals interact with each other and there is temporal summation or integration (the "integrator" part of the unit's name). In a TLU, the activation would, of course, just be equal to s. The value of the constants α and β govern the decay rate and rise-time respectively and, as they are increased, the decay rate increases and the rise-time falls. Keeping $\alpha = \beta$ and letting both become very large therefore allows a to rise and fall very quickly and to reach equilibrium at s. As these constants are increased further, the resulting behaviour of a becomes indistinguishable from that of a TLU, which can therefore be thought of as a special case of the leaky integrator with very large constants α, β (and, of course, very steep sigmoid).

Leaky integrators find their main application in self-organizing nets (Ch. 8). They have been studied extensively by Stephen Grossberg who provides a review in Grossberg (1988). What Grossberg calls the "additive STM model" is essentially the same as that developed here, but he also goes on to describe another – the "shunting STM" neuron – which is rather different.

This completes our first foray into the realm of artificial neurons. It is adequate for most of the material in the rest of this book but, to round out the story, Chapter 10 introduces some alternative structures.

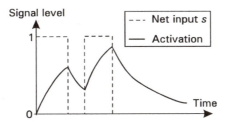

Figure 2.12 Leaky-integrator activation (solid line) for two square input pulses (dashed line).

2.6 Summary

The function of real neurons is extremely complex. However, the essential information processing attributes may be summarized as follows. A neuron receives input signals from many other (afferent) neurons. Each such signal is modulated (by the synaptic mechanism) from the voltage spike of an action potential into a continuously variable (graded) postsynaptic potential (PSP). PSPs are integrated by the dendritic arbors over both space (many synaptic inputs) and time (PSPs do not decay to zero instantaneously). PSPs may be excitatory or inhibitory and their integrated result is a change in the membrane potential at the axon hillock, which may serve to depolarize (excite or activate) or hyperpolarize (inhibit) the neuron. The dynamics of the membrane under these changes are complex but may be described in many instances by supposing that there is a membrane-potential threshold, beyond which an action potential is generated and below which no such event takes place. The train of action potentials constitutes the neural "output". They travel away from the cell body along the axon until they reach axon terminals (at synapses) upon which the cycle of events is initiated once again. Information is encoded in many ways in neurons but a common method is to make use of the frequency or rate of production of action potentials.

The integration of signals over space may be modelled using a linear weighted sum of inputs. Synaptic action is then supposed to be equivalent to multiplication by a weight. The TLU models the action potential by a simple threshold mechanism that allows two signal levels (0 or 1). The rate of firing may be represented directly in a semilinear node by allowing a continuous-valued output or (in the stochastic variant) by using this value as a probability for the production of signal pulses. Integration over time is catered for in the leaky-integrator model. All artificial neurons show robust behaviour under degradation of input signals and hardware failure.

2.7 Notes

1. The millivolt (mV) is one-thousandth of a volt.
2. After George Boole who developed a formal logic with two values denoting "True" and "False".
3. Scientific calculators should have this as one of their special purpose buttons.

Chapter Three

TLUs, linear separability and vectors

The simplest artificial neuron presented in the last chapter was the threshold logic unit or TLU. In this chapter we shall discuss a geometric context for describing the functionality of TLUs and their networks that has quite general relevance for the study of all neural networks. In the process it will be necessary to introduce some mathematical concepts about vectors. These are also of general importance and so their properties are described in some detail. Readers already familiar with this material may still wish to skim Section 3.2 to become acquainted with our notation.

3.1 Geometric interpretation of TLU action

In summary, a TLU separates its input patterns into two categories according to its binary response ("0" or "1") to each pattern. These categories may be thought of as regions in a multidimensional space that are separated by the higher dimensional equivalent of a straight line or plane.

These ideas are now introduced step by step and in a way that should help put to rest any concerns about "higher dimensionality" and "multidimensional spaces".

3.1.1 Pattern classification and input space

Consider a two-input TLU with weights $w_1 = 1$, $w_2 = 1$ and threshold 1.5, as shown in Figure 3.1. The responses to the four possible Boolean inputs are shown in Table 3.1. The TLU may be thought of as *classifying* its input patterns into two groups: those that give output "1" and those that give output "0". Each input pattern has two *components*, x_1, x_2. We may therefore represent these patterns in a two-dimensional space as shown in Figure 3.2.

Each pattern determines a point in this so-called *pattern space* by using its

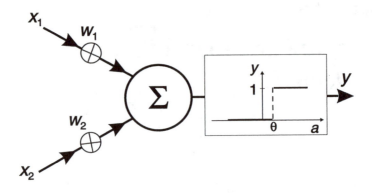

Figure 3.1 Two-input TLU.

Table 3.1 Functionality of two-input TLU example.

x_1	x_2	Activation	Output
0	0	0	0
0	1	1	0
1	0	1	0
1	1	2	1

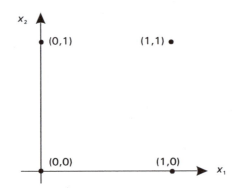

Figure 3.2 Two-input patterns in pattern space.

component values as space co-ordinates – just as grid references can locate points in physical space on a normal geographical map. In general, for n inputs, the pattern space will be n dimensional. Clearly, for $n > 3$ the pattern space cannot be drawn or represented in physical space. This is not a problem. The key is that all relationships between patterns can be expressed either geometrically, as in Figure 3.2, or algebraically using the notion of *vectors*. We can then gain insight into pattern relationships in two dimensions (2D), reformulate this in vector form and then simply carry over the results to higher dimensions. This process will become clearer after it has been put to use later. All the necessary tools for using vectors are introduced in this chapter; their appreciation will significantly increase any understanding of neural nets.

We now develop further the geometric representation of our two-input TLU.

3.1.2 The linear separation of classes

Since the critical condition for classification occurs when the activation equals the threshold, we will examine the geometric implication of this. For two inputs, equating θ and a gives

$$w_1 x_1 + w_2 x_2 = \theta \tag{3.1}$$

Subtracting $w_1 x_1$ from both sides

$$w_2 x_2 = -w_1 x_1 + \theta \tag{3.2}$$

and dividing both sides by w_2 gives

$$x_2 = -\left(\frac{w_1}{w_2}\right) x_1 + \left(\frac{\theta}{w_2}\right) \tag{3.3}$$

This is of the general form

$$x_2 = a x_1 + b \tag{3.4}$$

where a and b are constants. This equation describes a straight line with *slope a* and *intercept b* on the x_2 axis. This is illustrated in Figure 3.3 where the graph of the equation $y = ax + b$ has been plotted for two sets of values of a, b. In each case the slope is given by the change Δy that occurs in y when a positive change Δx is made in x ("Δ" is Greek upper case delta and usually signifies a change in a

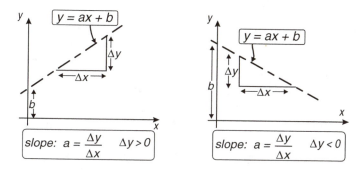

Figure 3.3 Straight line graphs.

quantity). As an example, in motoring, to describe a hill as having a "one-in-ten" slope implies you have to travel 10 metres to go up 1 metre and the hill therefore has a slope of magnitude 1/10. In the notation introduced here, there is a Δx of 10 associated with a Δy of 1. In the left hand part of the figure, y is increasing with x. Therefore, $\Delta y > 0$ when a positive change Δx is made, and so the slope a is positive. The right hand part of the figure shows y decreasing with x so that $\Delta y < 0$ when x is increased, resulting in a negative slope.

For the TLU example, inserting the values of w_1, w_2, θ in (3.3) we obtain $a = -1$, $b = 1.5$ as shown in Figure 3.4, which also shows the output of the TLU for each pattern. The two classes of TLU output are separated by the line produced in this way so that the 1s (there is only one of them) and 0s lie on opposite sides of the line; we therefore talk of this as the *decision line*. Clearly, it is always possible to partition the two classes in 2D by drawing some kind of line – the point here is that the line is a straight one having no kinks or bends. It turns out that this is not just a fortuitous result made possible by our choice of weights and threshold. It holds true for any two-input TLU. This distinction is clearer in 3D where, quite generally, we can define a *decision surface* that may have to be highly convoluted but a TLU will necessarily be associated with a flat *decision plane*.

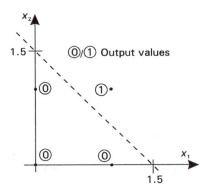

Figure 3.4 Decision line in two-input example.

Further, it is possible to generalize this result (in its algebraic form) to TLUs with an arbitrary number, n say, of inputs; that is, it is always possible to separate the two output classes of a TLU by the n-dimensional equivalent of a straight line in 2D or, in 3D, a plane. In n dimensions this is referred to as the *decision hyperplane*. (The "hyper-" is sometimes dropped even when $n > 3$). Because TLUs are intimately related to linear relations like (3.3) (and their generalization) we say that TLUs are *linear classifiers* and that their patterns are *linearly separable*. The converse of our result is also true: any binary classification that cannot be realized by a linear decision surface cannot be realized by a TLU.

We now try to demonstrate these results using the machinery of vectors. These ideas will also have general applicability in our discussion of nets throughout.

3.2 Vectors

Vectors are usually introduced as representations of quantities that have magnitude and direction. For example, the velocity of the wind is defined by its speed and direction. On paper we may draw an arrow whose direction is the same as that of the wind and whose length is proportional to its speed. Such a representation is the basis for some of the displays on televised weather reports, and we can immediately see when there will be high winds, as these are associated with large arrows. A single vector is illustrated in Figure 3.5, which illustrates some notation.

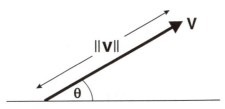

Figure 3.5 A vector.

Vectors are usually denoted in printed text by bold face letters (e.g. **v**), but in writing them by hand we can't use bold characters and so make use of an underline as in <u>v</u>. The magnitude (or length) of **v** will be denoted by $\|\mathbf{v}\|$ but is also sometimes denoted by the same letter in italic face (e.g. v). In accordance with our geometric ideas a vector is now defined by the pair of numbers ($\|\mathbf{v}\|$, θ) where θ is the angle the vector makes with some reference direction. Vectors are to be distinguished from simple numbers or *scalars*, which have a value but no direction.

In order to generalize to higher dimensions, and to relate vectors to the ideas of pattern space, it is more convenient to describe vectors with respect to a rectangular or *cartesian* co-ordinate system like the one used for the TLU example in 2D. That is, we give the projected lengths of the vector onto two perpendicular axes as shown in Figure 3.6.

The vector is now described by the pair of numbers v_1, v_2. These numbers are its *components* in the chosen co-ordinate system. Since they completely determine the vector we may think of the vector itself as a pair of component values and write $\mathbf{v} = (v_1, v_2)$. The vector is now an ordered list of numbers. Note that the ordering is important, since $(1,3)$ is in a different direction from $(3,1)$. It is this algebraic definition that immediately generalizes to more than 2D. An n-dimensional vector is simply an ordered list of n numbers, $\mathbf{v} = (v_1, v_2, \ldots, v_n)$. They become of interest when rules are defined for combining them and multiplying them by numbers or scalars (see below). To motivate the following technical material, we note that there are two vectors of immediate concern to us – the *weight vector* $(w_1, w_2, \ldots, w_n)$ and the *input vector* $(x_1, x_2, \ldots, x_n)$ for artificial neurons.

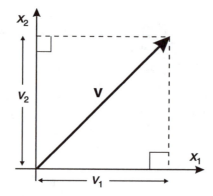

Figure 3.6 Vector components.

3.2.1 Vector addition and scalar multiplication

Multiplying a vector by a number (scalar) k simply changes the length of the vector by this factor so that if $k = 2$, say, then we obtain a vector of twice the length. Multiplying by a negative number results in a reversal of vector direction and a change in length required by the number's magnitude – see Figure 3.7. In component terms, if a vector in 2D, $\mathbf{v} = (v_1, v_2)$, is multiplied by k, then the result[1] $\mathbf{v}'$ has components (kv_1, kv_2). This can be seen in the right hand side of Figure 3.7 where the original vector $\mathbf{v}$ is shown stippled. Generalizing to n dimensions we *define* vector multiplication by $k\mathbf{v} = (kv_1, kv_2, \dots, kv_n)$.

Geometrically, two vectors may be added in 2D by simply appending one to

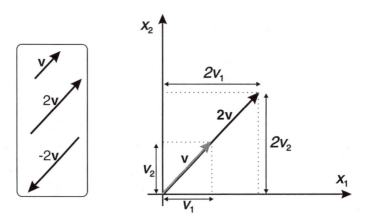

Figure 3.7 Scalar multiplication of a vector.

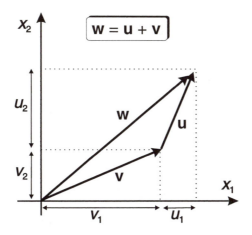

Figure 3.8 Vector addition.

the end of the other as shown in Figure 3.8. Notice that a vector may be drawn anywhere in the space as long as its magnitude and direction are preserved. In terms of the components, if $\mathbf{w} = \mathbf{u} + \mathbf{v}$, then $w_1 = u_1 + v_1$, $w_2 = u_2 + v_2$. This lends itself to generalization in n dimensions in a straightforward way. Thus, if $\mathbf{u}, \mathbf{v}$ are now vectors in n dimensions with sum $\mathbf{w}$, $\mathbf{w} = (u_1 + v_1, u_2 + v_2, \ldots, u_n + v_n)$. Note that $\mathbf{u} + \mathbf{v} = \mathbf{v} + \mathbf{u}$.

Vector subtraction is defined via a combination of addition and scalar multiplication so that we interpret $\mathbf{u} - \mathbf{v}$ as $\mathbf{u} + (-1)\mathbf{v}$, giving the addition of $\mathbf{u}$ and a reversed copy of $\mathbf{v}$ (see Fig. 3.9). The left hand side of the figure shows the original vectors $\mathbf{u}$ and $\mathbf{v}$. The construction for subtraction is shown in the centre and the right hand side shows how, by making use of the symmetry of the situation, the resulting vector $\mathbf{w}$ may be drawn as straddling $\mathbf{u}$ and $\mathbf{v}$ themselves.

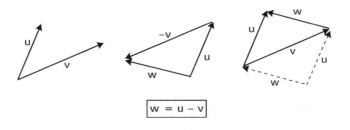

Figure 3.9 Vector subtraction.

3.2.2 The length of a vector

For our prototype in 2D, the length of a vector is just its geometrical length in the plane. In terms of its components, this is given by applying Pythagoras's theorem to the triangle shown in Figure 3.10, so that

$$\|\mathbf{v}\| = \sqrt{v_1^2 + v_2^2} \tag{3.5}$$

In n dimensions, the length is defined by the natural extension of this, so that

$$\|\mathbf{v}\| = \left[\sum_{i=1}^{n} v_i^2 \right]^{\frac{1}{2}} \tag{3.6}$$

where the exponent of $\frac{1}{2}$ outside the square brackets is a convenient way of denoting the operation of square root.

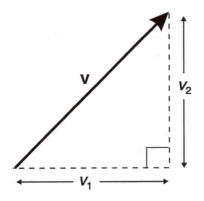

Figure 3.10 Obtaining the length of a vector.

3.2.3 Comparing vectors – the inner product

In several situations in our study of networks it will be useful to have some measure of how well aligned two vectors are – that is, to know whether they point in the same or opposite directions. The vector *inner product* allows us to do just this. This section relies on the trigonometric function known as the *cosine* and so, for those readers who may not be familiar with this, it is described in an appendix.

Inner product – geometric form

Suppose two vectors **v** and **w** are separated by an angle ϕ. Define the *inner product* **v** · **w** of the two vectors by the product of their lengths and the cosine of ϕ; that is,

$$\mathbf{v} \cdot \mathbf{w} = \|\mathbf{v}\|\|\mathbf{w}\| \cos \phi \tag{3.7}$$

This is pronounced "v dot w" and is also known as the scalar product since its result is a number (rather than another vector). Note that **v** · **w** = **w** · **v**.

What is the significance of this definition? Essentially (as promised) it tells us something about the way two vectors are aligned with each other, which follows from the properties of the cosine function. To see this, fix **w** but allow **v** to vary its direction (but not its lengths) as shown in Figure 3.11. Then, if the lengths are fixed, **v** · **w** can only depend on $\cos \phi$. When $0 < \phi < 90°$, the cosine is positive and so too, therefore, is the inner product. However, as the angle approaches 90°, the cosine diminishes and eventually reaches zero. The inner product follows in sympathy with this and, when the two vectors are at right angles they are said to be *orthogonal* with **v** · **w** = 0. Thus, if the vectors are well aligned or point in roughly the same direction, the inner product is close to its largest positive value of $\|\mathbf{v}\|\|\mathbf{w}\|$. As they move apart (in the angular sense) their inner product decreases until it is zero when they are orthogonal. As ϕ becomes greater than 90°, the cosine becomes progressively more negative until it reaches −1. Thus, $\|\mathbf{v}\|\|\mathbf{w}\|$ also behaves in this way until, when $\phi = 180°$, it takes on its largest negative value of $-\|\mathbf{v}\|\|\mathbf{w}\|$. Thus, if the vectors are pointing in roughly opposite directions, they will have a relatively large *negative* inner product.

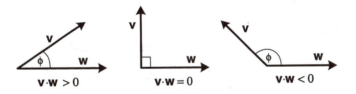

Figure 3.11 Inner product examples.

Note that we only need to think of angles in the range $0 < \phi < 180°$ because a value of ϕ between 180° and 360° is equivalent to an angle given by $360 - \phi$.

Inner product – algebraic form

Consider the vectors **v** = $(1, 1)$ and **w** = $(0, 2)$ shown in Figure 3.12 where the angle between them is 45°. An inset in the figure shows a right-angled triangle with its other angles equal to 45°. The hypotenuse, h, has been calculated from Pythagoras's theorem to be $\sqrt{1^2 + 1^2} = \sqrt{2}$ and, from the definition of the cosine (A.1), it can then be seen that $\cos 45° = 1/\sqrt{2}$. To find the inner product

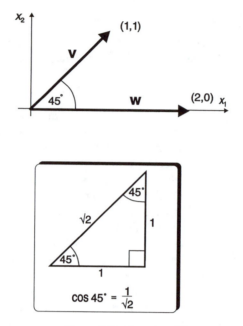

Figure 3.12 Vectors at 45°.

of the two vectors in Figure 3.12, we note that $\|\mathbf{v}\| = \sqrt{2}$, $\|\mathbf{w}\| = 2$, so that $\mathbf{v} \cdot \mathbf{w} = \sqrt{2} \times 2 \times 1/\sqrt{2} = 2$. We now introduce an equivalent, algebraic definition of the inner product that lends itself to generalization in n dimensions.

Consider the quantity $\mathbf{v} \circ \mathbf{w}$ defined in 2D by

$$\mathbf{v} \circ \mathbf{w} = v_1 w_1 + v_2 w_2 \tag{3.8}$$

The form on the right hand side should be familiar – substituting x for v we have the activation of a two-input TLU. In the example above, substituting the component values gives $\mathbf{v} \circ \mathbf{w} = 2$ which is the same as $\mathbf{v} \cdot \mathbf{w}$. The equivalence of what we have called $\mathbf{v} \circ \mathbf{w}$ and the geometrically defined inner product is not a chance occurrence resulting from the particular choice of numbers in our example. It is a general result (Rumelhart et al. 1986b) (which will not be proved here) and it means that we may write $\mathbf{v} \cdot \mathbf{w} = v_1 w_1 + v_2 w_2$ for any vectors $\mathbf{v}, \mathbf{w}$ in 2D. The form in (3.8) immediately lends itself to generalization in n dimensions so that we define the dot product of two n-dimensional vectors $\mathbf{v}, \mathbf{w}$ as

$$\mathbf{v} \cdot \mathbf{w} = \sum_{i=1}^{n} w_i v_i \tag{3.9}$$

We shall interpret the value obtained in this way just as we did in 2D. Thus, if it is positive then the two vectors are, in some sense, roughly "lined up" with each other, if it is negative then they are "pointing away from" each other and, if it is zero, the vectors are at "right angles". No attempt should be made to visualize this in n dimensions; rather, think of its analogue in 2D as a schematic or cartoon representation of what is happening. The situation is a little like using pictures in 2D to represent scenes in 3D – the picture is not identical to the objects it depicts in 3D, but it may help us think about their geometrical properties.

Finally, what happens if $\mathbf{v} = \mathbf{w}$? Then we have

$$\mathbf{v} \cdot \mathbf{v} = \sum_i v_i v_i = \|\mathbf{v}\|^2 \tag{3.10}$$

so that the square length of vector is the same as the inner product of the vector with itself.

Vector projection

There is one final concept that we will find useful. Consider the two vectors $\mathbf{v}, \mathbf{w}$ in Figure 3.13 and suppose we ask the question – how much of $\mathbf{v}$ lies in the direction of $\mathbf{w}$? Formally, if we drop a perpendicular from $\mathbf{v}$ onto $\mathbf{w}$ what is the length of the line segment along $\mathbf{w}$ produced in this way? This segment is called the *projection* v_w of $\mathbf{v}$ *onto* $\mathbf{w}$ and, using the definition of cosine, we have $v_w = \|\mathbf{v}\| \cos \phi$. We can reformulate this, using the inner product, in a way suitable for generalization. Thus, we write

$$
\begin{aligned}
v_w &= \frac{\|\mathbf{v}\|\|\mathbf{w}\| \cos \phi}{\|\mathbf{w}\|} \\
&= \frac{\mathbf{v} \cdot \mathbf{w}}{\|\mathbf{w}\|}
\end{aligned}
\tag{3.11}
$$

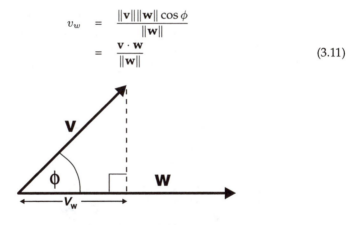

Figure 3.13 Vector projections.

3.3 TLUs and linear separability revisited

Our discussion of vectors was motivated by the desire to prove that the connection between TLUs and linear separability is a universal one, independent of the dimensionality of the pattern space. We are now in a position to show this, drawing on the ideas developed in the previous section. Using the definition of the inner product (3.9) the activation a of an n-input TLU may now be expressed as

$$a = \mathbf{w} \cdot \mathbf{x} \tag{3.12}$$

The vector equivalent to (3.1) now becomes

$$\mathbf{w} \cdot \mathbf{x} = \theta \tag{3.13}$$

As in the example in 2D, we expect deviations either side of those $\mathbf{x}$ that satisfy this relation to result in different output for the TLU. We now formalize what is meant by "either side" a little more carefully. Our strategy is to examine the case in 2D geometrically to gain insight and then, by describing it algebraically, to generalize to n dimensions.

In general, for an arbitrary $\mathbf{x}$, the projection of $\mathbf{x}$ onto $\mathbf{w}$ is given by

$$x_w = \frac{\mathbf{w} \cdot \mathbf{x}}{\|\mathbf{w}\|} \tag{3.14}$$

If, however, we impose the constraint implied by (3.13), we have

$$x_w = \frac{\theta}{\|\mathbf{w}\|} \tag{3.15}$$

So, assuming $\mathbf{w}$ and θ are constant, the projection x_w is constant and, in 2D, $\mathbf{x}$ must actually lie along the perpendicular to the weight vector, shown as a dashed line in Figure 3.14. Therefore, in 2D, the relation $\mathbf{w} \cdot \mathbf{x} = \theta$ defines a straight line. However, since we have used algebraic expressions that are valid in n dimensions throughout, we can generalize and use this to *define* the n-dimensional equivalent

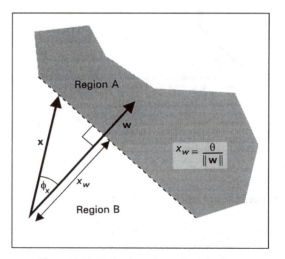

Figure 3.14 Projection of $\mathbf{x}$ as decision line.

of a straight line – a hyperplane – which is perpendicular to the weight vector **w**. When x lies on the hyperplane, $\mathbf{w} \cdot \mathbf{x} = \theta$, and the TLU output rule states that $y = 1$; it remains to see what happens on each side of the line.

Suppose first that $x_w > \theta/\|\mathbf{w}\|$; then the projection is longer than that in Figure 3.14 and **x** must lie in region A (shown by the shading). Comparison of (3.14) and (3.15) shows that, in this case, $\mathbf{w} \cdot \mathbf{x} > \theta$, and so $y = 1$. Conversely, if $x_w < \theta/\|\mathbf{w}\|$, the projection is shorter than that in Figure 3.14 and **x** must lie in region B. The implication is now that $\mathbf{w} \cdot \mathbf{x} < \theta$, and so $y = 0$. The diagram can only show part of each region and it should be understood that they are, in fact, of infinite extent so that any point in the pattern space is either in A or B. Again these results are quite general and are independent of the number n of TLU inputs.

To summarize: we have proved two things:

(a) The relation $\mathbf{w} \cdot \mathbf{x} = \theta$ defines a hyperplane (n-dimensional "straight line") in pattern space which is perpendicular to the weight vector. That is, any vector wholly *within* this plane is orthogonal to **w**.

(b) On one side of this hyperplane are all the patterns that get classified by the TLU as a "1", while those that get classified as a "0" lie on the other side of the hyperplane.

To recap on some points originally made in Section 3.1.2, the hyperplane is the decision surface for the TLU. Since this surface is the n-dimensional version of a straight line the TLU is a *linear* classifier. If patterns cannot be separated by a hyperplane then they cannot be classified with a TLU.

One assumption has been made throughout the above that should now be made explicit. Thus, Figure 3.14 shows a positive projection x_w, which implies a positive threshold. For a negative threshold θ, the projection constraint (3.15) now implies that $x_w < 0$, since $\|\mathbf{w}\|$ is always positive. Therefore $\mathbf{w} \cdot \mathbf{x} < 0$ for

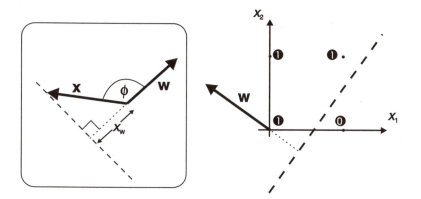

Figure 3.15 Projection with negative threshold.

those **x** that lie on the decision line and they must point away from **w** as shown in the left half of Figure 3.15. A typical instance of the use of a negative threshold is shown in the right hand part of the figure. Notice that the weight vector always points towards the region of 1s, which is consistent with the TLU rule: $\mathbf{w} \cdot \mathbf{x} > 0$ implies $y = 1$.

3.4 Summary

The function of a TLU may be represented geometrically in a pattern space. In this space, the TLU separates its inputs into two classes (depending on the output "1" or "0"), which may be separated by a hyperplane (the n-dimensional equivalent of a straight line in 1D or a plane in 2D). The formal description of neuron behaviour in pattern space is greatly facilitated by the use of vectors, which may be thought of as the generalization of directed arrows in 2D or 3D. A key concept is that of the dot product $\mathbf{w} \cdot \mathbf{x}$ of two vectors **w** and **x**. If the lengths of the two vectors are held fixed, then the dot product tells us something about the "angle" between the vectors. Vector pairs that are roughly aligned with each other have a positive inner product, if they point away from each other the inner product is negative, and if they are at right angles (orthogonal) it is zero. The significance of all this is that the activation of a TLU is given by the dot product of the weight and input vectors, $a = \mathbf{w} \cdot \mathbf{x}$, so that it makes sense to talk about a neuron computing their relative alignment. Our first application of this was to prove the linear separability of TLU classes. However, the geometric view (and the dot product interpretation of activation) will, quite generally, prove invaluable in gaining insight into network function.

3.5 Notes

1. The small dash symbol is pronounced "prime" so one reads **v**′ as "v-prime".

Chapter Four

Training TLUs:
the perceptron rule

4.1 Training networks

This chapter introduces the concept of training a network to perform a given task. Some of the ideas discussed here will have general applicability, but most of the time refer to the specifics of TLUs and a particular method for training them. In order for a TLU to perform a given classification it must have the desired decision surface. Since this is determined by the weight vector and threshold, it is necessary to adjust these to bring about the required functionality. In general terms, adjusting the weights and thresholds in a network is usually done via an iterative process of repeated presentation of examples of the required task. At each presentation, small changes are made to weights and thresholds to bring them more in line with their desired values. This process is known as *training* the net, and the set of examples as the *training set*. From the network's viewpoint it undergoes a process of learning, or adapting to, the training set, and the prescription for how to change the weights at each step is the *learning rule*. In one type of training (alluded to in Ch. 1) the net is presented with a set of input patterns or vectors $\{x_i\}$ and, for each one, a corresponding desired output vector or target $\{t_i\}$. Thus, the net is supposed to respond with t_k, given input x_k for every k. This process is referred to as *supervised* training (or learning) because the network is told or supervised at each step as to what it is expected to do.

We will focus our attention in this chapter on training TLUs and a related node, the *perceptron*, using supervised learning. We will consider a single node in isolation at first so that the training set consists of a set of pairs $\{v, t\}$, where v is an input vector and t is the target class or output ("1" or "0") that v belongs to.

4.2 Training the threshold as a weight

In order to place the adaptation of the threshold on the same footing as the weights, there is a mathematical trick we can play to make it look like a weight. Thus, we normally write $w \cdot x \geq \theta$ as the condition for output of a "1". Subtracting

θ from both sides gives $\mathbf{w} \cdot \mathbf{x} - \theta \geq 0$ and making the minus sign explicit results in the form $\mathbf{w} \cdot \mathbf{x} + (-1)\theta \geq 0$. Therefore, we may think of the threshold as an extra weight that is driven by an input constantly tied to the value -1. This leads to the negative of the threshold being referred to sometimes as the *bias*. The weight vector, which was initially of dimension n for an n-input unit, now becomes the $(n + 1)$-dimensional vector $w_1, w_2, \ldots, w_n, \theta$. We shall call this the *augmented* weight vector, in contexts where confusion might arise, although this terminology is by no means standard. Then for all TLUs we may express the node function as follows[1]:

$$\mathbf{w} \cdot \mathbf{x} \geq 0 \quad \Rightarrow \quad y = 1$$
$$\mathbf{w} \cdot \mathbf{x} < 0 \quad \Rightarrow \quad y = 0 \tag{4.1}$$

Putting $\mathbf{w} \cdot \mathbf{x} = 0$ now defines the decision hyperplane, which, according to the discussion in Chapter 3, is orthogonal to the (augmented) weight vector. The zero-threshold condition in the augmented space means that the hyperplane passes through the origin, since this is the only way that allows $\mathbf{w} \cdot \mathbf{x} = 0$. We now illustrate how this modification of pattern space works with an example in 2D, but it is quite possible to skip straight to Section 4.3 without any loss of continuity.

Consider the two-input TLU that outputs a "1" with input (1, 1) and a "0" for all other inputs so that a suitable (non-augmented) weight vector is (1/2, 1/2) with threshold 3/4. This is shown in Figure 4.1 where the decision line and weight vector have been shown quantitatively. That the decision line goes through the points $x_1 = (1/2, 1)$ and $x_2 = (1, 1/2)$ may be easily verified since according to (3.8) $\mathbf{w} \cdot \mathbf{x}_1 = \mathbf{w} \cdot \mathbf{x}_2 = 3/4 = \theta$. For the augmented pattern space we have to go to 3D as shown in Figure 4.2. The previous two components x_1, x_2 are now drawn in the horizontal plane while a third component x_3 has been introduced, which is shown as the vertical axis. All the patterns to the TLU now have the form $(x_1, x_2, -1)$ since the third input is tied to the constant value of -1. The augmented weight vector now has a third component equal to the threshold

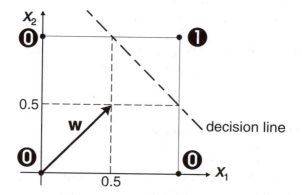

Figure 4.1 Two-dimensional TLU example.

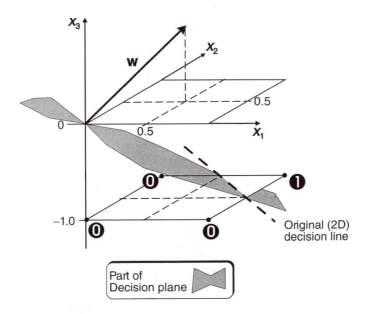

Figure 4.2 Two-dimensional example in augmented pattern space.

and is perpendicular to a decision plane that passes through the origin. The old decision line in 2D is formed by the intersection of the decision plane and the plane containing the patterns.

4.3   Adjusting the weight vector

We now suppose we are to train a single TLU with augmented weight vector **w** using the training set consisting of pairs like **v**, t. The TLU may have any number of inputs but we will represent what is happening in pattern space in a schematic way using cartoon diagrams in 2D.

Suppose we present an input vector **v** to the TLU with desired response or target $t = 1$ and, with the current weight vector, it produces an output of $y = 0$. The TLU has misclassified and we must make some adjustment to the weights. To produce a "0" the activation must have been negative when it should have been positive – see (4.1). Thus, the dot product **w** · **v** was negative and the two vectors were pointing away from each other as shown on the left hand side of Figure 4.3.

In order to correct the situation we need to rotate **w** so that it points more in the direction of **v**. At the same time, we don't want to make too drastic a change as this might upset previous learning. We can achieve both goals by adding a

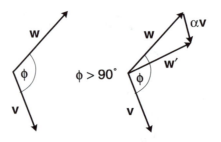

Figure 4.3 TLU misclassification 1–0.

fraction of **v** to **w** to produce a new weight vector **w**′, that is

$$\mathbf{w}' = \mathbf{w} + \alpha\mathbf{v} \tag{4.2}$$

where $0 < \alpha < 1$, which is shown schematically on the right hand side of Figure 4.3.

Suppose now, instead, that misclassification takes place with the target $t = 0$ but $y = 1$. This means the activation was positive when it should have been negative as shown on the left in Figure 4.4. We now need to rotate **w** *away* from **v**, which may be effected by *subtracting* a fraction of **v** from **w**, that is

$$\mathbf{w}' = \mathbf{w} - \alpha\mathbf{v} \tag{4.3}$$

as indicated on the left of the figure.

Both (4.2) and (4.3) may be combined as a single rule in the following way:

$$\mathbf{w}' = \mathbf{w} + \alpha(t - y)\mathbf{v} \tag{4.4}$$

This may be written in terms of the change in the weight vector $\Delta\mathbf{w} = \mathbf{w}' - \mathbf{w}$ as follows:

$$\Delta\mathbf{w} = \alpha(t - y)\mathbf{v} \tag{4.5}$$

or in terms of the components

$$\Delta w_i = \alpha(t - y)v_i : \quad i = 1 \text{ to } n + 1 \tag{4.6}$$

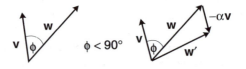

Figure 4.4 TLU misclassification 0–1.

where $w_{n+1} = \theta$ and $v_{n+1} = -1$ always. The parameter α is called the *learning rate* because it governs how big the changes to the weights are and, hence, how fast the learning takes place. All the forms (4.4, 4.5, 4.6) are equivalent and define the *perceptron training rule*. It is called this rather than the TLU rule because, historically, it was first used with a modification of the TLU known as the perceptron, described in Section 4.4. The learning rule can be incorporated into the overall scheme of iterative training as follows.

> repeat
> > for each training vector pair $(\mathbf{v}, t)$
> > > evaluate the output y when $\mathbf{v}$ is input to the TLU
> > > if $y \neq t$ then
> > > > form a new weight vector $\mathbf{w}'$ according to (4.4)
> > > else
> > > > do nothing
> > > end if
> > end for
> until $y = t$ for all vectors

The procedure in its entirety constitutes the perceptron *learning algorithm*. There is one important assumption here that has not, as yet, been made explicit: the algorithm will generate a valid weight vector for the problem in hand, if one exists. Indeed, it can be shown that this is the case and its statement constitutes the *perceptron convergence theorem*:

> If two classes of vectors X, Y are linearly separable, then application of the perceptron training algorithm will eventually result in a weight vector $\mathbf{w}_0$ such that $\mathbf{w}_0$ defines a TLU whose decision hyperplane separates X and Y.

Since the algorithm specifies that we make no change to $\mathbf{w}$ if it correctly classifies its input, the convergence theorem also implies that, once $\mathbf{w}_0$ has been found, it remains stable and no further changes are made to the weights. The convergence theorem was first proved by Rosenblatt (1962), while more recent versions may be found in Haykin (1994) and Minsky & Papert (1969).

One final point concerns the uniqueness of the solution. Suppose $\mathbf{w}_0$ is a valid solution to the problem so that $\mathbf{w}_0 \cdot \mathbf{x} = 0$ defines a solution hyperplane. Multiplying both sides of this by a constant k preserves the equality and therefore defines the same hyperplane. We may absorb k into the weight vector so that, letting $\mathbf{w}_0' = k\mathbf{w}_0$, we have $\mathbf{w}_0' \cdot \mathbf{x} = k\mathbf{w}_0 \cdot \mathbf{x} = 0$. Thus, if $\mathbf{w}_0$ is a solution, then so too is $k\mathbf{w}_0$ for any k and this entire family of vectors defines the same solution hyperplane.

We now look at an example of the training algorithm in use with a two-input TLU whose initial weights are 0, 0.4, and whose initial threshold is 0.3. It has to learn the function illustrated in Figure 4.1; that is, all inputs produce 0 except for the vector (1, 1). The learning rate is 0.25. Using the above algorithm, it is possible to calculate the sequence of events that takes place on presentation of all four training vectors as shown in Table 4.1.

Table 4.1 Training with the perceptron rule on a two-input example.

w_1	w_2	θ	x_1	x_2	a	y	t	$\alpha(t - y)$	δw_1	δw_2	$\delta\theta$
0.0	0.4	0.3	0	0	0	0	0	0	0	0	0
0.0	0.4	0.3	0	1	0.4	1	0	−0.25	0	−0.25	0.25
0.0	0.15	0.55	1	0	0	0	0	0	0	0	0
0.0	0.15	0.55	1	1	0.15	0	1	0.25	0.25	0.25	−0.25

Each row shows the quantities required for a single vector presentation. The columns labelled w_1, w_2, θ show the weights and threshold just prior to the application of the vector with components in columns x_1, x_2. The columns marked a and y show the activation and output resulting from input vector (x_1, x_2). The target t appears in the next column and takes part in the calculation of the quantity $\alpha(t - y)$, which is used in the training rule. If this is non-zero then changes are effected in the weights δw_1, δw_2, and threshold $\delta\theta$. Notice that the lower case version of delta, δ, may also be used to signify a change in a quantity as well as its upper case counterpart, Δ. These changes should then be added to the original values in the first three columns to obtain the new values of the weights and threshold that appear in the next row. Thus, in order to find the weight after all four vectors have been presented, the weight changes in the last row should be added to the weights in the fourth row to give $w_1 = 0.25$, $w_2 = 0.4$, $\theta = 0.3$.

4.4 The perceptron

This is an enhancement of the TLU introduced by Rosenblatt (Rosenblatt 1962) and is shown in Figure 4.5. It consists of a TLU whose inputs come from a set of preprocessing *association units* or simply A-units. The input pattern is supposed to be Boolean, that is a set of 1s and 0s, and the A-units can be assigned any arbitrary Boolean functionality but are fixed – they do not learn. The depiction of the input pattern as a grid carries the suggestion that the input may be derived from a visual image, which is the subject of Section 4.6. The rest of the node functions just like a TLU and may therefore be trained in exactly the same way. The TLU may be thought of as a special case of the perceptron with a trivial set of A-units, each consisting of a single direct connection to one of the inputs. Indeed, sometimes the term "perceptron" is used to mean what we have defined as a TLU. However, whereas a perceptron always performs a linear separation with respect to the output of its A-units, its function of the input space may not be linearly separable if the A-units are non-trivial.

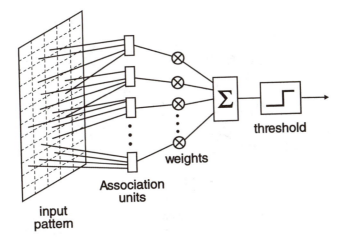

Figure 4.5 The perceptron.

4.5 Multiple nodes and layers

4.5.1 Single-layer nets

Using the perceptron training algorithm. we are now in a position to use a single perceptron or TLU to classify two linearly separable classes A and B. Although the patterns may have many inputs, we may illustrate the pattern space in a schematic or cartoon way as shown in Figure 4.6. Thus the two axes are not labelled, since they do not correspond to specific vector components, but are merely indicative that we are thinking of the vectors in their pattern space.

It is possible, however, to train multiple nodes on the input space to achieve a set of linearly separable dichotomies of the type shown in Figure 4.6. This might

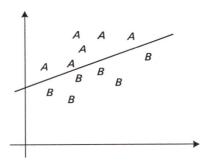

Figure 4.6 Classification of two classes A, B.

45

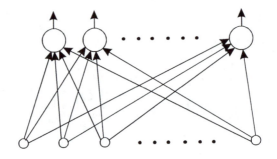

Figure 4.7 Single-layer net.

occur, for example, if we wish to classify handwritten alphabetic characters where 26 dichotomies are required, each one separating one letter class from the rest of the alphabet – "A"s from non-"A"s, "B"s from non-"B"s, etc. The entire collection of nodes forms a *single-layer net* as shown in Figure 4.7. Of course, whether each of the above dichotomies is linearly separable is another question. If they are, then the perceptron rule may be applied successfully to each node individually.

4.5.2   Nonlinearly separable classes

Suppose now that there are four classes A, B, C, D and that they are separable by two planes in pattern space as shown in Figure 4.8. Once again, this diagram is a schematic representation of a high-dimensional space. It would be futile trying to use a single-layer net to separate these classes since class A, for example, is not linearly separable from the others taken together. However, although the problem (identifying the four classes A, B, C, D) is not linearly separable, it is possible to solve it by "chopping" the pattern space into linearly separable regions and looking for particular combinations of overlap within these regions.

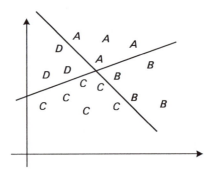

Figure 4.8 Pattern space for classification of four classes A, B, C, D.

The initial process of pattern space division may be accomplished with a first layer of TLUs and the combinations evaluated by a subsequent layer. This strategy is now explained in detail.

We start by noting that, although no single class (such as A, for example) is linearly separable from the others, the higher order class consisting of A and B together *is* linearly separable from that consisting of C and D together. To facilitate talking about these classes, let AB be the class consisting of all patterns that are in A or B. Similarly, let CD be the class containing all patterns in C or D, etc. Then our observation is that AB and CD are linearly separable as are AD and BC.

We may now train two units U_1, U_2 with outputs y_1, y_2 to perform these two dichotomies as shown in Table 4.2.

Table 4.2 y_1, y_2 outputs.

Class	y_1	Class	y_2
AB	1	AD	1
CD	0	BC	0

Suppose now a member of the original class A is input to each of U_1, U_2. From the table, this results in outputs $y_1 = y_2 = 1$. Conversely, suppose an unknown vector **x** is input and both outputs are 1. As far as U_1 is concerned **x** is in AB, and U_2 classifies it as in AD. The only way it can be in both is if it is in A. We conclude therefore that $y_1 = 1$ and $y_2 = 1$ if, and only if, the input vector **x** is in A. Proceeding with the other three possibilities, we obtain a unique code, in terms of y_1, y_2, for each of the classes, as shown in Table 4.3.

Table 4.3 y_1, y_2 codes.

y_1	y_2	Class
0	0	C
0	1	D
1	0	B
1	1	A

These codes may now be decoded by a set of four two-input TLUs, each connected to both U_1 and U_2 as shown in Figure 4.9. Thus, to signal class A we construct a two-input TLU that has output "1" for input (1, 1) and output "0" for all other inputs. To signal class B the TLU must output "1" only when presented with (1, 0), and so on for C and D. These input–output relations are certainly linearly separable since they each consist, in pattern space, of a line that "cuts away" one of the corners of the square (refer back to Fig. 3.4 for an example that corresponds to the A-class node). Notice that only one of the four TLU *output*

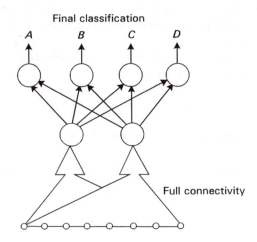

Figure 4.9 Two-layer net for four-class classification

units is "on" (output "1") at any one time so that the classification is signalled in an unambiguous way.

Two important points need to be made here. First, the output units were not trained; each one has been assigned the appropriate weights by inspection of their pattern space. Secondly, if we had chosen to use the groupings AC or DB then we would have failed, since neither of these can take part in a linearly separable dichotomy. There were therefore two pieces of information required in order to train the two units.

(a) The four classes may be separated by two hyperplanes.

(b) AB was linearly separable from CD and AD was linearly separable from BC.

It would be more satisfactory if we could dispense with (b) and train the entire two-layer architecture in Figure 4.9 as a whole *ab initio*. The less information we have to supply ourselves, the more useful a network is going to be. In order to do this, it is necessary to introduce a new training algorithm based on a different approach, which obviates the need to have prior knowledge of the pattern space.

Incidentally, there is sometimes disagreement in the literature as to whether the network in Figure 4.9 is a two- or three-layer net. Most authors (as I do) would call it a two-layer net because there are two layers of artificial neurons, which is equivalent to saying there are two layers of weights. Some authors, however, consider the first layer of input distribution points as units in their own right, but since they have no functionality it does not seem appropriate to place them on the same footing as the TLU nodes.

4.6 Some practical matters

We have spoken rather glibly so far about training sets without saying how they may originate in real applications. The training algorithm has also been introduced in the abstract with little heed being paid to how it, and the network, are implemented. This is a suitable point to take time out from the theoretical development and address these issues.

4.6.1 Making training sets

We will make this concrete by way of an example which assumes a network that is being used to classify visual images. The sequence of events for making a single training pattern in this case is shown in Figure 4.10.

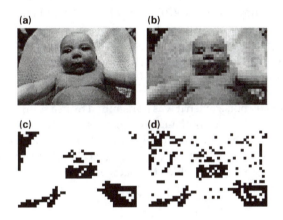

Figure 4.10 Making training sets from images.

Part (a) shows the original scene in monochrome. Colour information adds another level of complexity and the image shown here was, in fact, obtained by first converting from a colour picture. Our goal is somehow to represent this image in a way suitable for input to a TLU or perceptron. The first step is shown in part (b) in which the image has been divided into a series of small squares in a grid-like fashion. Within each square, the luminance intensity is averaged to produce a single grey level. Thus, if a square is located in a region that is mainly dark, it will contain a uniform dark grey, whereas squares in lighter regions will contain uniform areas of pale grey. Each square is called a *pixel* and may now be assigned a number, based on the darkness or lightness of its grey content. One popular scheme divides or *quantizes* the grey-scale into 256 discrete levels and assigns 0 to black and 255 to white. In making the assignment of scale values to pixels, we have to take the value closest to the pixel's grey level. This will

49

result in small *quantization errors*, which will not be too large, however, if there are enough levels to choose from.

If we know how many pixels there are along each side of the picture the rows (or columns) of the grid may now be concatenated to obtain a vector of numbers. This is adequate as it stands for input to a TLU, which does not necessarily need Boolean vectors, but is not suitable for the perceptron. To convert to a Boolean vector we must use only two values of grey, which may be taken to be black and white. This conversion is accomplished by thresholding at some given grey level. For example, if we set the threshold at 50 per cent and are using the 0–255 labelling scheme, all pixels with values between 0 and 127 will be assigned the value 0 (white), while all those between 128 and 255 will be given the label 1 (black). This has been done in part (c) of the figure, which shows the *binarized* version of the image with threshold 50 per cent. The rows (or columns) may now be concatenated to produce a Boolean vector suitable for use as input to the perceptron. Another way of thinking of the binarized image is that it is a direct result of grey-level quantization but with only two (instead of 256) grey levels. Image vectors like those in Figure 4.10b,c may be stored for later use in computer memory or *framestore*, or on disk in a file.

Before leaving our example, we can use it to help illustrate a typical task that our network may be expected to perform. In Figure 4.10d is shown a copy of the original binarized image of part (c) but with some of the pixels having their values inverted. This may have occurred, for example, because the image became corrupted by noise when it was transmitted from a source to a destination machine. Alternatively, we might imagine a more structured alteration in which, for example, the child has moved slightly or has changed facial expression. We would expect a well-trained network to be able to classify these slightly altered images along with the original, which is what we mean by its ability to generalize from the training set.

4.6.2   Real and virtual networks

When we build a neural network do we go to our local electronic hardware store, buy components and then assemble them? The answer, in most cases, is "no". Usually we simulate the network on a conventional computer such as a PC or workstation. What is simulation? The entries in Table 4.1 could have been filled out by pencil and paper calculation, by using a spreadsheet, or by writing a special purpose computer program. All these are examples of simulations of the TLU, although the first method is rather slow and is not advised for general use. In the parlance of computer science, when the net is being simulated on a general purpose computer, it is said to exist as a *virtual machine* (Tanenbaum 1990). The term "virtual reality" has been appropriated for describing simulations of spatial environments – however, the virtual machines came first.

Instead of writing a computer program from scratch, one alternative is to use a general purpose neural network simulator that allows network types and algorithms to be chosen from a set of predetermined options. It is also often the case that they include a set of visualization tools that allow one to monitor the behaviour of the net as it adapts to the training set. This can be extremely important in understanding the development and behaviour of the network; a machine in which the information is distributed in a set of weights can be hard to understand. Examples of this type of simulator are available both commercially and as freely distributed software that may be downloaded via an Internet link. For a survey, see Murre (1995).

Large neural networks can often require many thousands of iterations of their training algorithm to converge on a solution, so that simulation can take a long time. The option, wherever possible, should be to use the most powerful computer available and to limit the network to a size commensurate with the available computing resources. For example, in deciding how large each pixel should be in Figure 4.10, we have to be careful that the resulting vector is not so large that there are too many weights to deal with in a reasonable time at each iteration of the learning algorithm.

In Chapter 1, one of the features of networks that was alluded to was their ability to compute in parallel. That is, each node may be regarded as a processor that operates independently of, and concurrently with, the others. Clearly, in simulation as a virtual machine, networks cannot operate like this. The computation being performed by any node has to take place to the exclusion of the others and each one must be updated in some predefined sequence. In order to take advantage of the latent parallelism, the network must be realized as a physical machine with separate hardware units for each node and, in doing this, there are two aspects that need attention. First, there needs to be special purpose circuitry for implementing the node functionality, which includes, for example, multiplying weights by inputs, summing these together and a nonlinearity output function. Secondly, there needs to be hardware to execute the learning algorithm. This is usually harder to achieve and many early physical network implementations dealt only with node functionality. However, it is the learning that is computer intensive and so attention has now shifted to the inclusion of special purpose learning hardware.

Distinction should also be made between network hardware accelerators and truly parallel machines. In the former, special circuitry is devoted to executing the node function but only one copy exists so that, although there may be a significant speed-up, the network is still operating as a virtual machine in some way. Intermediate structures are also possible in which there may be several node hardware units, allowing for some parallelism, but not sufficient for an entire network. Another possibility is to make use of a general purpose parallel computer, in which case the node functionality and training may be shared out amongst individual processors. Some accounts of special purpose chips for neural networks may be found in two special issues of the *IEEE Transactions on Neural Nets* (Sánchez-Sinencio & Newcomb 1992a,b).

4.7 Summary

By building on the insights gained using the geometric approach introduced in the last chapter, we have demonstrated how TLU-like nodes (including perceptrons) can adapt their weights (or learn) to classify linearly separable problems. The resulting learning rule is incorporated into a training algorithm that iteratively presents vectors to the net and makes the required changes. The threshold may be adapted on the same basis using a simple trick that makes it appear like a weight. We have seen how nonlinearly separable problems may be solved in principle using a two-layer net, but the method outlined so far relies heavily on prior knowledge and the hand crafting of weights. More satisfactory schemes are the subject of subsequent chapters. Finally, the general idea of a "training vector" was made more concrete with reference to an example in vision, and issues concerning the implementation of networks in software and hardware were discussed.

4.8 Notes

1. The symbol $\Rightarrow$ is read as "implies".

Chapter Five

The delta rule

At the end of the last chapter we set out a programme that aimed to train all the weights in multilayer nets with no a priori knowledge of the training set and no hand crafting of the weights required. It turns out that the perceptron rule is not suitable for generalization in this way so that we have to resort to other techniques. An alternative approach, available in a supervised context, is based on defining a measure of the difference between the actual network output and target vector. This difference is then treated as an error to be minimized by adjusting the weights. Thus, the object is to find the minimum of the sum of errors over the training set where this error sum is considered to be a function of (depends on) the weights of the network. This paradigm is a powerful one and, after introducing some basic principles and their application to single-layer nets in this chapter, its generalization to multilayer nets is discussed in Chapter 6.

5.1 Finding the minimum of a function: gradient descent

Consider a quantity y that depends on a single variable x – we say that y is a function of x and write $y = y(x)$. Suppose now that we wish to find the value x_0 for which y is a minimum (so that $y(x_0) \leq y(x)$ for all x) as shown in Figure 5.1. Let x^* be our current best estimate for x_0; then one sensible thing to do in order to obtain a better estimate is to change x so as to follow the function "downhill"

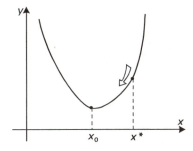

Figure 5.1 Function minimization.

as it were. Thus, if increasing x (starting at x^*) implies a decrease in y then we make a small positive change, $\Delta x > 0$, to our estimate x^*. On the other hand, if decreasing x results in decreasing y then we must make a negative change, $\Delta x < 0$. The knowledge used to make these decisions is contained in the *slope* of the function at x^*; if increasing x increases y, the slope is positive, otherwise it is negative.

We met the concept of slope in Section 3.1.2 in connection with straight lines. The extension to general functions of a single variable is straightforward, as shown in Figure 5.2. The slope at any point x is just the slope of a straight line, the *tangent*, which just grazes the curve at that point. There are two ways to find the slope. First, we may draw the function on graph paper, draw the tangent at the required point, complete the triangle as shown in the figure and measure the sides Δx and Δy. It is possible, however, to calculate the slope from $y(x)$ using a branch of mathematics known as the differential calculus. It is not part of our brief to demonstrate or use any of the techniques of the calculus but it is possible to understand what is being computed, and where some of its notation comes from.

Figure 5.3 shows a closeup of the region around point P in Figure 5.2. The slope at P has been constructed in the usual way but, this time, the change Δx used to construct the base of the triangle is supposed to be very small. If δy is

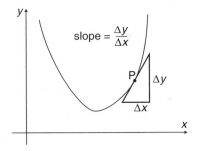

Figure 5.2 Slope of $y(x)$.

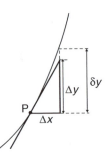

Figure 5.3 Small changes used in computing the slope of $y(x)$.

the change in the value of the function y due to Δx then, if the changes are small enough, δy is approximately equal to Δy. We write this symbolically as $\delta y \approx \Delta y$.

Now, dividing Δy by Δx and then multiplying by Δx leaves Δy unchanged. Thus we may write

$$\Delta y = \frac{\Delta y}{\Delta x} \Delta x \tag{5.1}$$

This apparently pointless manipulation is, in fact, rather useful, for the fraction on the the right hand side is just the slope. Further since $\delta y \approx \Delta y$ we can now write

$$\delta y \approx \text{slope} \times \Delta x \tag{5.2}$$

We now introduce a rather more compact and suggestive notation for the slope and write

$$\delta y \approx \frac{dy}{dx} \times \Delta x \tag{5.3}$$

We have already come across this kind of symbol used to denote the "rate of change" of a quantity. Informally, the ideas of "rate of change" and "slope" have a similar meaning since if a function is rapidly changing it has a large slope, while if it is slowly varying its slope is small. This equivalence in ordinary language is mirrored in the use of the same mathematical object to mean both things. It should once again be emphasized that dy/dx should be read as a *single* symbol – although its form should not now be so obscure since it stands for something that may be expressed as a ratio. The key point here is that there are techniques for calculating dy/dx, given the form of $y(x)$, so that we no longer have to resort to graphical methods. By way of terminology dy/dx is also known as the *differential* or *derivative* of y with respect to x.

Suppose we can evaluate the slope or derivative of y and put

$$\Delta x = -\alpha \frac{dy}{dx} \tag{5.4}$$

where $\alpha > 0$ and is small enough to ensure $\delta y \approx \Delta y$; then, substituting this in (5.3),

$$\delta y \approx -\alpha \left(\frac{dy}{dx} \right)^2 \tag{5.5}$$

Since taking the square of anything gives a positive value the $-\alpha$ term on the right hand side of (5.5) ensures that it is always negative and so $\delta y < 0$; that is, we have "travelled down" the curve towards the minimal point as required. If we keep repeating steps like (5.5) iteratively, then we should approach the value x_0 associated with the function minimum. This technique is called, not surprisingly, *gradient descent* and its effectiveness hinges, of course, on the ability to calculate, or make estimates of, the quantities like dy/dx.

We have only spoken so far of functions of one variable. If, however, y is a function of more than one variable, say $y = y(x_1, x_2, \ldots, x_n)$, it makes sense to talk about the slope of the function, or its rate of change, with respect to each of these variables independently. A simple example in 2D is provided by considering a valley in mountainous terrain in which the height above sea level is a function that depends on two map grid co-ordinates x_1 and x_2. If x_1, say, happens to be parallel to a contour line at some point then the slope in this direction is zero; by walking in this direction we just follow the side of the valley. However, the slope in the other direction (specified by x_2) may be quite steep as it points to the valley floor (or the top of the valley face). The slope or derivative of a function y with respect to the variable x_i is written $\partial y / \partial x_i$ and is known as the *partial derivative*. Just as for the ordinary derivatives like dy/dx, these should be read as a single symbolic entity standing for something like "slope of y when x_i alone is varied". The equivalent of (5.4) is then

$$\Delta x_i = -\alpha \frac{\partial y}{\partial x_i} \tag{5.6}$$

There is an equation like this for each variable and all of them must be used to ensure that $\delta y < 0$ and there is gradient descent. We now apply gradient descent to the minimization of a network error function.

5.2 Gradient descent on an error

Consider, for simplicity, a "network" consisting of a single TLU. We assume a supervised regime so that, for every input pattern p in the training set, there is a corresponding target t^p. The behaviour of the network is completely character-ized by the augmented weight vector $\mathbf{w}$, so that any function E, which expresses the discrepancy between desired and actual network output, may be considered a function of the weights, $E = E(w_1, w_2, \ldots, w_{n+1})$. The optimal weight vector is then found by minimizing this function by gradient descent as shown schemati-cally in Figure 5.4. By applying (5.6) in this case we obtain

$$\Delta w_i = -\alpha \frac{\partial E}{\partial w_i} \tag{5.7}$$

It remains now to define a suitable error E. One way to proceed is to assign equal importance to the error for each pattern so that, if e^p is the error for training pattern p, the total error E is just the average or mean over all patterns

$$E = \frac{1}{N} \sum_{p=1}^{N} e^p \tag{5.8}$$

where there are N patterns in the training set. Clearly, just as for E, any e^p will also be completely determined by the weights. As a first attempt to define e^p we might simply use the difference, $e^p = t^p - y^p$, where y^p is the TLU output in response to p. This definition falls within the general remit since y^p, and hence e^p, may be written as a function of the weights.

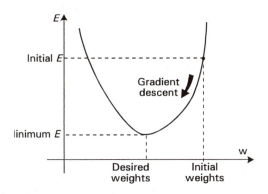

Figure 5.4 Gradient descent for a network.

The problem here, however, is that the error is then smaller for the combination $t^p = 0$, $y^p = 1$, than it is for $t^p = 1$, $y^p = 0$, whereas both are as "wrong" as each other. The way around this is to work with the purely positive quantity obtained by squaring the difference, so an improvement is

$$e^p = (t^p - y^p)^2 \qquad (5.9)$$

There remains, however, a more subtle problem. In applying gradient descent, it is assumed that the function to be minimized depends on its variables in a smooth, continuous fashion. In the present context, we require e^p to be a smooth function of the weights w_i. To see how e^p depends on the weights, it is necessary to substitute for the output y^p in terms of the weights and inputs. This occurs in two stages. First, the activation a^p is simply the weighted sum of inputs, which is certainly smooth and continuous. Secondly, however, the output depends on a^p via the discontinuous step function. This weak link in the chain of dependencies therefore prevents e^p, in its current form, from being a suitable candidate for gradient descent. One way to remedy the situation is simply to remove this part of the causal chain so that the error is defined with respect to the activation

$$e^p = (t^p - a^p)^2 \qquad (5.10)$$

We must be careful now how we define the targets. So far they have been referenced to the unit output, which is either 1 or 0. It is necessary, however, in using (5.10), to reference them to the activation. Recall that, when using the augmented weight vector, the output changes as the activation changes sign; $a \geq 0 \Rightarrow y = 1$. Therefore, as long as the activation takes on the correct sign, the target output is guaranteed and we are free to choose two arbitrary numbers, one positive and one negative, as the activation targets. It is often conventional, however, to use 1 and -1, which is the choice adopted here. One last finesse that is usually added to the expression for the error is a factor of $1/2$ and has to do with the simplification of the resulting slopes or derivatives. Thus our final form for e^p looks like

$$e^p = \frac{1}{2}(t^p - a^p)^2 \tag{5.11}$$

The full error E is then given by substituting this in (5.8).

5.3 The delta rule

Since E depends on all the patterns, the same can be said for its derivatives, so that the whole training set needs to be presented in order to evaluate the gradients $\partial E/\partial w_i$. This *batch training* results in true gradient descent but is rather computationally intensive. It can be avoided by adapting the weights based on the gradients found on presentation of each pattern individually. That is, we present the net with a pattern p, evaluate $\partial e^p/\partial w_i$ and use this as an *estimate* of the true gradient $\partial E/\partial w_i$. Using (5.11) and expressing a^p in terms of the weights w_i and inputs x_i^p, it can be shown that

$$\frac{\partial e^p}{\partial w_i} = -(t^p - a^p)x_i^p \tag{5.12}$$

where x_i^p is the ith component of pattern p. Although a proof of this will not be given here, it is possible to make this result plausible in the following way. First, the gradient must depend in some way on the discrepancy $(t^p - a^p)$; the larger this is, the larger we expect the gradient to be and, if this difference is zero, then the gradient should also be zero, since then we have found the minimum value of e_p and are at the bottom of the curve in the error function. Secondly, the gradient must depend on the input x_i^p for, if this is zero, then the ith input is making no contribution to the activation for the pth pattern and cannot affect the error – no matter how w_i changes it makes no difference to e_p. Conversely, if x_i^p is large then the ith input is correspondingly sensitive to the value of w_i.

Using the gradient estimate of (5.12) in (5.7) we obtain the new learning rule

$$\Delta w_i = \alpha(t^p - a^p)x_i^p \tag{5.13}$$

The resulting training now works in a so-called *pattern training* regime in which weight changes are made after each vector presentation. Because we are using *estimates* for the true gradient, the progress in the minimization of E is noisy so that weight changes are sometimes made which effect an increase in E. On average, however, the result is a systematic decrease in the error – a phenomenon that is explored further in Section 5.4.

Training based on (5.13) was first proposed by Widrow & Hoff (1960), who used it to train nodes called ADALINEs (ADAptive LINear Elements), which were identical to TLUs except that they used input and output signals of 1, −1 instead of 1, 0. The training rule in (5.13) was therefore originally known as the Widrow–Hoff rule. More recently it is more commonly known as the *delta rule* (or δ-rule) and the term $(t^p - a^p)$ is referred to as "the δ" (since this involves a difference). The original reference for the delta rule (Widrow & Hoff 1960) is a very brief summary by a third party reporting on a conference meeting and is largely of historical interest. More complete accounts are available in Widrow et al. (1987) and Widrow & Stearns (1985).

To see the significance of using the signal labels ± 1 (read "plus or minus 1") in ADALINEs, consider what happens when, in the normal Boolean representation, $x_i^p = 0$. Then, from (5.13), the change in the weight is zero. The use of -1 instead of 0 enforces a weight change, so that inputs like this influence the learning process on the same basis as those with value 1. This symmetric representation will crop up again in Chapter 7.

It can be shown (Widrow & Stearns 1985) that if the learning rate α is sufficiently small, then the delta rule leads to convergent solutions; that is, the weight vector approaches the vector $\mathbf{w}_0$ for which the error is a minimum, and E itself approaches a constant value. Of course, a solution will not exist if the problem is not linearly separable, in which case $\mathbf{w}_0$ is the best the TLU can do and some patterns will be incorrectly classified. This is one way in which the delta and perceptron rules differ. If a solution doesn't exist then, under the perceptron rule, the weights will continually be altered by significant amounts so that the weight vector oscillates. On the other hand, the delta rule always converges (with sufficiently small α) to some weight vector $\mathbf{w}_0$ at which the error is a minimum. Further, the perceptron rule engenders no change in the weights if the output and target agree and, if a solution exists, there will come a point when no more weight changes are made. The delta rule, however, will always make some change to the weights, no matter how small. This follows because the target activation values ± 1 will never be attained exactly, so that, even when correct classification has been achieved, the weights will continue to adapt, albeit at an ever decreasing rate. The training algorithm which uses the delta rule is similar, therefore, to that in Section 4.3 but now there is no option of "do nothing" and the stopping criterion is different.

> repeat
> > for each training vector pair $(\mathbf{v}, t)$
> > > evaluate the activation a when $\mathbf{v}$ is input to the TLU
> > > adjust each of the weights according to (5.13)
> > end for
> until the rate of change of the error is sufficiently small

The stopping criterion is not as well defined as it might be and often relies on experience with using the algorithm. More will be said about this in the next chapter.

An example of using the delta rule is provided by the worked simulation in Table 5.1. Its layout and interpretation are similar to those for the example with the perceptron rule (Table 4.1) except that no output needs to be computed

Table 5.1 Training with the delta rule on a two-input example.

w_1	w_2	θ	x_1	x_2	a	t	$\alpha\delta$	δw_1	δw_2	$\delta\theta$
0.00	0.40	0.30	0	0	-0.30	-1.00	-0.17	-0.00	-0.00	0.17
0.00	0.40	0.48	0	1	-0.08	-1.00	-0.23	-0.00	-0.23	0.23
0.00	0.17	0.71	1	0	-0.71	-1.00	-0.07	-0.07	-0.00	0.07
-0.07	0.17	0.78	1	1	-0.68	1.00	0.42	0.42	0.42	-0.42

here (since we are working with the activation directly) and the key column in determining weight changes is now labelled $\alpha\delta$. The problem is the same: train a two-input TLU with initial weights $(0, 0.4)$ and threshold 0.3, using a learn rate of 0.25.

Comparison of the delta rule (5.13) and the perceptron rule (4.6) shows that formally they look very similar. However, the latter uses the output for comparison with a target, while the delta rule uses the activation. They were also obtained from different theoretical starting points. The perceptron rule was derived by a consideration of hyperplane manipulation while the delta rule is given by gradient descent on the square error.

In deriving a suitable error measure e^p for the delta rule, our first attempt (5.9) used the TLU output y. This had to be abandoned, however, because of the discontinuous relation between y and the weights arising via the step-function output law. If this is replaced with a smooth squashing function, then it is possible to reinstate the output in the definition of the error so that for semilinear units we may use $e^p = 1/2(t^p - y^p)^2$. In this case there is an extra term in the delta rule that is the derivative of the sigmoid $d\sigma(a)/da$. It is convenient occasionally to denote derivatives by a dash or prime symbol so putting $d\sigma(a)/da = \sigma'(a)$ we obtain

$$\Delta w_i = \alpha\sigma'(a)(t^p - y^p)x_i^p \tag{5.14}$$

It is not surprising that the slope of the activation–output function (the sigmoid) crops up here. Any changes in the weights alter the output (and hence the error) via the activation. The effect of any such changes depends, therefore, on the sensitivity of the output with respect to the activation. To illustrate this, the sigmoid and its slope are shown in Figure 5.5. Suppose, first, that the activation is either very large or very small, so that the output is close to 1 or 0 respectively. Here, the graph of the sigmoid is quite flat or, in other words, its gradient $\sigma'(a)$ is very small. A small change Δa in the activation (induced by a weight change Δw_i) will result in a very small change Δy in the output, and a correspondingly small change Δe^p in the error. Suppose now that the activation is close to the threshold θ at which the sigmoid takes the value 0.5. Here, the function is changing most rapidly – its gradient is maximal. The same change Δa in the activation (induced by the same weight change) now results in a much larger change in the output Δy, and a correspondingly larger change in the error Δe^p. Thus the rate of change, or gradient, of the error with respect to any weight is governed by the slope of the sigmoid.

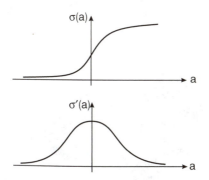

Figure 5.5 The sigmoid and its slope.

So far we have considered training a single node. In the case of a single-layer net with M nodes the error has to be summed over all nodes

$$e^p = \frac{1}{2}\sum_{j=1}^{M}(t_j^p - y_j^p)^2 \tag{5.15}$$

which is reasonable since each node is acting independently and there are no between-node interactions. In a similar way, the error gradient for the ith weight of the jth node only involves the error term $(t_j^p - y_j^p)$ for that node. Thus for semilinear nodes the learning rule is the same as that in (5.14), except for a unit or node index

$$\Delta w_{ji} = \alpha\sigma'(a_j)(t_j^p - y_j^p)x_{ji}^p \tag{5.16}$$

5.4 Watching the delta rule at work

Consider a TLU with a single input x so that it has two trainable parameters, a weight w and threshold θ, which are components of the augmented weight vector $\mathbf{w} = (w, \theta)$. Suppose the TLU is to learn simply to transmit its Boolean input so that there are two training patterns ($x = 0, a = -1$), ($x = 1, a = 1$). This example can be used to demonstrate some of the properties of gradient descent with the delta rule, in spite of its apparent triviality, because the error is a function of two variables, $E = E(w, \theta)$, and can be represented in a three-dimensional surface plot as shown in Figure 5.6. Thus, E is the height above a plane that contains two axes, one each for w and θ. Now let the weights undergo a series of adaptive changes and let $\mathbf{w}(n)$ be the weight vector after the nth update and $\mathbf{w}(0)$ the initial vector. Further, let $E(n)$ be the error after the nth update; then we may plot $E(n)$ as the height above the plane at the point $\mathbf{w}(n)$.

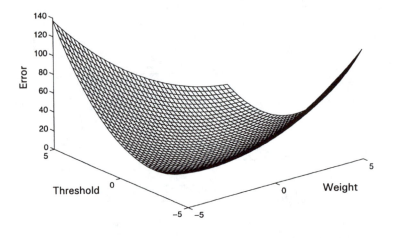

Figure 5.6 Error surface for example in 1D.

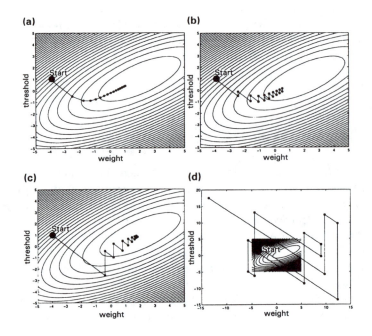

Figure 5.7 Training in the example in 1D.

Suppose we now perform a true gradient descent using batch training by evaluating the gradient of E over both training patterns. Starting with $\mathbf{w}(0) = (-4, 1)$ and using a learning rate α of 0.25, we obtain the series $E(n)$, $\mathbf{w}(n)$ shown by the dots in Figure 5.7a. The error surface has been shown as a contour map this time, but has the same profile as that in Figure 5.6. The larger dot indicates the location of $\mathbf{w}(0)$ and successive weight vectors are joined by line segments. There is a steady decrease in the error so that $E(n + 1) < E(n)$ for all n and the direction of descent is down the steepest trajectory, as indicated by the inter-weight lines being perpendicular to the contours. Notice that, as the surface becomes shallower, the size of the change in the weight vector becomes smaller since the surface gradient and $\Delta\mathbf{w}$ are directly related under gradient descent training.

Figure 5.7b shows the same TLU being trained with the same value of α but, this time, using sequential pattern update under the delta rule. The progress down the error slope is clearly more erratic since we are using an estimate, $\partial e_p / \partial w_i$, for the error gradient based on evidence provided by pattern p alone. In fact, there are as many steps taken "uphill" as there are down, although the mean direction is downwards.

Increasing the learning rate to 0.6 results in bigger steps being taken at each update (Fig. 5.7c) so that the error decreases, on average, more rapidly. Increasing α even further to 1.6 results, however, in an unstable situation (Fig. 5.7d) where the steps are so large that the weight vector roams erratically around the error landscape and there is no convergence towards the valley floor. The axes for w and θ have had to be rescaled to show all the updates (we have "zoomed out") and the region of the error surface shown in the previous diagrams has now receded into the distance.

5.5 Summary

This chapter introduced a powerful, general technique for supervised learning in neural networks. It is based on the concept of minimizing a network error E, defined in terms of the discrepancy between the desired target and network output. Since the network is completely defined by its weight set, the error may be written as a function of the weights and the problem couched in terms of attempting to "move downhill" over the error "surface" – considered as a function of the weights – until a minimum is reached. This movement requires knowledge of the gradient or slope of E and is therefore known as gradient descent. An examination of the local behaviour of the function under small changes showed explicitly how to make use of this information. The delta rule has superficial similarities with the perceptron rule but they are obtained from quite different starting points (vector manipulation versus gradient descent). Technical difficulties with the TLU required that the error be defined with respect to the node activation using suitably defined (positive and negative) targets.

Semilinear nodes allow a rule to be defined directly using the output but this has to incorporate information about the slope of the output squashing function. The learning rate must be kept within certain bounds if the network is to be stable under the delta rule.

Chapter Six

Multilayer nets and backpropagation

Recall that our goal is to train a two-layer net *in toto* without the awkwardness incurred by having to train the intermediate layer separately and hand craft the output layer. This approach also required prior knowledge about the way the training patterns fell in pattern space. A training rule was introduced – the *delta rule* – which, it was claimed, could be generalized from the single-unit/layer case to multilayer nets. Our approach is to try and understand the principles at work here, rather than simply use the brute force of the mathematics, and many of the fundamental ideas have already been introduced in the last chapter. A full derivation may be found, for example, in Haykin (1994). The training algorithm to be developed is called *backpropagation* because, as will be shown, it relies on signalling errors backwards (from output to input nodes) through the net.

6.1 Training rules for multilayer nets

A network that is typical of the kind we are trying to train is shown in Figure 6.1. It consists of a set of input distribution points (shown in black) and two layers of semilinear nodes shown as circles. The second, or output, layer signals the network's response to any input, and may have target vectors t_i applied to it in a supervised training regime. The other half, v_i, of the training patterns are applied to the inputs of an intermediate layer of *hidden* nodes, so called because we do not have direct access to their outputs for the purposes of training and they must develop their own representation of the input vectors.

The idea is still to perform a gradient descent on the error E considered as a function of the weights, but this time the weights for two layers of nodes have to be taken into account. The error for nets with semilinear nodes has already been established as the sum of pattern errors e_p defined via (5.15). Further, we assume the serial, pattern mode of training so that gradient estimates based on information available at the presentation of each pattern are used, rather than true gradients available only in batch mode. It is straightforward to calculate the error gradients for the output layer; we have direct access to the mismatch

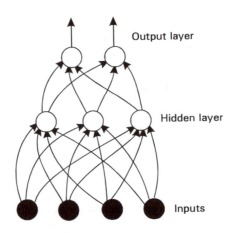

Figure 6.1 Two-layer net example.

between target and output and so they have the same form as those given in (5.16) for a single-layer net in the delta rule. This is repeated here for convenience:

$$\Delta w_{ji} = \alpha \sigma'(a_j)(t_j^p - y_j^p)x_{ji}^p \qquad (6.1)$$

where the unit index j is supposed to refer to one of the output layer nodes. The problem is now to determine the gradients $\partial e^p/\partial w_i k$ for nodes (index k) in the hidden layer. It is sometimes called the *credit assignment problem* since one way of thinking about this is to ask the question – how much "blame" or responsibility should be assigned to the hidden nodes in producing the error at the output? Clearly, if the hidden layer is feeding the output layer poor information then the output nodes can't sensibly aspire to match the targets.

Our approach is to examine (6.1) and see how this might generalize to a similar expression for a hidden node. The reasoning behind the appearance of each term in (6.1) was given in Section 5.3 and amounted to observing that the sensitivity of the error to any weight change is governed by these factors. Two of these, the input and sigmoid slope, are determined solely by the structure of the node and, since the hidden nodes are also semilinear, these terms will also appear in the expression for the hidden unit error-weight gradients. The remaining term, $(t^p - y^p)$, which has been designated the "δ", is specific to the output nodes and our task is therefore to find the hidden-node equivalent of this quantity.

It is now possible to write the hidden-node learning rule for the kth hidden unit as

$$\Delta w_{ki} = \alpha \sigma'(a_k)\delta^k x_{ki}^p \qquad (6.2)$$

where it remains to find the form of δ^k. The way to do this is to think in terms of the credit assignment problem. Consider the link between the kth hidden node and the jth output node as shown in Figure 6.2. The effect this node has on the error depends on two things: first, how much it can influence the output of

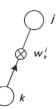

Figure 6.2 Single hidden-output link.

node j and, via this, how the output of node j affects the error. The more k can affect j, the greater the effect we expect there to be on the error. However, this will only be significant if j is having some effect on the error at its output. The contribution that node j makes towards the error is, of course, expressed in the "δ" for that node δ^j. The influence that k has on j is given by the weight w_{jk}. The required interaction between these two factors is captured by combining them multiplicatively as $\delta^j w_{jk}$. However, the kth node is almost certainly providing input to (and therefore influencing) many output nodes so that we must sum these products over all j giving the following expression for δ^k:

$$\delta^k = \sum_{j \in I_k} \delta^j w_{jk} \tag{6.3}$$

Here, I_k is the set of nodes that take an input from the hidden node k. For example, in a network that is fully connected (from layer to layer) I_k is the whole of the output layer. Using (6.3) in (6.2) now gives the desired training rule for calculating the weight changes for the hidden nodes since the δ^j refer to the output nodes and are known quantities.

The reader should be careful about the definition of the "δ" in the literature. We found it convenient to split off the slope of the sigmoid $\sigma'(a_k)$, but it is usually absorbed into the corresponding δ term. In this scheme then, for any node k (hidden or output) we may write

$$\Delta w_{ki} = \alpha \delta^k x_{ki}^p \tag{6.4}$$

where for output nodes

$$\delta_k = \sigma'(a_k)(t_k^p - y_k^p) \tag{6.5}$$

and for hidden nodes

$$\delta_k = \sigma'(a_k) \sum_{j \in I_k} \delta^j w_{jk} \tag{6.6}$$

In line with convention, this is the usage that will be adopted subsequently. It remains to develop a training algorithm around the rules we have developed.

6.2   The backpropagation algorithm

This basic algorithm loop structure is the same as for the perceptron rule or delta rule

> initialize weights
> repeat
> > for each training pattern
> > > train on that pattern
> > end for loop
> until the error is acceptably low

Algorithm outline

The first step is to initialize the weights to small random values. Criteria that help define "small" have been given by Lee et al. (1991) and essentially require that no training pattern causes any node to reach an output close to one of its extreme values (usually 0 or 1). If this does occur then the node is said to have reached *premature saturation* and may be considered to have been pretrained to some arbitrary value for that pattern. Such nodes may then have to undergo a process of *unlearning* before being retrained to give useful outputs.

One iteration of the for loop results in a single presentation of each pattern in the training set and is sometimes referred to as an *epoch*. What constitutes an "acceptably low" error is treated in Section 6.4 but for the moment we expand the main step of "train on that pattern" into the following steps.

1. Present the pattern at the input layer.

2. Let the hidden units evaluate their output using the pattern.

3. Let the output units evaluate their output using the result in step 2 from the hidden units.

4. Apply the target pattern to the output layer.

5. Calculate the δs on the output nodes.

6. Train each output node using gradient descent (6.4).

7. For each hidden node, calculate its δ according to (6.6).

8. For each hidden node, use the δ found in step 7 to train according to gradient descent (6.2).

The steps 1–3 are collectively known as the *forward pass* since information is flowing forward through the network in the natural sense of the nodes' input–output relation. Steps 4–8 are collectively known as the *backward pass*.

Step 7 involves *propagating* the δs *back* from the output nodes to the hidden units – hence the name *backpropagation*. The backpropagation (BP) algorithm is also known as *error backpropagation* or *back error propagation* or the *generalized delta rule*. The networks that get trained like this are sometimes known as *multilayer perceptrons* or MLPs.

6.3 Local versus global minima

In drawing the error–weight relation schematically in Figure 5.4 we made a simplification, which now needs to be addressed. A more realistic view is taken in Figure 6.3. The error is a more complex function of the weights and it is now possible to converge on one of several weight vectors. Suppose we start with a weight set for the network corresponding to point P. If we perform gradient descent, the minimum we encounter is the one at M_l, not that at M_g. Gradient descent is a local algorithm in that it makes use of information which is immediately available at the current weight vector. As far as the training process is concerned it cannot "know" of the existence of a smaller error at M_g and it simply proceeds downhill until it finds a place where the error gradient is zero. M_l is called a *local minimum* and corresponds to a partial solution for the network in response to the training data. M_g is the *global minimum* we seek and, unless measures are taken to escape from M_l, the global minimum will never be reached.

One way of avoiding getting stuck in local minima would be sometimes to allow uphill steps against the gradient. In this way, it might be possible to jump over intervening bumps between points like M_l and M_g. This is exactly what occurs in the pattern update regime in which we perform a noisy descent based on approximate gradient estimates (recall Fig. 5.7). This is therefore one advantage of the pattern update procedure over its batched counterpart. Noise

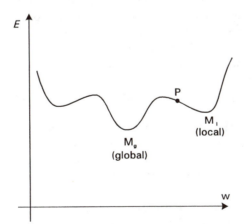

Figure 6.3 Local and global minima.

is also introduced when the learning rule is modified to include the so-called momentum term (Sect. 6.5), since this deviates from the exact requirements of gradient descent.

Another factor that can play a role here is the order of pattern presentation. In pattern update training during a single epoch it is possible to present vectors in a fixed sequence, or by selecting a random permutation of the pattern set each time; that is, all vectors are presented once and only once but their order is changed from epoch to epoch in a random way. If the latter option is chosen, there is a greater diversity of possible paths across the error–weight landscape and so this tends to favour escape from local minima.

6.4   The stopping criterion

In the algorithm outlined above, what constitutes an acceptably low error? One possible definition for Boolean training sets might be to accept any error for which all output nodes have responses to all patterns that are closest to the correct Boolean value, as defined by the target, since then, if we were to replace the sigmoid with a hard-limiting threshold, the correct Boolean response would be guaranteed.

Another definition might simply prescribe some very low value ϵ (Greek epsilon) for the mean pattern error $\langle e_p \rangle$[1]. This must be interpreted carefully for the following reason. Consider a net with N output nodes and M training patterns and suppose a single output node in response to a single training pattern is in error with the delta taking its maximum value of 1. We then say there is a single *bit-error* and $\langle e_p \rangle = 1/MN$. Clearly for large values of M and N this becomes insignificant and may easily satisfy the ϵ criterion, while for smaller nets and training sets it may not. However, it may be that we are interested in the number of such bit-errors and should decrease ϵ accordingly for the larger net. One problem with this approach is that it assumes the net can decrease its mean error below the given value of ϵ, which is not necessarily the case if the net does not have enough resources (nodes and connections) to approximate the required function to the desired degree. This might also occur if the net becomes trapped in a local minimum but, in any case, we would carry on training to no avail without ever stopping.

An alternative stopping criterion that is always valid is to halt when the rate of change of the error is sufficiently small. This is reasonable since, as an error minimum is approached (either local or global), the error surface becomes shallower and so the change in error at each epoch becomes ever smaller (see Fig. 5.7).

Finally, it is possible to base the termination of training on the network's ability to generalize, a topic discussed further in Section 6.10.1.

6.5 Speeding up learning: the momentum term

The speed of learning is governed by the learning rate α. If this is increased too much, learning becomes unstable; the net oscillates back and forth across the error minimum or may wander aimlessly around the error landscape. This was illustrated in Section 5.4 for a simple single-node case but the behaviour is quite typical of any gradient descent and so applies equally well to backpropagation. It is evident, however, that although a small learning rate will guarantee stability it is rather inefficient. If there is a large part of the error surface that runs consistently downhill then it should be possible to increase the learning rate here without danger of instability. On the other hand, if the net finds itself in a region where the error surface is rather "bumpy", with many undulations, then we must proceed carefully and make small weight changes.

One attempt to achieve this type of adaptive learning utilizes an additional term in the learning rule. Thus, if $\Delta w(n)$ is the nth change in weight w (indices have been dropped for clarity) then

$$\Delta w(n) = \alpha \delta^j(n)x(n) + \lambda \Delta w(n-1) \tag{6.7}$$

The *momentum term* $\lambda \Delta w(n-1)$ is just the *momentum constant* λ (Greek lambda) multiplied by the previous weight change. The momentum constant is greater than zero and, to ensure convergence, is also less than 1. By using this relation recursively it is possible to express $\Delta w(n)$ as a sum of gradient estimates evaluated at the current and previous training steps. Therefore, if these estimates are consistently of the same sign over a "run" of updates (we are on a large, uniform slope) then the weight change will grow larger as previous gradient estimates contribute cumulatively and consistently towards the current update. It is in this sense that the net "gathers momentum". However, if successive gradient estimates are of opposite sign (we are undulating up and down) then successive changes will tend to cancel each other and the latest update will be smaller than it would without any momentum term.

6.6 More complex nets

Although the net shown in Figure 6.1 is a typical multilayer perceptron net, it does not exhaust the kind of net we may train with backpropagation. First, it is possible to have more than one hidden layer as shown in Figure 6.4, which shows a net with two hidden layers. This is trained in exactly the same way with the δs of each layer (apart from the output nodes) being expressed in terms of those in the layer above. Thus, the δs for the first hidden layer are expressed in terms of those of the second hidden layer, which are, in turn, calculated using those of the output nodes. It is quite possible to have more than two hidden layers but the training time increases dramatically as the number of layers is increased and, as

71

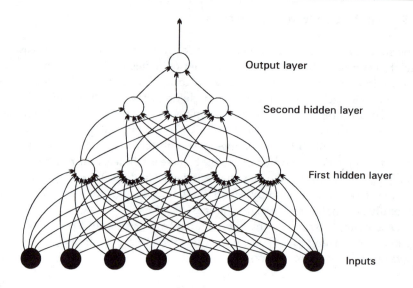

Figure 6.4 Network with two hidden layers.

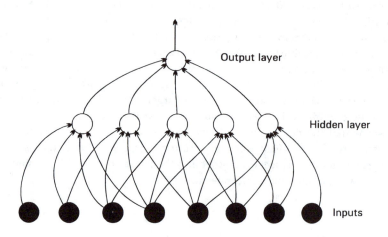

Figure 6.5 Network with non-full connectivity.

discussed in Section 6.7, there are good reasons to suppose we don't ever need more than three layers altogether.

All the nets exhibited so far have been fully connected layer to layer so that each node has inputs from all nodes in the previous layer. This is not necessarily the case and the speed of learning may be increased if we can restrict the connectivity in some way, as shown in Figure 6.5 in which each hidden node is connected to only four of the inputs. Connectivity may be restricted if we have prior knowledge of the problem domain as, for example, in the case of visual tasks. Here, points

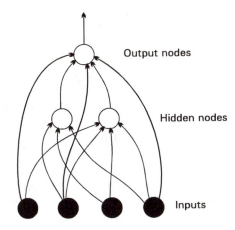

Figure 6.6 Non-layered network.

that are physically close to each other in the image are often highly correlated and so it makes sense to sample the image locally over small patches. This is just what is done in the animal visual system in which each neuron in the visual cortex is stimulated by a small part of the visual stimulus called the neuron's *receptive field* (Bruce & Green 1990).

Finally, we have assumed so far that the nets have a *layered* structure in which any path from input to output has to pass through the same number of nodes. Once again this is not necessary and a non-layered network is shown in Figure 6.6 in which the connections shown by heavier lines bypass the hidden nodes altogether. It is quite possible to train such nets using backpropagation but most networks tend to be of the layered type.

In spite of the variations just described, all the nets dealt with in this chapter have one thing in common: there are no signal paths that loop back on themselves. In other words, starting from an input, say, signals are processed by a finite series of nodes (some of which may be hidden) before contributing to a final output response, and there is no feedback loop from output to input. Such nets are therefore designated *feedforward* nets in contrast with *feedback* or *recurrent* nets, which allow signals to propagate around closed paths; more will be said about these in Chapter 7.

6.7 The action of well-trained nets

6.7.1 Operation in pattern space

The two-layer net that was partially hand crafted in Section 4.5.2 to solve the four-way classification problem can now be retrained *in toto* using backpropagation.

Further, the same problem may be recast to demonstrate the power of our new algorithm to classify a nonlinearly separable pattern space. Thus, consider the situation in pattern space shown on the left in Figure 6.7. The two classes A and B cannot be separated by a single hyperplane. In general we require an arbitrarily shaped *decision surface* and, in this case, it may be approximated by two plane segments. Extending these segments, it can be seen that the situation is similar to that in Figure 4.8 except the labelling of the patterns is different. The network solution, therefore, again consists of two hidden nodes h_1, h_2 (one for each plane) but this time with a single output node that will signal "1" for class A and "0" for class B. Of course, the output node can never actually supply these values, but we assume that the weights are sufficiently large that the sigmoid can operate close to its extremes. The hidden nodes are also assumed to operate close to saturation. The required output node function y is indicated on the right of the figure. Since it has two inputs its pattern space may be represented in 2D and, assuming for simplicity perfect Boolean hidden outputs, its inputs will be the corners of the square. All inputs induce a "1" except for that at the corner $(0,0)$ and so it is linearly separable.

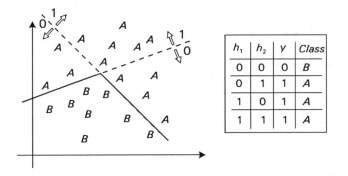

h_1	h_2	y	Class
0	0	0	B
0	1	1	A
1	0	1	A
1	1	1	A

Figure 6.7 Two classes nonlinearly separable.

Using more hidden nodes it is possible to generate more complex regions in pattern space and, in order to discuss this more fully, it is useful to invoke a couple of new concepts. A region R in pattern space is said to be *connected* if, for any two points P_1, P_2 there exists a path connecting P_1, P_2 that lies wholly within R. Informally, R consists of a single unbroken area, as shown at the top of Figure 6.8. The areas of pattern space dealt with so far have all been connected. A connected region of pattern space R is said to be *convex* if, for all pairs of points P_1, P_2 in R, the straight line between P_1 and P_2 lies wholly within R, as shown in the lower half of Figure 6.8. This is the formalization of the requirement that, in 2D, there are no indentations in R.

Now consider a net with a single output node that signals whether we are in some region R of pattern space or in the remainder (or *complement*) $\bar{R}$, where it is assumed that R is the smaller of the two. The situation in Figure 6.7 is typical

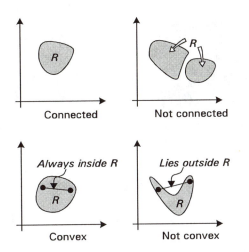

Figure 6.8 Connectedness and convexity.

and represents a case of a convex, connected R, with R being the part of the space containing class B. In this example, R extends infinitely in pattern space – schematically it is unbounded in the bottom half of the diagram. Using a third hidden node, however, it would be possible to implement the problem shown in Figure 6.9 in which R is still convex and connected, but is now finite. We may continue adding sides to the region's circumference in this way by adding more hidden nodes. How far, then, can we proceed in this way using a single hidden layer? Lippmann (1987) states that, with this type of network, R is necessarily connected and convex. However, Wieland & Leighton (1987) have demonstrated the ability of a single hidden layer to allow a non-convex decision region and Makhoul et al. (1989) extended this result to disconnected regions. In general, therefore, any region R may be picked out using a single hidden layer.

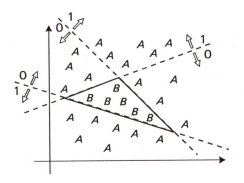

Figure 6.9 Finite region in pattern space.

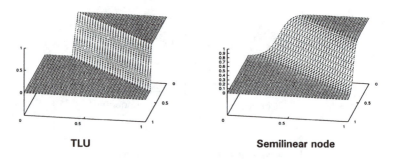

Figure 6.10 TLU versus semilinear boundaries.

Notice that the existence of regions with perfectly sharp boundaries presupposes a threshold function instead of a sigmoid at the output. This is not the case with semilinear nodes and so the sharp boundaries become blurred. These two cases are illustrated in Figure 6.10, which shows surface plots in pattern space of the output for a TLU and semilinear node. Both units have weight vector (1/2, 1/2) and threshold 3/4 so that the TLU case is the same as that in Figure 4.1 and shows the sharp decision line between the "0" and "1" regions. The semilinear node, however, has a smooth sigmoidal rise across the decision line which now constitutes a contour at a height of 0.5.

6.7.2 Networks and function fitting

Up till now our analysis of the way networks operate has been exclusively in the geometric context of pattern space. An alternative explanation may be offered that has its basis in thinking of the net as implementing a mathematical function of its inputs, and is especially pertinent if we are dealing with continuous input and output signals (not restricted to the Boolean values 0, 1). For example, if we wanted to make a forecast p_n of a stock value based on k previous values of the price $p_{n-1}, p_{n-2}, \ldots, p_{n-k}$, we would want to train a net to discover the functional relation (if any) between these quantities; that is, to discover the underlying function $p_n = p_n(p_{n-1}, p_{n-2}, \ldots, p_{n-k})$.

This way of thinking may be illustrated with the following simple example whose network is shown in Figure 6.11.

There is a single input x and two hidden nodes h_1, h_2 with weights and thresholds $w_1 = 1$, $\theta_1 = 2$, $w_2 = 1$, $\theta_2 = -2$, respectively. These provide input for a single output node with weights 5, −5 and threshold 2. The way this network functions is shown in Figure 6.12. The horizontal axis is the input and the vertical axis the output of the network nodes. Curve 1 shows the output y_1 of h_1, and curve 2 the *negative* output $-y_2$ of h_2. The activation a of the output node is $5(y_1 - y_2)$, which is just a scaled copy of the sum of the two quantities represented by these two curves. The sigmoid of the output node will work to compress the activation into the interval $(0, 1)$ but its output y (curve 3) will have the same basic shape as a.

Notice first that, for very large positive and negative values of x, the activation a is almost constant and equal to zero, which means that y will also be approximately constant. At first, as x increases from large negative values, the output y_1 of the first hidden node increases while y_2 remains close to zero. Thus, a (and hence y) for the output node also increase. As x increases still further, however, h_2 starts to come into play and it makes its negative contribution to a. This starts to make a decrease and eventually, when y_1 and y_2 are almost equal, effectively cancels out the input from h_1 making a almost zero.

Moving the thresholds θ_1, θ_2 apart would make the output "hump" wider, while increasing the weights of the output node makes it more pronounced. Also, making these weights differ in magnitude would allow the levels either side of

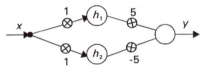

Figure 6.11 Simple network to illustrate function fitting in 1D.

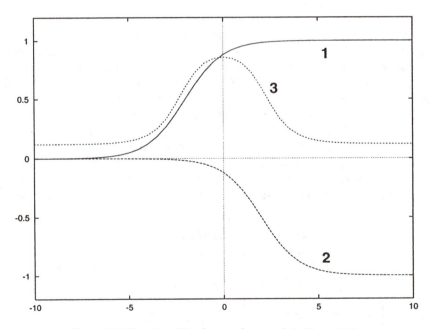

Figure 6.12 Functionality of network example in Figure 6.11.

the hump to be different. We may think of the network's output y as a function of the input x (we write $y = y(x)$) and, by suitable choice of the net parameters, implement any one of a wide range of "single-humped" or *unimodal* functions. Introducing another hidden node h_3 would enable the appearance of a second hump and so on for further nodes h_4, h_5 .... In this way it is possible to train networks to solve problems with intricate functional relationships $y = y(x)$.

In most cases, of course, the net will have many inputs x_1, x_2, ..., x_n and outputs y_1, y_2, ..., y_m, in which case·it may be thought of as implementing m functions of the form $y_j = y_j(x_1, x_2, \ldots, x_n)$. For $n = 2$ we may represent these relations graphically as surface plots but their exact visualization becomes impossible for $n > 3$. The best we can hope to do is hold all but two (p and q, say) of the inputs constant and explore the variation of y_j as a function of x_p, x_q.

Just as, in the geometric setting, it is important to know how complex the decision surface may be for a given number of hidden layers, it is pertinent to ask in the functional context what class of functions may be implemented in each such case. This time it can be shown (Funahashi 1989, Hornik et al. 1989) that, using a single hidden layer, it is possible to approximate any continuous function as closely as we please. This is consistent with the discussion of pattern space analysis in which it was noted that a single hidden layer is sufficient to encode arbitrary decision surfaces.

6.7.3   Hidden nodes as feature extractors

Consider the four 11-input, single-output training patterns shown in Table 6.1. What are the "features" in this training set? At first, we might say that vector components like x_3 and x_6 through to x_9 are features since these components always take the value "1". However, a more meaningful interpretation would be that these are really just "background" components since their value doesn't change and they tell us nothing about the classification of each vector. Better candidates for features are components like x_1 or x_{11} in which each value (0 or 1) is correlated with the output (y) in some way. In the case of x_1, for example, $y = x_1$ always, so that input x_1 is a very informative feature which completely determines the output. Thus a "feature" in this context is a subset of the input space that helps us to discriminate the patterns by its examination

Table 6.1 Vectors for feature detection.

x_1	x_2	x_3	x_4	x_5	x_6	x_7	x_8	x_9	x_{10}	x_{11}	y
1	1	1	1	1	1	1	1	1	0	0	1
1	1	1	0	0	1	1	1	1	0	0	1
0	0	1	1	1	1	1	1	1	1	1	0
0	0	1	1	0	1	1	1	1	1	1	0

without recourse to the entire pattern. This, of itself, is important but there is a further significance in that we can think of features as containing the essential information content in the pattern set. Of course, in more complex problems, we may need to combine evidence from several features to be sure about a given pattern classification.

If the vectors in this example were used to train a single semilinear node then we would expect a large positive weight to develop on input 1 so that it becomes influential in forcing the activation to positive values. On the other hand x_{11}, although correlated with the output, takes on an opposing value. This is captured by developing a negative weight on input 11 since then, when $x_{11} = 1$, it will force the output to be zero.

Is it possible to formalize these ideas mathematically? Suppose we replace each "0" in Table 6.1 with "-1" to give new components $\bar{x}_i$ and output $\bar{y}$. Now, for each pattern p and each component $\bar{x}_i^p$, form $\bar{x}_i^p \bar{y}^p$. This gives some measure of the input–output correlation since, if the input and the output are the same, the expression is $+1$; if they are different it is -1. Notice that this property is lost if we use the original Boolean notation (0 instead of -1), for then the product is zero if either of x_i or y is zero, irrespective whether the two are equal or not. Now consider the mean correlation c_i on the ith component

$$c_i = \frac{1}{4} \sum_p \bar{x}_i^p \bar{y}^p \tag{6.8}$$

For a feature like x_1 this evaluates to $+1$. For a background component, however, it is 0 since there are as many input–output similarities ($+1$s) as there are differences (-1s). For components like x_{11} that anti-correlate with the output, $c_{11} = -1$. This, then, seems to mesh quite nicely with our informal idea of what constitutes a feature.

In Figure 6.13 the correlation coefficients c_i are plotted against i and are shown by the lines terminated with small square symbols. Also plotted are the weights that evolve as a result of training a single semilinear node on the patterns using the delta rule. There is a very close match between the weights and the coefficients (or features) so that, in this sense, the node has learnt to detect the features in the training set.

Of particular interest is x_4, which, for three of the patterns, takes on the opposite value to the output, but for one is the same. This then is an anti-correlated feature but not of the same strength as x_{11}.

6.8 Taking stock

To summarize the power of the tools that have now been developed: we can train a multilayer net to perform categorization of an arbitrary number of classes and with an arbitrary decision surface. All that is required is that we have a set of inputs and targets, that we fix the number of hyperplanes (hidden units)

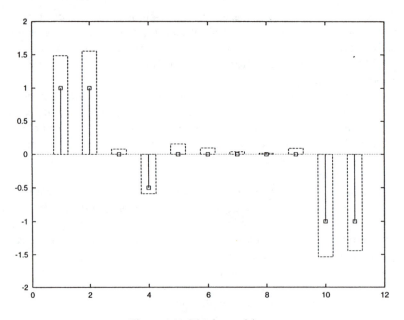

Figure 6.13 Weights and features.

that are going to be used, and that we perform gradient descent on the error with the backpropagation algorithm. There are (as always), however, subtleties that emerge which make life difficult. One of these concerned the presence of local minima but we hope that, by using noisy, pattern–serial training and/or momentum these may be avoided. Another, more serious problem concerns the number of hidden units used and can result in inadequate *training set generalization*. If this occurs then we have lost most of the benefit of the connectionist approach.

6.9 Generalization and overtraining

Consider the dichotomy in pattern space shown schematically in Figure 6.14. The training patterns are shown by circular symbols and the two classes distinguished by open and filled symbols. In the right hand diagram, there are two line segments indicating two hyperplane fragments in the decision surface, accomplished using two hidden units. Two members of the training set have been misclassified and it may appear at first sight that this net has performed poorly since there will be some residual error. However, suppose that some previously unseen *test patterns* are presented, as shown by the square symbols. The colouring scheme corresponds to that used for the training set so that filled and open squares are from the same classes as filled and open circles respectively. These have been

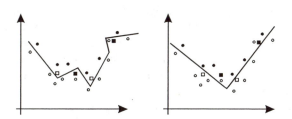

Figure 6.14 Generalization and overtraining in pattern space.

classified correctly and the net is said to have *generalized* from the training data. This would seem to vindicate the choice of a two-segment hyperplane for the decision surface since it may be that the two misclassified training patterns result from noisy data or outliers. In this case the net has implemented a good *model* of the data, which captures the essential characteristics of the data in pattern space.

Consider now the left hand diagram in which there are six line segments associated with the use of six hidden units. The training set is identical to that used in the previous example and each one has been successfully classified, resulting in a significantly smaller error. However, all four test patterns have been incorrectly classified so that, even though the training data are all dealt with correctly, there may be many examples, especially those close to the decision boundary from each class (see below), that are misclassified. The problem here is that the net has too much freedom to choose its decision surface and has *overfitted* it to accommodate all the noise and intricacies in the data without regard to the underlying trends.

It is suggested in these diagrams that there is some sense in which input vectors are "close" to one another so that, for example, the two training patterns that fail to get classified correctly using two hidden units are still, nevertheless, close to the decision surface. The geometric approach associated with the use of pattern space does indeed imply some measure of distance $d(\mathbf{u}, \mathbf{v})$, between two vectors $\mathbf{u}, \mathbf{v}$. We might, for instance, use the length of the vector difference $\mathbf{u} - \mathbf{v}$ with the length defined via (3.6) giving

$$d = \left[\sum_{i=1}^{n} (u_i - v_i)^2 \right]^{\frac{1}{2}} \tag{6.9}$$

Of special interest is the case when the patterns are Boolean so that u_i, v_i are all 0 or 1. Then, if we omit the square root we obtain a measure known as the Hamming distance h

$$h = \sum_{i=1}^{n} (u_i - v_i)^2 \tag{6.10}$$

Since $(u_i - v_i) = \pm 1$ or 0 the square term may be replaced with the absolute value of the difference

$$h = \sum_{i=1}^{n} |u_i - v_i| \tag{6.11}$$

which is just the number of places where the two vectors differ. For example $(1, 1, 0, 0)$ and $(1, 0, 1, 0)$ are Hamming distance 2 apart because they differ in the second and third places. For Boolean vectors, the network is therefore performing Hamming distance generalization so that, unless we are very close to the decision surface, vectors that are close to each other tend to be given the same classification.

It is possible to describe generalization from the viewpoint adopted in Section 6.7.2, which dealt with nets as function approximators. Figure 6.15 shows two examples of the output y of a net as a function of its input x. This is only a schematic representation since both y and x may be multidimensional. The circles and squares are supposed to represent training and test data respectively, while the curves show the functions implemented by each network. On the right hand side is a network function that is comparatively simple and may be realized with few hidden units (recall that adding units allows more undulations or "bumps" in the function's graph). It does not pass exactly through the training data and so there will be some residual error. However, it appears to have captured quite well the underlying function from which the training data were sampled since the test data are reasonably close to the curve; the net has generalized well.

On the other hand, the left hand figure shows the function realized by a network with more hidden units giving rise to a correspondingly more complex function. The training data are the same as those used in the previous example but, this time, the net has learned these patterns with almost no error. However, the test data (squares) are poorly represented because the net has been given too much freedom to fit a function to the training set. In trying to obtain an ever increasingly accurate fit, the net has introduced spurious variations in the function that have nothing to do with the underlying input–output relation from which the data were sampled. This is clearly analogous to the situation in pattern space shown in Figure 6.14.

One of the questions that remained unanswered at the end of our development of the backpropagation algorithm was how to determine the number of hidden units to use. At first, this might not have seemed a problem since it appears that we can always use more hidden units than are strictly necessary; there would simply be redundancy with more than one hidden node per hyperplane. This is the "more of a good thing is better" approach. Unfortunately, as we have discovered here,

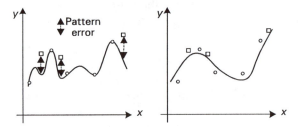

Figure 6.15 Generalization and overtraining in the context of function approximation.

things aren't so easy. Too many hidden nodes can make our net a very good lookup table for the training set at the expense of any useful generalization. In the next section, techniques are described that attempt to overcome this problem. It turns out that it is not always necessary to determine an optimum number of hidden nodes and that it is possible to limit the eventual freedom allowed for the net to establish a decision surface in other ways.

6.10 Fostering generalization

6.10.1 Using validation sets

Consider again networks with too many hidden units like those associated with the left hand side of Figures 6.14 and 6.15. The diagrams show the decision surface and function respectively after exhaustive training, but what form do these take in the early stages of learning? It is reasonable to suppose that the smoother forms (indicated on the right hand side of the respective figures) or something like them may be developed as intermediates at this time. If we then curtail the training at a suitable stage it may be possible to "freeze" the net in a form suitable for generalization.

A striking graphical demonstration that this is indeed what happens in pattern space was provided by Rosin & Fierens (1995). They trained a net on two classes in a pattern space in 2D (to allow easy visualization), each of which consisted of a circularly symmetric cluster of dots in the plane. The two classes overlapped and so the error-free decision boundary for the training set was highly convoluted. However, in terms of the underlying statistical distributions from which the training set was drawn they should be thought of as being separated optimally by a straight line. On training, a straight line did emerge at first as the decision boundary but, later, this became highly convoluted and was not a useful reflection of the true situation.

How, then, are we to know when to stop training the net? One approach is to divide the available training data into two sets: one training set proper T, and one so-called *validation set* V. The idea is to train the net in the normal way with T but, every so often, to determine the error with respect to the validation set V. This process is referred to as *cross-validation* and a typical network behaviour is shown in Figure 6.16. One criterion for stopping training, therefore, is to do so when the validation error reaches a minimum, for then generalization with respect to the unseen patterns of V is optimal. Cross-validation is a technique borrowed from regression analysis in statistics and has a long history (Stone 1974). That such a technique should find its way into the "toolkit" of supervised training in feedforward neural networks should not be surprising because of the similarities between the two fields. Thus, feedforward nets are performing a smooth function fit to some data, a process that can be thought of as a kind of

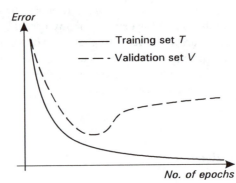

Figure 6.16 Cross-validation behaviour.

nonlinear regression. These similarities are explored further in the review article by Cheng & Titterington (1994).

6.10.2 Adequate training set size

If, in Figures 6.14 and 6.15, the test data had originally been part of the training set, then they would have forced the network to classify them properly. The problem in the original nets is that they were *underconstrained* by the training data. In particular, if there are too few patterns near the decision surface then this may be allowed to acquire spurious convolutions. If, however, pattern space is filled to a sufficient density with training data, there will be no regions of "indecision" so that, given a sufficiently large training set of size N, generalization can be guaranteed. Such a result has been established for single output nets by Baum & Haussler (1989), who showed that the required value of N increased with the number of weights W, the number of hidden units H and the fraction f of correctly classified training patterns; in this sense W and H are the network "degrees of freedom". The only problem here is that, although this result provides theoretical lower bounds on the size of N, it is often unrealistic to use sets of this size. For example, for a single output net with ten hidden units, each of 30 weights, and with $f = 0.01$ (1 per cent misclassified in the training set) N is more than 10.2 million; increasing f to 0.1 reduces this to 0.8 million but, either way, these are usually not realizable in practice. Baum and Haussler's result has subsequently been extended and sharpened for a special class of nets with internal symmetries by Shawe-Taylor (1992).

6.10.3   Net pruning

The last section introduced the idea that poor generalization may result from a large network being underconstrained by the training set. The other side of this coin is that there are too many internal parameters (weights) to model the data that are supplied. The number of weights is, of course, partly determined by the number of hidden units and we set out by showing that this must be kept to a minimum for good generalization. However, rather than eliminate complete units, it may be possible to place constraints on the weights across the network as a whole so that some of the network's freedom of configuration is removed. One way to achieve this is to extend the network error function to incorporate a term that takes on small values for simple nets and large values for more complex ones. The utility of this hinges, of course, on what we mean by "complex" and one definition is that nets with many weights close to zero should be favoured in contrast to those with weights that all take significant numerical values. It transpires that there is a very simple way of enforcing this (Hinton 1987). Thus, define

$$E_c = \sum_i w_i \qquad (6.12)$$

where the sum is over all weights in the net, and let E_t be the error used so far based on input–output differences (5.15). Now put $E = E_t + \lambda E_c$ and perform gradient descent on this total *risk E*. The new term E_c is a *complexity penalty* and will favour nets whose weights are all close to zero. However, the original *performance measure E_t* also has to be small, which is favoured by nets with significantly large weights that enable the training set to be correctly classified. The value of λ determines the relative importance attached to the complexity penalty. With $\lambda = 0$ we obtain the original backpropagation algorithm while very large values of λ may force the net to ignore the training data and simply assume small weights throughout. With the right choice of λ the result is a compromise; those weights that are important for the correct functioning of the net are allowed to grow, while those that are not important decay to zero, which is exactly what is required. In effect, each very small weight is contributing nothing and represents a non-connection; it has been "pruned" from the network. In this way connections that simply fine-tune the net – possibly to outliers and noise in the data – are removed, leaving those that are essential to model the underlying data trends.

Many variations have been tried for the form of E_c, and other heuristics, not based on a cost function like E_c, have been used to prune networks for better generalization; see Reed (1993) for a review.

6.10.4 Constructing topologies

So far it has been assumed that the network topology (the number of layers and number of nodes in each layer) is fixed. Our initial analysis, however, showed that the obvious thing to try is to determine a suitable number of hidden nodes. This may be done in one of two ways. We can try to determine an optimum topology at the outset and then proceed to train using backpropagation, or alter the topology dynamically in conjunction with the normal gradient descent. Either way, the resulting algorithms tend to be fairly complex and so we only give the barest outline of two examples, one for each approach.

Weymare & Martens (1994) provide an example of the topology initialization technique in which the data are first sent through a conventional clustering algorithm to help determine candidate hyperplanes, and hence hidden units. These candidate units are then used in a network construction algorithm to estimate the optimal topology. Finally the net is fine tuned with a limited number of backpropagation epochs. This algorithm is perhaps best considered as a hybrid technique in which the hidden units are trained in part via the initial data clustering, as well as the normal gradient descent.

In the method of Nabhan & Zomaya (1994) nodes are dynamically added or subtracted from a network that is concurrently undergoing training using backpropagation. Their algorithm is based on the hypothesis that nets which model the data well will train in such a way that the root mean square (rms) value of the weight changes ($[\sum_i \Delta w_i^2]^2$) decreases from epoch to epoch. If this fails to take place then structural changes are made to the network by selecting what they call "promising" structures – nets that start to decrease their rms weight change.

Other constructive algorithms, such as the cascade–correlation procedure (Fahlman & Lebiere 1990), make use of cost-function optimization but do not use gradient descent *per se* and are therefore only distantly related to backpropagation.

6.11 Applications

It is not the intention here to give an exhaustive list of the areas in which multilayer perceptrons have found application; any problem that can be framed as one of classification or prediction is a candidate for treatment in this way. Rather, it is more instructive to take a couple of case studies that highlight some of the aspects of implementing a problem using an MLP.

6.11.1   Psychiatric patient length of stay

Our first example (Davis et al. 1993) is taken from the area of medical diagnosis with a network that predicts the length of stay of psychiatric patients in hospital based on demographic, social and clinical information recorded at their time of admission. This is an important problem since patient admission may be contingent on financial resources, which will be better allocated if probable length of stay is known in advance.

In contrast to the previous net, which had only three continuously variable inputs, this one uses many tri-valued inputs (0, 0.5, 1) representing two-valued categorical data with the value 0.5 reserved for missing data. For example, the rating for social impairment is usually given on a nine-point scale from 0 (none) to 8 (severe) but was collapsed into two values – 0 for "low" and 1 for "high". If this was not assessed for some reason then it is set to 0.5. The net had 49 inputs, 500 hidden units and four outputs to represent the four categories of length of stay T: (I) $T \leq 7$ days, (II) $T > 7$ days but ≤ 30 days, (III) $T > 30$ days but ≤ 6 months, (IV) $T > 6$ months but ≤ 1 year.

The data for the training set were gathered over a 3.5 year period with a view to controlling for factors such as health policy changes, economic factors and resource availability. The main point to emerge here is that the network modeller should be aware of any underlying assumptions concerning the variability of the data. The training patterns included information about age, sex, population of town of residence, previous admission history, family support systems, severity of illness, length of stay in the community, and clinical psychiatric metrics formalized in a standard psychiatric reference (*Diagnostic and statistical manual*, 3rd edn). As noted above, all these quantities have been reduced to one of two values (or 0.5 if the data were missing). The authors also tried using analogue values but found that the performance was not as good. In binarizing the data, information is discarded and there are two possible outcomes. Either important information that can be used by the net is thrown away, or irrelevant variation (noise) that would present the net with a much harder problem to solve is avoided. It appears, on the whole, that in this case the latter situation prevailed. One way in which noise can enter the clinical data is in the reliability of assessment; thus two doctors may assign different values to diagnostic parameters since these are established by subjective (albeit expert) judgement on rating scales.

One of the problems to be overcome in using MLPs lies in interpreting the output. Assuming that each class is encoded by a single node, it is clear what category is being indicated if one of the output units has a value close to 1 while the others have small values. However, it is not so clear what to do if two or more outputs are very close to each other. There are theoretical grounds (Haykin 1994: 164–5) for supposing that, no matter how small the difference between output values, we should adopt the class indicated by the maximal output. In interpreting their network output, Davis et al. used this technique for reporting one set of results. Another set, however, were based on what they called "extended tolerance" in which, if all outputs were below 0.2, they deemed that the network was unable to make a firm categorical estimate for T. It was then assumed that the net was unable to distinguish between classes I and II, and between III and IV, so that the only classification possible is "short stay" ($T \leq 30$ days) or "long stay" ($T > 6$ months). This is still useful since 30 days is a common dividing point in hospital reimbursement schemes.

In all, 958 patient records were used for training and 106 for testing. The net predicted the length of stay correctly in 47 per cent of cases in the test set, which grew to 60 per cent on using the extended tolerance criterion. A second, larger test of 140 patients was then taken and used to compare the net's performance with that of a multidisciplinary team of clinicians and mental health experts. The network scored 46 per cent on exact classification and 74 per cent under extended tolerance. The treatment team attempted a classification of only 85 patients out of this group but, of those classified, they scored 54 per cent and 76 per cent for exact and extended tolerance respectively. It is not clear whether the other cases were not attempted owing to uncertainty or lack of time. If the former, then the net is performing better than the team; if the latter, it is showing comparable performance. It should be emphasized that the clinical team had access to the patients over a 72 hour period and spent a significant amount of time with them before making their assessments.

6.11.2 Stock market forecasting

The next example is taken from the work by Refenes et al. (1994) on predicting the performance of stock returns in the capital markets. Although their work is introduced in the context of other models of stock returns, we shall focus here only on the core of the problem as presented to the network in order to draw out the network-dependent issues. Thus, Refenes et al. seek to predict the so-called "outperformance" Y of each stock as a function of three parameters A, B and C, which are extracted from the balance sheets of the companies that contribute to the portfolio of stocks. The authors do not give details of what these factors are – they presumably constitute commercially sensitive data – and, in any case, their exact nature is not critical for understanding the network problem. The outperformance is a measure of relative success of the stock 6 months after the data for the input factors A, B and C are gathered so that the value of Y for January, say, refers to something measured in June of the same year. Therefore, the net is effectively being trained to predict the stock 6 months into the future, given current information about factors that are believed to determine its behaviour. This is in contrast with the previous example in which it was explicitly assumed that there is no temporal variation in the data, or that we are supposed to ignore any such change. The dataset was obtained from 143 stocks, each one having an input triplet and outperformance assigned every month. Training was done using 6 months' data and so used $143 \times 6 = 858$ vectors.

One of the questions addressed concerned the optimal topology. They found that better results on the training set and generalization on test data[2] were obtained using two layers of hidden units. To help describe network topologies, let $(I\text{-}H_1\text{-}H_2\text{-}V)$ denote a three-layer net with I, H_1, H_2, V units in the input, first hidden, second hidden and output layers respectively; for this problem $I = 3$, $V = 1$. The best performance was obtained with a net of structural type (3–32–16–1), with similar results provided by nets of type (3–26–13–1) and (3–24–12–1). Two-layer nets gave errors on the training and test data that were typically about twice as great. They conclude that the net shows stability with respect to the number of nodes in each layer, with the number of layers being the most important factor. Further, the performance with the training data was significantly better than that obtained with a multivariate linear regression (MLR) model currently in use.

The three-layer nets took typically 25 000 epochs to train while the single-layer nets converged after about 5000 epochs. It is not surprising that it should take longer to train three- rather than two-layer nets, but what is not clear is why they should perform better on this problem. Now, the inputs and output are continuous variables rather than Boolean valued. Thus, there may be a complex, nonlinear relation between Y and each of A, B and C, so that the net has to "track" relatively small variations in each input. We therefore speculate that the first hidden layer acts to recode the three-dimensional input in a higher dimensional (H_1-D) space in which these differences are amplified in some way. The units in the second hidden layer may then act on the recoded input in the normal way as some kind of feature detectors. There is a theorem due to Cover (1965) that provides some theoretical support for this idea. The theorem states that a complex classification problem recast in a higher dimensional space via a nonlinear transform is more likely to be linearly separable. Although the stock prediction net is not performing classification as such, we could repose it in this way by dividing the outperformance Y into "low" and "high" values and merely asking for a decision into these course categories. These two problems, although not equivalent, are obviously closely related.

In assessing the net's ability to generalize, it is necessary to test using data from a different timeframe, since each stock has only a single input vector for each month. Thus, testing took place using a subsequent 6 month period from that used in training. Two conclusions were drawn. First, the mean error on the test data was about one-half that obtained with the MLR model. Secondly, the error increased slowly from month to month in the 6 month period whereas the MLR model showed no temporal variation. That there may be some variation is to be expected since the environment in which stock prices vary changes over time according to government economic policy, general market confidence, etc. However, it is not clear over what time period we should expect such variations and this is formalized in a hypothesis of the so-called DynIM[3] model, which posits a slow change characterized by 6 month periods of relative stability. The net performance is consistent with this hypothesis, being subject to slow temporal change, and is therefore superior to the MLR model, which is insensitive to time.

One of the criticisms sometimes levelled at neural nets is that, although they may generate good models of the data, it is difficult to then analyze the structure of the resulting model or to discover the relative importance of the inputs. Refenes et al. tackled the second of these by a *sensitivity analysis*. By holding two of the inputs constant, it is possible to plot the output against the remaining variable. This was done for each variable while holding the other two at their mean values and it was apparent that, while there was a complex, nonlinear relation between Y and the inputs A and B, the output was less sensitive to C, with Y remaining fairly low over much of its range and only increasing when C took on large values.

6.12   Final remarks

Backpropagation is probably the most well-researched training algorithm in neural nets and forms the starting point for most people looking for a network-based solution to a problem. One of its drawbacks is that it often takes many hours to train real-world problems and consequently there has been much effort directed to developing improvements in training time. For example, in the *delta-bar–delta* algorithm of Jacobs (1988) adaptive learning rates are assigned to each weight to help optimize the speed of learning. More recently Yu et al. (1995) have developed ways of adapting a single, global learning rate to speed up learning.

Historically, backpropagation was discovered by Werbos (1974) who reported it in his PhD thesis. It was later rediscovered by Parker (1982) but this version languished in a technical report that was not widely circulated. It was discovered again and made popular by Rumelhart et al. (1986b,c,d) in their well-known book *Parallel distributed processing*, which caught the wave of resurgent interest in neural nets after a comparatively lean time when it was largely overshadowed by work in conventional AI.

6.13   Summary

We set out to use gradient descent to train multilayer nets and obtain a generalization of the delta rule. This was made possible by thinking in terms of the credit assignment problem, which suggested a way of assigning "blame" for the error to the hidden units. This process involved passing back error information from the output layer, giving rise to the term "backpropagation" for the ensuing training algorithm. The basic algorithm may be augmented with a momentum term that effectively increases the learning rate over large uniform regions of the error–weight surface.

One of the main problems encountered concerned the existence of local minima in the error function, which could lead to suboptimal solutions. These may be avoided by injecting noise into the gradient descent via serial update or momentum. Backpropagation is a quite general supervised algorithm that may be applied to incompletely connected nets and nets with more than one hidden layer. The operation of a feedforward net may be thought of in several ways. The original setting was in pattern space and it may be shown that a two-layer net (one hidden layer) is sufficient to achieve any arbitrary partition in this space. Another viewpoint is to consider a network as implementing a mapping or function of its inputs. Once again, any function may be approximated to an arbitrary degree using only one hidden layer. Finally, we may think of nets as discovering features in the training set that represent information essential for describing or classifying these patterns.

Well-trained networks are able to classify correctly patterns unseen during training. This process of generalization relies on the network developing a decision surface that is not overly complex but captures the underlying relationships in the data. If this does not occur the net is said to have overfitted the decision surface and does not generalize well. Overfitting can occur if there are too many hidden units and may be prevented by limiting the time to train and establishing this limit using a validation set. Alternatively, by making the training set sufficiently large we may minimize the ambiguities in the decision surface, thereby helping to prevent it from becoming too convoluted. A more radical approach is to incorporate the construction of the hidden layer as part of the training process.

Example applications were provided that highlighted some of the aspects of porting a problem to a neural network setting. These were typical of the kind of problems solved using backpropagation and helped expand the notion of how training vectors originate in real situations (first introduced via the visual examples in Fig. 4.10).

6.14   Notes

1. Angled brackets usually imply the average or mean of the quantity inside.
2. Training and test data are referred to as *in-sample* and *out-of-sample* data respectively in the paper.
3. DynIM (Dynamic multi-factor model of stock returns) is a trademark of County NatWest Investment Management Ltd.

Chapter Seven

Associative memories: the Hopfield net

7.1 The nature of associative memory

In common parlance, "remembering" something consists of *associating* an idea or thought with a sensory cue. For example, someone may mention the name of a celebrity, and we immediately recall a TV series or newspaper article about the celebrity. Or, we may be shown a picture of a place we have visited and the image recalls memories of people we met and experiences we enjoyed at the time. The sense of smell (olfaction) can also elicit memories and is known to be especially effective in this way.

It is difficult to describe and formalize these very high-level examples and so we shall consider a more mundane instance that, nevertheless, contains all the aspects of those above. Consider the image shown on the left of Figure 7.1. This is supposed to represent a binarized version of the letter "T" where open and filled circular symbols represent 0s and 1s respectively (Sect. 4.6.1). The pattern in the centre of the figure is the same "T" but with the bottom half replaced by noise – pixels have been assigned a value 1 with probability 0.5. We might imagine that the upper half of the letter is provided as a cue and the bottom half has to be recalled from memory. The pattern on the right hand side is obtained from the original "T" by adding 20 per cent noise – each pixel is inverted with probability 0.2. In this case we suppose that the whole memory is available but in an imperfectly recalled form, so that the task is to "remember" the original letter in its uncorrupted state. This might be likened to our having a "hazy" or inaccurate memory of some scene, name or sequence of events in which the whole may be pieced together after some effort of recall.

Figure 7.1 Associative recall with binarized letter images.

The common paradigm here may be described as follows. There is some underlying collection of stored data which is ordered and interrelated in some way; that is, the data constitute a stored pattern or memory. In the human recollection examples above, it was the cluster of items associated with the celebrity or the place we visited. In the case of character recognition, it was the parts (pixels) of some letter whose arrangement was determined by a stereotypical version of that letter. When part of the pattern of data is presented in the form of a sensory cue, the rest of the pattern (memory) is recalled or *associated* with it. Alternatively, we may be offered an imperfect version of the stored memory that has to be associated with the true, uncorrupted pattern. Notice that it doesn't matter which part of the pattern is used as the cue; the whole pattern is always restored.

Conventional computers (von Neumann machines) can perform this function in a very limited way using software usually referred to as a database. Here, the "sensory cue" is called the *key* or *index* term to be searched on. For example, a library catalogue is a database that stores the authors, titles, classmarks and data on publication of books and journals. Typically we may search on any one of these discrete items for a catalogue entry by typing the complete item after selecting the correct option from a menu. Suppose now we have only the fragment "ion, Mar" from the encoded record "Vision, Marr D." of the book *Vision* by D. Marr. There is no way that the database can use this fragment of information even to start searching. We don't know if it pertains to the author or the title, and, even if we did, we might get titles or authors that start with "ion". The input to a conventional database has to be very specific and complete if it is to work.

7.2   Neural networks and associative memory

Consider a feedforward net that has the same number of inputs and outputs and that has been trained with vector pairs in which the output target is the same as the input. This net can now be thought of as an associative memory since an imperfect or incomplete copy of one of the training set should (under generalization) elicit the true vector at the output from which it was obtained. This kind of network was the first to be used for storing memories (Willshaw et al. 1969) and its mathematical analysis may be found in Kohonen (1982). However, there is a potentially more powerful network type for associative memory which was made popular by John Hopfield (1982), and which differs from that described above in that the net has feedback loops in its connection pathways. The relation between the two types of associative network is discussed in Section 7.9. The Hopfield nets are, in fact, examples of a wider class of dynamical physical systems that may be thought of as instantiating "memories" as stable states associated with minima of a suitably defined system energy. It is therefore to a description of these systems that we now turn.

7.3   A physical analogy with memory

To illustrate this point of view, consider a bowl in which a ball bearing is allowed to roll freely as shown in Figure 7.2.

Figure 7.2 Bowl and ball bearing: a system with a stable energy state.

Suppose we let the ball go from a point somewhere up the side of the bowl. The ball will roll back and forth and around the bowl until it comes to rest at the bottom. The physical description of what has happened may be couched in terms of the energy of the system. The energy of the system is just the *potential* energy of the ball and is directly related to the height of the ball above the bowl's centre; the higher the ball the greater its energy. This follows because we have to do work to push the ball up the side of the bowl and, the higher the point of release, the faster the ball moves when it initially reaches the bottom. Eventually the ball comes to rest at the bottom of the bowl where its potential energy has been dissipated as heat and sound that are lost from the system. The energy is now at a minimum since any other (necessarily higher) location of the ball is associated with some potential energy, which may be lost on allowing the bowl to reach equilibrium. To summarize: the ball–bowl system settles in an energy minimum at equilibrium when it is allowed to operate under its own dynamics. Further, this equilibrium state is the same, regardless of the initial position of the ball on the side of the bowl. The resting state is said to be *stable* because the system remains there after it has been reached.

There is another way of thinking about this process that ties in with our ideas about memory. It may appear a little fanciful at first but the reader should understand that we are using it as a metaphor at this stage. Thus, we suppose that the ball comes to rest in the same place each time because it "remembers" where the bottom of the bowl is. We may push the analogy further by giving the ball a co-ordinate description. Thus, its position or *state* at any time t is given by the three co-ordinates $x(t)$, $y(t)$, $z(t)$ with respect to some cartesian reference frame that is fixed with respect to the bowl. This is written more succinctly in terms of its position vector, $\mathbf{x}(t) = (x(t), y(t), z(t))$ (see Fig. 7.3). The location of the bottom of the bowl, $\mathbf{x}_p$, represents the pattern that is stored. By writing the ball's vector as the sum of $\mathbf{x}_p$ and a displacement $\Delta\mathbf{x}$, $\mathbf{x} = \mathbf{x}_p + \Delta\mathbf{x}$, we may think of the ball's initial position as representing the partial knowledge or cue for recall, since it approximates to the memory $\mathbf{x}_p$.

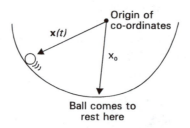

Figure 7.3 Bowl and ball bearing with state description.

If we now use a corrugated surface instead of a single depression (as in the bowl) we may store many "memories" as shown in Figure 7.4. If the ball is now started somewhere on this surface, it will eventually come to rest at the local depression that is closest to its initial starting point. That is, it evokes the stored pattern which is closest to its initial partial pattern or cue. Once again, this corresponds to an energy minimum of the system. The memories shown correspond to states x_1, x_2, x_3 where each of these is a vector.

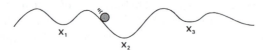

Figure 7.4 Corrugated plane with ball bearing: several stable states.

There are therefore two complementary ways of looking at what is happening. One is to say that the system falls into an energy minimum; the other is that it stores a set of patterns and recalls that which is closest to its initial state. The key, then, to building networks that behave like this is the use of the state vector formalism. In the case of the corrugated surface this is provided by the position vector $x(t)$ of the ball and those of the stored memories x_1, x_2, ..., x_n. We may abstract this, however, to any system (including neural networks) that is to store memories.

(a) It must be completely described by a *state vector* $\mathbf{v}(t) = (v_1(t), v_2(t), \ldots, v_n(t))$ which is a function of time.

(b) There are a set of *stable states* $\mathbf{v}_1$, $\mathbf{v}_2$, $\mathbf{v}_1$, ..., $\mathbf{v}_n$, which correspond to the stored patterns or memories.

(c) The system evolves in time from any arbitrary starting state $\mathbf{v}(0)$ to one of the stable states, which corresponds to the process of memory recall.

As discussed above, the other formalism that will prove to be useful makes use of the concept of a system energy. Abstracting this from the case of the corrugated surface we obtain the following scheme, which runs in parallel to that just described.

(a) The system must be associated with a scalar variable $E(t)$, which we shall call the "energy" by analogy with real, physical systems, and which is a function of time.

(b) The stable states $\mathbf{v}_i$ are associated with energy minima E_i. That is, for each i, there is a neighbourhood or *basin of attraction* around $\mathbf{v}_i$ for which E_i is the smallest energy in that neighbourhood (in the case of the corrugated surface, the basins of attraction are the indentations in the surface).

(c) The system evolves in time from any arbitrary initial energy $E(0)$ to one of the stable states E_i with $E(0) > E_i$. This process corresponds to that of memory recall.

Notice that the energy of each of the equilibria E_i may differ, but each one is the lowest available *locally* within its basin of attraction. It is important to distinguish between this use of local energy minima to store memories, in which each minimum is as valid as any other, and the unwanted local error minima occurring during gradient descent in previous chapters. This point is discussed further in Section 7.5.3.

7.4 The Hopfield net

We now attempt to apply the concepts outlined above to the construction of a neural network capable of performing associative recall. Consider the network consisting of three TLU nodes shown in Figure 7.5. Each node is connected to every other node (but not to itself) and the connection strengths or weights are symmetric in that the weight from node i to node j is the same as that from node j to node i. That is, $w_{ij} = w_{ji}$ and $w_{ii} = 0$ for all i, j. Additionally, the thresholds are all assumed to be zero. Notice that the flow of information in this type of

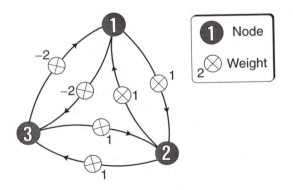

Figure 7.5 Three-node Hopfield net.

net is not in a single direction, since it is possible for signals to flow from a node back to itself via other nodes. We say there is feedback in the network or that it is *recurrent* because nodes may be used repeatedly to process information. This is to be contrasted with the feedforward nets that have been used exclusively so far.

Networks of this type and their energy-based analysis were described elegantly by John Hopfield in 1982 so that his name is usually associated with this type of net. In fact something very close to the "Hopfield model" had been introduced previously by Little in 1974 but here there was less emphasis on the energy-based description. Little also made extensive use of a quantum mechanical formalism, which may have made his work less accessible to readers from non-physics backgrounds.

The state of the net at any time is given by the vector of the node outputs[1] (x_1, x_2, x_3). Suppose we now start this net in some initial state, choose a node at random and let it update its output or "fire". That is, the chosen node evaluates its activation in the normal way and outputs a "1" if this is greater than or equal to zero and a "0" otherwise. The net now finds itself either in the same state as it started in, or in a new state that is at Hamming distance 1 from the old one. We now choose another node at random, let it update or fire, and repeat this many times. This process defines the dynamics of the net and it is now pertinent to ask what the resulting behaviour of the net will be.

In describing these state transitions it is convenient to attach a numeric label to each state and the most natural way of doing this is to interpret the Boolean state vector as a binary number, so that state (x_1, x_2, x_3) is labelled with $4x_1 + 2x_2 + x_3$. For example, $(1, 1, 0)$ is state 6, and state $(0, 1, 1)$ is state 3. For each network state, there are three possible outcomes for the next state depending on which of the three nodes is chosen to fire. Suppose, for example, the net starts in state $(1, 0, 1)$ (label 5) and node 1 fires. The activation a of this node is given by $a = w_{13}x_3 + w_{12}x_2 = -2 \times 1 + 1 \times 0 = -2$. Then, since this is less than 0, the new output is also 0 and the new state is $(0, 0, 1)$ (label 1); in summary, state 5 goes to state 1 when node 1 fires. Repeating this working for nodes 2 and 3 firing, the new states are 7 and 4 respectively. By working through all initial states and node selections it is possible to evaluate every state transition of the net as shown in Table 7.1. Notice that a state may or may not change when a node fires. This information may also be represented in graphical form as a *state transition diagram*, shown in Figure 7.6. States are represented by triangles with their associated state number, directed arcs represent possible transitions between states and the number along each arc is the probability that each transition will take place (given that any of the three nodes are chosen at random to fire). For example, starting in state 5 we see from the diagram that there is an equal probability of 1/3 of going to states 1, 7, or 4, which is reflected in the three arcs emanating from state 5 in the diagram. Again, starting in state 1 and updating nodes 1 or 3 results in no state change, so there is a probability of 2/3 that state 1 stays as it is; however, choosing node 2 to update (probability 1/3) results in a transition to state 3. The "no-change" condition gives an arc that starts and ends at the same state.

Table 7.1 State transition table for three-node net.

Initial state				Next state (number labels)		
Components			Number	After node 1	After node	After node 3
x_1	x_2	x_3	label	has fired	2 has fired	has fired
0	0	0	0	4	2	1
0	0	1	1	1	3	1
0	1	0	2	6	2	3
0	1	1	3	3	3	3
1	0	0	4	4	6	4
1	0	1	5	1	7	4
1	1	0	6	6	6	6
1	1	1	7	3	7	6

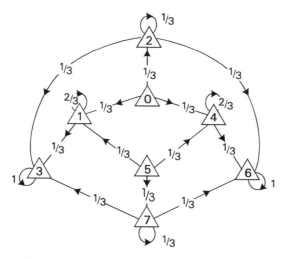

Figure 7.6 State transition diagram for three-node net.

The important thing to notice at this stage is that, no matter where we start in the diagram, the net will eventually find itself in one of the states 3 or 6, which re-enter themselves with probability 1. That is, they are stable states; once the net finds itself in one of these it stays there. The state vectors for 3 and 6 are $(0,1,1)$ and $(1,1,0)$ respectively and so these are the patterns or "memories" stored by the net.

The collection of states, together with possible transitions, is referred to as the *state space* of the network and is analogous to the physical space in which the corrugated surface and ball reside. The set of states that can result in state 3 being retrieved are $1, 2, 0, 5, 7$ and the corresponding set for state 6 are $4, 2, 0, 5, 7$. These are therefore the basins of attraction for these two stable states and there is, in this case, a strong overlap between the two. Basins of attraction are also known simply as *attractors* or *confluents*, which also reflect mental images we might have of the behaviour of the net in state space as being attracted to, or flowing towards, the state cycles.

As the network moves towards a stored pattern its state becomes ever closer (in Hamming distance) to that pattern. For example, in the case of the stored "T" pattern of Figure 7.1, starting in a state like the one on the left, we would see the degree of noise decrease gradually and the pattern on the left of the figure emerge. This is illustrated in Figure 7.7 in which the numbers indicate how many nodes have been selected for update.

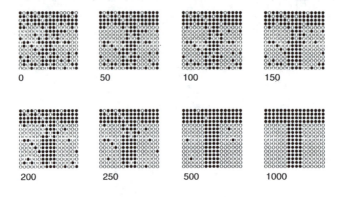

Figure 7.7 Dynamic evolution of states.

7.4.1 Defining an energy for the net

The dynamics of the net are described completely by the state transition table or diagram. It has demonstrated the existence of stable states (crucial to the associative memory paradigm) but it is not clear that we are guaranteed to obtain such states always. The alternative, energy-based formalism will, however, prove more fruitful in this respect. Our approach will be to think of each member of a pair of nodes as exercising a constraint on the other member via the internode weight. The use of the energy concept in this context may be introduced using an analogy with a simple physical system. Thus, consider a pair of objects joined by a spring as shown in Figure 7.8. The left hand part of the figure shows the use of a tension spring, which tends to pull the objects together. Since work has to be done to draw the objects apart, the energy minimum of this system occurs when the objects are close to each other or, in other words, tend towards the *same* position in space. The right hand part of the figure shows a compression spring whose energy minimum occurs when the objects are far apart or take *different* positions in space.

Now consider two nodes i, j in a Hopfield net connected by a positive weight

100

Tension   Compression

Figure 7.8 Pairwise energy between objects joined by springs.

$+w$, as shown on the left hand part of Figure 7.9. We claim that positive and negative weights are analogous to the tension and compression springs respectively, since positive weights tend to make the nodes take on the same output values while negative weights tend to force different values. This viewpoint has led to the name *constraint satisfaction network* being used occasionally for recurrent nets with symmetric weights. To make this claim plausible, consider first the case of a positive weight $+w$ (with $w > 0$) and suppose, in fact, the two nodes had opposite values with the outputs of i and j being 1 and 0 respectively. If j were given the chance to update or fire, the contribution to its activation from i is positive, which helps to bring j's activation above threshold, thereby inducing an output of "1". Of course, the contribution from i on its own may be insufficient, the point being that node i is trying to drive node j above threshold, so that the state[2] 1, 0 is not stable with respect to these nodes. The same argument applies to state 0, 1 since the weight is the same for both nodes. Suppose now that both nodes have 1 on their outputs. The contributions to each other's activity are positive, which tends to reinforce or stabilize this state. The state 0, 0 is neutral with respect to the sign of the weight since no contribution to the activation is made by either node.

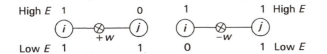

Figure 7.9 Pairwise energy in a Hopfield net.

Now consider the case of a negative weight $-w$ (shown on the right hand side of Fig. 7.9). The situation is now reversed and opposite output values are stabilized. Thus, if i and j have outputs 1 and 0 respectively and j fires, then i inhibits j and reinforces its negative activation. Similarly with both outputs equal to 1, each node inhibits the other, which tends to destabilize this state.

The constraint description may now be set within the energy framework by assigning high energies to states that tend to get destabilized and low energies to those that are reinforced. One way of doing this is to define the internode energy e_{ij} by

$$e_{ij} = -w_{ij}x_i x_j \tag{7.1}$$

This results in values for e_{ij} as given in Table 7.2. To see how this works, consider first the case where the weight is positive. The last energy entry in the table $(-w_{ij})$ is then negative and, since it is the only non-zero value, is therefore the

Table 7.2 Pairwise energies.

x_i	x_j	e_{ij}
0	0	0
0	1	0
1	0	0
1	1	$-w_{ij}$

lowest energy available. Further, it occurs when both units are "on", which is consistent with the arguments above. On the other hand, if the weight is negative the non-zero energy state (state $1, 1$) is positive, has the highest energy available, and is therefore not favoured, which is again in line with the requirements.

The energy of the whole network E is found by summing over all pairs of nodes

$$E = \sum_{\text{pairs}} e_{ij} = - \sum_{\text{pairs}} w_{ij} x_i x_j \tag{7.2}$$

This may be written

$$E = -\frac{1}{2} \sum_{i,j} w_{ij} x_i x_j \tag{7.3}$$

since the sum includes each pair twice (as $w_{ij} x_i x_j$ and $w_{ji} x_j x_i$, where $w_{ij} = w_{ji}$) and $w_{ii} = 0$.

In order to demonstrate the existence of stable network states, it is necessary to see what the change in energy is when a node fires. Suppose node k is chosen to be updated. Write the energy E in a form that singles out the terms involving this node:

$$E = -\frac{1}{2} \sum_{\substack{i \neq k \\ j \neq k}} w_{ij} x_i x_j - \frac{1}{2} \sum_i w_{ki} x_k x_i - \frac{1}{2} \sum_i w_{ik} x_i x_k$$

The first term here contains no references to node k, which are all contained in the second two terms. Now, because $w_{ik} = w_{ki}$, these last two sums may be combined

$$E = -\frac{1}{2} \sum_{\substack{i \neq k \\ j \neq k}} w_{ij} x_i x_j - \sum_i w_{ki} x_k x_i$$

For ease of notation, denote the first sum by S and, in the second sum, take x_k outside the summation since it is constant throughout. Then

$$E = S - x_k \sum_i w_{ki} x_i$$

The sum following x_k is just the activation of the kth node so that

$$E = S - x_k a^k \tag{7.4}$$

Let the energy after k has updated be E' and the new output be x'_k. Then

$$E' = S - x'_k a^k \tag{7.5}$$

Denote the change in energy $E' - E$ by ΔE and the change in output $x'_k - x_k$ by Δx_k; then subtracting (7.4) from (7.5)

$$\Delta E = -\Delta x_k a^k \tag{7.6}$$

There are now two cases to consider:

(a) $a^k \geq 0$. The output then goes from 0 to 1 or stays at 1. In either case $\Delta x_k \geq 0$. Therefore $\Delta x_k a^k \geq 0$ and so $\Delta E \leq 0$.

(b) $a^k < 0$. The output then goes from 1 to 0 or stays at 0. In either case $\Delta x_k \leq 0$. Therefore, once again, $\Delta x_k a^k \geq 0$ and $\Delta E \leq 0$.

Thus, for any node selected to fire, we always have $\Delta E \leq 0$ so that the energy of the net decreases or stays the same. However, the energy cannot continue decreasing indefinitely – it is bounded below by a value obtained by putting all the $x_i, x_j = 1$ in (7.3). Thus E must reach some fixed value and then stay the same. However, we have not quite guaranteed stable states yet for, once E is constant, it is still possible for further changes in the network's state to take place as long as $\Delta E = 0$. State changes imply $\Delta x_k \neq 0$ but, in order that $E = 0$, (7.6) necessitates that $a^k = 0$. This, in turn, implies the change must be of the form $0 \to 1$. There can be at most N of these changes, where N is the number of nodes in the net. After this there can be no more change to the net's state and a stable state has been reached.

7.4.2 Alternative dynamics and basins of attraction

Up to now it has been assumed that only a single node updates or fires at any time step. All nodes are possible candidates for update and so they operate *asynchronously*; that is, there is no co-ordination between their dynamical action over time. The other extreme occurs if we make all nodes fire at the same time, in which case we say there is *synchronous* update. In executing this process, each node must use inputs based on the current state, so that it is necessary to retain a copy of the network's state as the new one is being evaluated. Unlike asynchronous dynamics, the behaviour is now deterministic. Given any state, a state transition occurs to a well-defined next state leading to a simplified state transition diagram in which only a single arc emerges from any state vertex. The price to pay is that the energy-based analysis of the previous section no longer applies. However, this is not a problem since the deterministic dynamics lead to a simple description of the state space behaviour. Thus, since the net is finite there is a finite number of states and, starting from any initial state, we must eventually

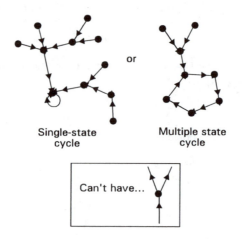

Figure 7.10 State space for synchronous dynamics.

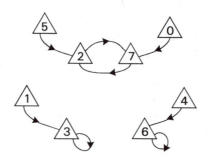

Figure 7.11 Confluent structure of three-node net.

reach a state that has been visited before. In particular, single-state cycles occur again but now there is the possibility for *multiple-state cycles*. The result is that the state space is divided into a set of discrete regions, each one being associated with a state cycle as shown in Figure 7.10. Each of these is, of course, a basin of attraction but, unlike the state space under asynchronous dynamics, the attractors are non-overlapping. Multiple-state cycles cannot occur under asynchronous dynamics and may be useful for storing sequences of events or patterns.

It is of interest to compare the synchronous–dynamical confluent structure of the three-node net used earlier in the chapter with its asynchronous behaviour in Figure 7.6. This is shown in Figure 7.11 and consists of three basins of attraction, two of which have single-state cycles and another a two-cycle. The single-state cycles are the same as those under asynchronous dynamics and it can be shown that this is a general result; the single stored patterns remain the same under both dynamics.

7.4.3   Ways of using the net

So far it has been assumed that the net is started in some initial state and the whole net allowed to run freely (synchronously or asynchronously) until a state cycle is encountered. As indicated in the central pattern of Figure 7.1, there is another possibility in which some part of the net has its outputs fixed while the remainder is allowed to update in the normal way. The part that is fixed is said to be *clamped* and, if the clamp forms part of a state cycle, the remainder (unclamped) part of the net will complete the pattern stored at that cycle. This process is illustrated in Figure 7.12, in which the top half of the "T" has been clamped and the bottom half initially contains 50 per cent noise. Which mode is used will depend on any prior knowledge about parts of the pattern being uncorrupted or noise free.

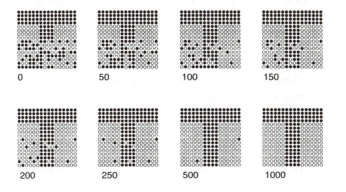

Figure 7.12 Evolution under clamp.

7.5   Finding the weights

Although we have established the existence of stable states, nothing has been said so far about how the net can be made to store patterns from a training set. In his original paper, Hopfield (1982) did not give a method for "training" the nets under an incremental, iterative process. Rather he gave a *prescription* for making a weight set as a given set of patterns to be stored, which, in spite of this, we will still refer to as a "training set". In Section 7.5.2 we shall relate the storage prescription to a biologically inspired learning rule – the Hebb rule – and show that the nodes may also be trained in the normal, incremental way.

7.5.1 The storage prescription

The rationale behind the prescription is based on the observations made in Section 7.4.1 about the way in which weights constrain the outputs of node pairs. Consider, for example, two nodes that tend, on average, to take on the same value over the training set so that the pairs 0, 0 or 1, 1 dominate; we say that the nodes are *correlated*. The pair 1, 1 will be reinforced by there being a positive internode weight (although the 0, 0 pairing is not affected). If, on the other hand, the two nodes tend, on average, to take on opposite values (they are *anti-correlated*) with pairs 0, 1 or 1, 0, then this will be reinforced by a negative internode weight.

We now proceed to formalize these ideas mathematically. First, it is convenient to introduce an alternative way of representing binary quantities. So far these have been denoted by 0 and 1 but in the *polarized* or *spin* representation they are denoted by -1 and 1 respectively. This name is derived from the fact that Hopfield nets have many similarities with so-called *spin glasses* in physics, which are used to model magnetic materials; each local magnetic domain is either aligned with ($+1$) or against (-1) an external field. The connection between spin glasses and other systems is explored by Kirkpatrick et al. (1983). Now let v_i^p, v_j^p be components of the pth pattern to be stored as given in the spin representation. Consider what happens if the weight between the nodes i and j is given by

$$w_{ij} = \sum_p v_i^p v_j^p \qquad (7.7)$$

where the sum is over all patterns p in the training set. If, on average, the two components take on the same value then the weight will be positive since we get terms like 1×1 and -1×-1 predominating. If, on the other hand, the two components tend to take on opposite values we get terms like -1×1 and 1×-1 predominating, giving a negative weight. This is just what is required according to the discussion given above, so that (7.7) is a suitable storage prescription for Hopfield nets. This discussion of output correlation should be compared with that of feature detection in Section 6.7.3. Note that the same weights would result if we had tried to learn the inverse of the patterns, formed by taking each component and changing it to the opposite value. The net, therefore, always learns the patterns *and* their inverses; more will be said about these *spurious states* in Section 7.5.3.

The storage prescription has a long history. Willshaw et al. (1969) proposed a correlational scheme for use in their feedforward net, which is a simplified precursor to that described above, while Anderson (1972) trained single-layer feedforward nets using essentially the same rule as that used by Hopfield.

7.5.2 The Hebb rule

The use of (7.7), which is a recipe for fixing the weights without incremental adaptation, may appear to run counter to the ideas being promoted in the connectionist cause. It is possible, however, to view the storage prescription as a shortcut to obtain weights that would result from the following process of adaptation

1. Choose a pattern from the training set at random.

2. Present the components of this pattern at the outputs of the corresponding nodes of the net.

3. If two nodes have the same value then make a small positive increment to the internode weight. If they have opposite values then make a small negative decrement to the weight.

Iteration of these three steps many times constitutes a training algorithm whose learning rule (step 3) may be written mathematically as

$$\Delta w_{ij} = \alpha v_i^p v_j^p \tag{7.8}$$

where, as usual, α is a rate constant and $0 < \alpha < 1$. It is clear that, as the number of iterations increases, the pattern of weights developed will approximate ever more closely to those given by the storage prescription up to some overall scaling factor. As a variation on (7.8), suppose we had used the usual Boolean representation for the components x_i^p so that x_i^p is 0 or 1. The rule would now be

$$\Delta w_{ij} = \alpha x_i^p x_j^p \tag{7.9}$$

Interpreting this, we see that the change in weight is only ever positive and only occurs if both nodes are firing (output "1"). This is essentially the same as a rule posited by the neuropsychologist D. O. Hebb in 1949 as a possible way that biological neurons learn. In his book *The organization of behaviour* Hebb postulated that

> When an axon of cell A is near enough to excite a cell B and repeatedly or persistently takes part in firing it, some growth process or metabolic change takes place in one or both cells such that A's efficiency, as one of the cells firing B, is increased.

The rules in (7.8) and (7.9) are examples of a family that involve the product of a pair of node activations or outputs. They are known collectively as Hebb rules even though the mathematical formulation of Hebb's proposal is most closely captured by (7.9).

7.5.3 Spurious states

As well as storing the required training set patterns, the storage prescription has the undesirable side effect of creating additional, spurious stable states together with their associated basins of attraction. It has already been noted that the inverse patterns are also stored. In some sense, however, these are not "spurious" since the original labelling of pattern components is arbitrary (renaming the set of "0" components as "1" and vice versa doesn't really change the pattern). Apart from these there is always a large number of other states that are mixtures of the training patterns. Amit (1989) has classified these and found that there are more than 3^p spurious states where p is the size of the training set.

However, things are not as bad as they seem at first glance. It transpires that the energies of the training set states (and their inverses) are all equal and less than any of the spurious states. It is possible to take advantage of this to help the net settle into a stable state corresponding to one of the prescribed patterns. Thus, suppose we replace the hard-limiter in the node output function with a sigmoid and interpret its value as the probability of outputting a 1. That is, the units are now stochastic semilinear nodes (Sect. 2.4). Now, when a node updates there is some possibility that the output will be the inverse of its TLU value so that the energy *increases*. In this way it is possible for the net to move away from a spurious minimum, across an energy boundary in state space, and find itself in the basin of attraction of a member of the training set. The price to pay is that we have to work a little harder at interpreting the network output since, in this noisy regime, the state of the net is continually fluctuating. We can then choose to interpret the retrieved state as the mean of each node output or the state that has, on average, greatest overlap with the network state. This approach, together with a quantitative analysis of the effect of noise, is given in the book by Amit (1989).

7.6   Storage capacity

The storage prescription attempts to capture information about the *mean* correlation of components in the training set. As such, it must induce a weight set that is a compromise as far as any *individual* pattern is concerned. Clearly, as the number m of patterns increases, the chances of accurate storage must decrease since more trade-offs have to be made between pattern requirements. In some empirical work in his 1982 paper, Hopfield showed that about half the memories were stored accurately in a net of N nodes if $m = 0.15N$. The other patterns did not get stored as stable states. In proving rigorously general results of this type, it is not possible to say anything about particular sets of patterns so that all results deal with probabilities and apply to a randomly selected training set. Thus McEliece et al. (1987) showed that for $m < N/2 \log N$, as N becomes very large, the probability that there is a single error in storing any one of the patterns becomes ever closer to zero. To give an idea of what this implies, for $N = 100$ this result gives $m = 11$.

7.7 The analogue Hopfield model

In a second important paper (Hopfield 1984) Hopfield introduced a variant of the discrete time model discussed so far that uses leaky-integrator nodes. The other structural difference is that there is provision for external input. The network dynamics are now governed by the system of equations (one for each node) that define the node dynamics and require computer simulation for their evaluation.

In the previous TLU model, the possible states are vectors of Boolean-valued components and so, for an N-node network, they have a geometric interpretation as the corners of the N-dimensional hypercube. In the new model, because the outputs can take any values between 0 and 1, the possible states now include the interior of the hypercube. Hopfield defined an energy function for the new network and showed that, if the inputs and thresholds were set to zero, as in the TLU discrete time model, and if the sigmoid was quite "steep", then the energy minima were confined to regions close to the corners of the hypercube and these corresponded to the energy minima of the old model. The use of a sigmoid output function in this model has the effect of smoothing out some of the smaller, spurious minima in a similar way to that in which the Boolean model can escape spurious minima by using a sigmoid.

There are two further advantages to the new model. The first is that it is possible to build the new neurons out of simple, readily available hardware. In fact, Hopfield writes the equation for the dynamics as if it were built from such components (operational amplifiers and resistors). This kind of circuit was the basis of several implementations – see for example Graf et al. (1987). The second is a more philosophical one in that the use of the sigmoid and time integration make greater contact with real, biological neurons.

7.8 Combinatorial optimization

Although we have concentrated exclusively on their role in associative recall, there is another class of problems that Hopfield nets can be used to solve, which are best introduced by an example. In the so-called travelling salesman problem (TSP) a salesman has to complete a round trip of a set of cities visiting each one only once and in such a way as to minimize the total distance travelled. An example is shown in Figure 7.13 in which a set of ten cities have been labelled from A through to J and a solution indicated by the linking arrows. This kind of problem is computationally very difficult and it can be shown that the time to compute a solution grows exponentially with the number of cities N.

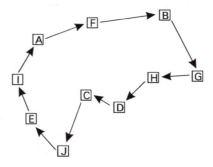

Figure 7.13 Travelling salesman problem: an example.

In 1985, Hopfield and Tank showed how this problem can be solved by a recurrent net using analogue nodes of the type described in the previous section. The first step is to map the problem onto the network so that solutions correspond to states of the network. The problem for N cities may be coded into an N by N network as follows. Each row of the net corresponds to a city and the ordinal position of the city in the tour is given by the node at that place outputting a high value (nominally 1) while the rest are all at very low values (nominally 0). This scheme is illustrated in Figure 7.14 for the tour of Figure 7.13. Since the trip is a closed one it doesn't matter which city is labelled as the first and this has been chosen to be A. This corresponds in the net to the first node in the row for A being "on" while the others in this row are all "off". The second city is F, which is indicated by the second node in the row for F being "on" while the rest are "off". Continuing in this way, the tour eventually finishes with city I in tenth position.

The next step is to construct an energy function that can eventually be rewritten in the form of (7.3) and has minima associated with states that are valid solutions. When this is done, we can then identify the resulting coefficients with the weights w_{ij}. We will not carry this through in detail here but will give an example of

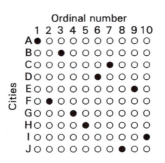

Figure 7.14 Network state for TSP solution.

the way in which constraints may be captured directly via the energy. The main condition on solution states is that they should represent valid tours; that is, there should be only one node "on" in each row and column. Let nodes be indexed according to their row and column so that y_{Xi} is the output of the node for city X in tour position i and consider the sum

$$\sum_{X} \sum_{i} \sum_{j \neq i} y_{Xi} y_{Xj} \qquad (7.10)$$

Each term is the product of a pair of single city outputs with different tour positions. If all rows contain only a single "on" unit, this sum is zero, otherwise it is positive. Thus, this term will tend to encourage rows to contain at most a single "on" unit. Similar terms may be constructed to encourage single units being "on" in columns, the existence of exactly ten units "on" in the net and, of course, to foster a shortest tour. When all these terms are combined, the resulting expression can indeed be written in the form of (7.3) and a set of weights extracted[3]. The result is that there are negative weights (inhibition) between nodes in the same row, and between nodes in the same column. The path-length criterion leads to inhibition between adjacent columns (cities in a path) whose strength is proportional to the path length between the cities for those nodes. By allowing the net to run under its dynamics, an energy minimum is reached that should correspond to a solution of the problem. What is meant by "solution" here needs a little qualification. The net is not guaranteed to produce the shortest tour but only those that are close to this; the complexity of the problem does not vanish simply because a neural net has been used.

The TSP is an example of a class of problems that are *combinatorial* in nature since they are defined by ordering a sequence or choosing a series of combinations. Another example is provided from graph theory. A *graph* is simply a set of vertices connected by arcs; the state transition diagram in Figure 7.6 is a graph, albeit with the extra directional information on the arcs. A *clique* is a set of vertices such that every pair is connected by an arc. The problem of finding the largest clique in a graph is one of combinatorial optimization and also takes time which is exponentially related to the number of vertices. Jagota (1995) has demonstrated the possibility of using a Hopfield net to generate near optimal solutions using a network with the same number of nodes as graph vertices.

7.9 Feedforward and recurrent associative nets

Consider the completely connected, feedforward net shown in Figure 7.15a. It has the same number of inputs and outputs and may therefore be used as an associative memory as discussed in Section 7.2 (for greater realism we might suppose the net has more than three nodes and that the diagram is schematic and indicative of the overall structure). Suppose now that the net processes an input pattern. We imagine that, although the net may not have managed to restore the pattern to its original form (perfect recall), it has managed to produce something that is closer to the stored memory pattern than the original input. Now let this pattern be used as a new input to the net. The output produced now will, in general, be even closer to a stored memory and, iterating in this way, we might expect eventually to restore the pattern exactly to one of the stored templates.

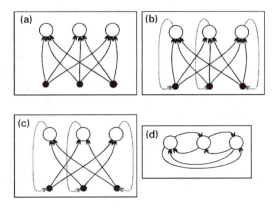

Figure 7.15 Relation between feedforward and recurrent associative nets.

To see how this is related to the recurrent nets discussed in this chapter, consider Figure 7.15b, which shows the network output being fed back to its input (the feedback connections are shown stippled). Making the process explicit in this way highlights the necessity for some technical details: there must be some mechanism to allow either the feedback or external input to be sent to the nodes and, during feedback, we must ensure that new network outputs about to be generated do not interfere with the recurrent inputs. However, this aside, the diagram allows for the iterative recall described above. Figure 7.15c shows a similar net, but now there are no feedback connections from a node to itself; as a result, we might expect a slightly different performance.

Now, each input node may be thought of as a distribution point for an associated network output node. Part (d) of the figure shows the input nodes having been subsumed into their corresponding output nodes while still showing the essential network connectivity. Assuming a suitable weight symmetry, we now clearly have a recurrent net with the structure of a Hopfield net. Since, in the supposed dynamics, patterns are fed back *in toto*, the recurrent net must be using synchronous dynamics (indeed the mechanism for avoiding signal conflict in the "input nodes" above may be supplied by sufficient storage for the previous and next states, a requirement for such nets as discussed in Sect. 7.4.3).

In summary we see that using a feedforward net in an *iterated* fashion for associative recall may be automated in an equivalent recurrent (feedback) net. Under suitable assumptions (no self-feedback, symmetric weights) this becomes a

Hopfield net under asynchronous dynamics. Alternatively, we could have started with the Hopfield net and "unwrapped" it, as it were, to show how it may be implemented as a succession of forward passes in an equivalent feedforward net.

7.10   Summary

Associative memory may be described as a process of recalling stored patterns or templates from a partial or noisy version of the original pattern. This is a much more general paradigm than that used by conventional computers when working with databases. Although feedforward nets may be used to perform this task, a more powerful tool is provided by a class of recurrent nets. These may be thought of as iteratively processing their input pattern to provide new versions that grow progressively closer to a stored memory. Such nets may also be thought of as examples of a larger class of dynamical systems that can be described in terms of an "energy" function. The system energy decreases as the system evolves and we identify stable states (energy minima) with stored memories. The Hopfield net is an example of this type of net. It consists of a set of TLUs with zero threshold in which every node takes input from all other nodes (except itself) and where the interunit weights are symmetric.

Under asynchronous operation, each node evaluates its inputs and "fires" accordingly. This induces a state transition and it is possible (in principle) to describe completely the network dynamics by exhaustively determining all possible state transitions. Alternative dynamics are offered by running the net synchronously, so that the net operation is deterministic. The stable states are, however, the same as under asynchronous dynamics. For nets of any significant size the problem of finding the state transition table is intractable but, since we are only interested in equilibrium states, this is not too important. It is here that the energy formalism comes into its own and enables us to demonstrate the general existence of stable states. The energy is defined by thinking of the net as instantiating a series of pairwise constraints (via the weights) on the current network state. If these constraints (the weights) are imposed by the pairwise statistics of the training set, then these will tend to form the stable states of the net and, therefore, constitute stored memories. Although the weights may be calculated directly, they may also be thought of as evolving under incremental learning according to a rule based on a description of biological synaptic plasticity due to Hebb.

Hopfield nets always store unwanted or spurious states as well as those required by the training set. In most cases this is not a problem since their energy is much higher than that of the training set. As a consequence their basins of attraction are smaller and they may be avoided by using a small amount of noise in the node operation. In order to store a given number of patterns reliably the net must exceed a certain size determined by its storage capacity.

Hopfield developed an analogue version of the binary net and also showed how problems in combinatorial optimization may be mapped onto nets of this type.

7.11 Notes

1. Since the Hopfield net is recurrent, any output serves as input to other nodes and so this notation is not inconsistent with previous usage of x as node input.
2. In this discussion the term "state" refers to the arrangement of outputs of i and j rather than the net as a whole.
3. The analogue net has, in fact, an extra linear component due to the external input.

Chapter Eight

Self-organization

In this chapter we explore the possibility that a network can discover *clusters* of similar patterns in the data without supervision. That is, unlike the MLPs, there is no target information provided in the training set. A typical dataset to be dealt with is illustrated schematically in Figure 8.1. Here, points appear to fall naturally into three clusters with two smaller, more tightly bound ones on the left, and one larger, more loosely bound on the right. Note that no mention has been made here of class labels; the relation between classes and clusters is discussed further in Section 8.2.1. If the network can encode these types of data, by assigning nodes to clusters in some way, then it is said to undergo both *self-organization* and *unsupervised* learning.

A key technique used in training nets in this way concerns establishing the most responsive node to any pattern. One way of doing this is simply to search the net for the largest activity. This, however, displaces the responsibility for this process onto some kind of supervisory mechanism that is not an integral part of the net. An alternative is to supply extra resources to the network that allow this

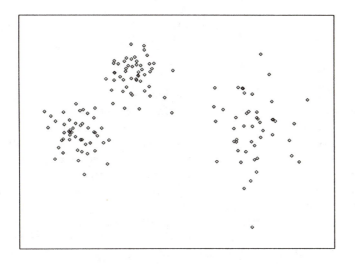

Figure 8.1 Clusters in a training set.

search to take place within the net itself. This distinction will become clearer later but we introduce it here to motivate the next section, which deals with a search mechanism intrinsic to the network.

8.1 Competitive dynamics

Consider a network layer of units as shown in Figure 8.2. Each unit is governed by leaky-integrator dynamics and receives the same set of inputs from an external input layer. Additionally there are intra-layer or *lateral* connections such that each node j is connected to itself via an excitatory (positive) weight $v_j^{(+)}$, and inhibits all other nodes in the layer with negative weights $v_{ij}^{(-)}$ which are symmetric, so that $v_{ij}^{(-)} = v_{ji}^{(-)}$. The connections from only one node have been shown in the diagram for the sake of clarity. This lateral connection scheme is sometimes referred to as *on-centre, off-surround* since it aptly describes the sign of the weights with respect to any neuron as centre.

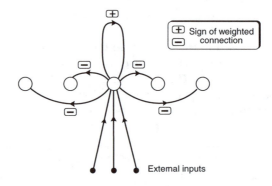

Figure 8.2 Competitive layer.

Now suppose a vector $\mathbf{x}$ is presented at the input. Each unit computes its external input s, as a weighted sum of the components of $\mathbf{x}$, formed using an input weight vector $\mathbf{w}$. This may be written in vector notation using the dot product as $s = \mathbf{w} \cdot \mathbf{x}$ and is the most expressive way of writing this for our purposes since we wish to view the situation from a geometric perspective. One of the nodes, labelled k say, will have a value of s larger than any other in the layer. It is now claimed that, under the influence of the lateral connections, the activation a_k of node k will increase towards its limiting value while that of the other units in the layer gets reduced. The total input to each node j consists of the "external" input s_j, together with a contribution l_j from other nodes within the layer. Thus, if $y_j = \sigma(a_j)$ is the node's output, l_j may be written

$$l_j = v_j^{(+)} y_j + \sum_{i \neq j} v_{ij}^{(-)} y_i \tag{8.1}$$

and, using (2.6) (with the constants relabelled c_1 and c_2),

$$\frac{da_j}{dt} = c_1(s_j + l_j) - c_2 a_j \qquad (8.2)$$

What happens is that node k has its activation stimulated directly from the external input more strongly than any other node. This is then reinforced indirectly via the self-excitatory connection. Further, as the output y_k grows, node k starts to inhibit the other nodes more than they can inhibit node k. The growth and decay processes are limited, however (Sect. 2.5), so that the layer gradually reaches a point of equilibrium or stability. If the net is a one-dimensional string of nodes (rather than a two-dimensional layer) its activity may be represented graphically in profile as shown in Figure 8.3. An initial situation, shown in the lower part of the figure, will evolve into that shown at the top. Each asterisk plots the activation of a node and dashed lines have been fitted to the spatial profiles merely to help show their arrangement. The final output profile of the net reflects that of the final activation (since $y = \sigma(a)$) and will have the same shape as that in the upper half of the figure, albeit with an even higher contrast in values.

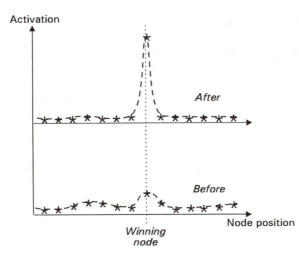

Figure 8.3 Competitive dynamics: network before and after reaching equilibrium.

The transition from initial state to equilibrium occurs as if there is a limited amount of activity to be shared amongst the nodes under some competition. The net is said to evolve via *competitive dynamics* and it is the node with the largest external input (the one with the initial advantage) that wins the competition by grabbing the bulk of the activity for itself. These nets and their dynamics are therefore sometimes referred to as "winner-takes-all". Thus, competitive dynamics can be used to enhance the activation "contrast" over a network layer and single out the node that is responding most strongly to its input.

117

To obtain the kind of situation shown in Figure 8.3 where there is a distinct and unique winning node, three conditions must be met. First, there should only be one excitatory weight emanating from any node that is connected to itself. Some lateral connections schemes allow for a small excitatory neighbourhood around each node so that nearby units are fed via positive rather than negative weights. In this case there will be a "winning neighbourhood" or localized region of high activity in the layer rather than a single, most active unit. Secondly, the lateral connections must be sufficiently strong so that the resulting equilibrium is well defined; small intra-layer weights will give a lower maximum and larger residual activities in the rest of the net. Finally, the inhibitory connections from each node must extend to all other nodes otherwise the competition takes place only within local regions of the net and several local activity maxima can then be supported. Depending on the requirements it may, in fact, be advantageous to allow any of these situations to occur by suitable choice of lateral weights (Sect. 8.3.2). However, focusing on the winner-takes-all situation, we now examine how competitive dynamics may be useful in a learning situation.

8.2 Competitive learning

Consider a training set whose vectors all have the same unit length, that is $\|x\| = 1$ for all x. If the vector set does not originally have unit length it is possible to convert or *normalize* it to a new one that does, by multiplying each vector by the reciprocal of its original length. Thus, if x' is the new vector formed from the original x,

$$x' = \left(\frac{1}{\|x\|} \right) x \tag{8.3}$$

In 2D the vectors all fall on the unit circle as shown in Figure 8.4. In general, they fall on the n-dimensional equivalent – the unit hypersphere – in which case the figure is a schematic representation of the true situation.

Figure 8.4 Normalized vectors on unit sphere.

Suppose that a competitive neural layer has a set of normalized weight vectors for connection to external input. These vectors may also be represented on the unit sphere as shown for a three-node net on the left hand side of Figure 8.5.

What we require for this net is that each node responds strongly to vectors in one of the clusters in the training set. Since there are three nodes and, apparently, three clusters, we should expect to be able to encode each cluster with a single node. Then, when a vector is presented to the net, there will be a single node that responds maximally to the input.

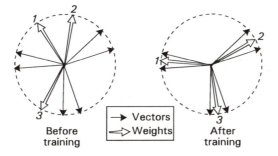

| → | Vectors |
| ⇒ | Weights |

Before training / After training

Figure 8.5 Normalized weights and vectors.

Clearly, for this process to take place, it is necessary to understand the relation that must pertain between a weight vector $\mathbf{w}$ and an input pattern $\mathbf{x}$ if a node is to respond "strongly" to $\mathbf{x}$. The key is provided by using the inner product expression for the node's external input, $s = \mathbf{w} \cdot \mathbf{x}$. Using the geometric viewpoint of the inner product developed in Chapter 3, s will be large and positive if the weight and input vectors are well aligned. Then, if the "angle" between $\mathbf{w}$ and $\mathbf{x}$ becomes larger, s becomes smaller, passing through zero before becoming negative. Corresponding with these changes, the output starts at comparatively large values and decreases towards zero.

Further, if the weight and pattern vectors are all of unit length, then s gives a *direct* measure of the alignment of each node's weight vector with a particular pattern. To see this, write the external input using the geometric form of the inner product, $s = \|\mathbf{w}\| \|\mathbf{x}\| \cos \theta$, where this defines the angle θ between $\mathbf{w}$ and $\mathbf{x}$. The appearance of the vector lengths in this expression means that, in general, they are confounded with the angular term and can lead to a misinterpretation of the angular separation; large external inputs can arise, not because θ is small but simply through large values of $\|\mathbf{w}\|$, $\|\mathbf{x}\|$. However, if all vectors are normalized, the lengths are both one, so that $s = \cos \theta$ and is therefore a true measure of the angular proximity between weight and pattern vectors. If we do not use normalized vectors, it would be possible for a single weight vector to give the largest response to several clusters simply by virtue of its having a large length, which is contrary to the proposed encoding scheme.

The ideal network will therefore have its three weight vectors aligned with the three pattern clusters as shown on the right hand side of Figure 8.5. This is brought about most efficiently by "rotating" each weight vector so that it becomes aligned with the cluster that is initially its nearest neighbour. This has been indicated in the figure by attaching labels to the weight vectors, which they retain throughout training.

The desired state may be effected by iteratively applying vectors and adjusting the weights of the node whose external input is largest. According to the above discussion, this is indeed the node whose weight vector is closest to the current pattern $\mathbf{x}$ and, under competitive dynamics, is identified as the node with the largest output at equilibrium. Let the "winning node" have index k and weight vector $\mathbf{w}_k$ (note that $\mathbf{w}_k$ is the kth weight vector, not the kth component of $\mathbf{w}$, which is w_k). Then $\mathbf{w}_k$ should now be rotated towards $\mathbf{x}$, which may be accomplished by adding a fraction of the difference vector $\mathbf{x} - \mathbf{w}_k$, as shown in Figure 8.6. This gives the learning rule for an arbitrary node j

$$\Delta\mathbf{w}_j = \begin{cases} \alpha(\mathbf{x} - \mathbf{w}_j) : j = k \\ 0 \qquad\quad : j \neq k \end{cases} \tag{8.4}$$

Suppose now the net is truly winner-takes-all, so that node k has its output y close to one while all the others have values close to zero. After letting the net reach equilibrium, the learning rule in (8.4) may be expressed without any special conditional information as

$$\Delta\mathbf{w}_j = \alpha(\mathbf{x} - \mathbf{w}_j)y \tag{8.5}$$

This may now be incorporated into a training algorithm as follows:

1. Apply a vector at the input to the net and evaluate s for each node.

2. Update the net according to (8.2) until it reaches equilibrium.

3. Train all nodes according to (8.5).

In practice, the number of updates in the second step will be predetermined to ensure a network state close to equilibrium in most cases.

As learning progresses, the best responding node to any pattern will change as the weight vectors reorganize themselves. If the training patterns are well clustered then it is usually the case that a stable weight set will be found (in the

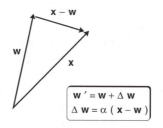

Figure 8.6 Competitive learning rule.

sense that the most responsive node for any pattern remains the same, although its exact response value may continue to change). If the patterns are not so well clustered and if there are many more patterns than nodes, then the weight coding may be unstable. This issue is addressed further in Chapter 9.

If a stable solution is found, then the weight vector for each cluster represents, in some sense, an average or typical vector from the cluster, since it has been directed towards each of them during training. Thus we may think of the weight vectors as archetypal patterns or *templates* for the cluster, a theme that is also taken up again in Chapter 9.

There remains a problem concerning the normalization that has not been addressed because, although the weights are initially of unit length, it is to be expected that as they adapt their length will change. One way around this is to renormalize the updated weight vector after each training step. However, this is computationally demanding and there is a simpler way that allows for a good approximation to true normalization while being automatically implemented in the learning rule. Thus, if we restrict ourselves to positive inputs, the condition

$$\sum_i w_i = 1 \tag{8.6}$$

is approximately equivalent to the normalization given by the *Euclidean* length that has been used so far. To see this we note that, because the (Euclidean) length is one, the squared length is also one and so, under the normalization used so far,

$$\sum_i w_i^2 = 1 \tag{8.7}$$

While (8.7) defines points on a unit sphere, (8.6) defines points on a plane (since it is a linear relation). This is illustrated in 3D in Figure 8.7, which shows the surfaces that weight or input vectors must lie on in the two normalization schemes. Since quantities are restricted to be positive, these surfaces are constrained to the positive quadrant of the space. According to how closely the distance of the plane from the origin approximates to one, the two schemes may be said to be equivalent. Now suppose that we do indeed use

$$l = \sum_i w_i \tag{8.8}$$

as an alternative definition of the the "length" of a vector so that normalization of both weights and inputs implies (8.6). The change in length of a weight vector is now just the sum of the changes in the weight components. If these changes take place under the training rule (8.5) then

$$\sum_i \Delta w_i = \alpha y \left(\sum_i x_i - \sum_i w_i \right) \tag{8.9}$$

For $y = 0$ there is no change. If $y = 1$ the first sum in the brackets on the right hand side is always one since the training patterns don't change. If the weight vector was normalized according to (8.6) prior to learning update then the second sum is also one and so the right hand side is zero. Thus, the change in the length of the weight vector is zero and normalization is automatically preserved. The use of normalization based on (8.8) turns out under most circumstances to be adequate although it should be emphasized that it relies on the input patterns having positive components. This is conceptually, at least, not a difficulty since, if we interpret the inputs as having come from a previous layer of sigmoidal output units, they must all be positive.

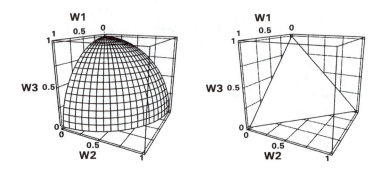

Figure 8.7 Normalization surfaces

It is of interest to rewrite the learning rule in a slightly different way as the sum of two terms

$$\Delta \mathbf{w} = \alpha xy - \alpha \mathbf{w} y \tag{8.10}$$

The first of these looks like a Hebb term while the second is a weight decay. Thus competitive self-organization may be thought of as Hebb learning but with a decay term that guarantees normalization. This latter property has a biological interpretation in terms of a conservation of metabolic resources; the sum of synaptic strengths may not exceed a certain value, which is governed by the physical characteristics of the cell to support synaptic and postsynaptic activity.

A good introduction to competitive learning is given by Rumelhart & Zipser (1985) who also provide several examples, one of which is discussed in the next section.

8.2.1 Letter and "word" recognition

Rumelhart and Zipser trained a competitive net using pairs of alphabetic characters A and B, each one being based on a 7 by 5 pixel array and inserted into one-half of a larger, 7 by 14, grid as shown in Figure 8.8. In a first set of experiments the input patterns were the letter pairs AA, AB, BA, BB. With just two units in the net, each one learned to detect either A or B in a particular serial position. Thus, in some experiments, one unit would respond if there was an A in the first position while the other would respond if there was a B in the first position. Alternatively the two units could learn to respond to the letter in the second position. Note that these possibilities are, indeed, the two "natural" pairwise groupings of these letter strings leading to the clusters $\{AA, AB\}$, $\{BA, BB\}$ or $\{AA, BA\}$, $\{AB, BB\}$. Rumelhart and Zipser call the two-unit net a "letter detector". With four units each node can learn to respond to one of the four letter pairs; each training pattern is then a separate "cluster" and the net is a "word detector". In making these distinctions, it is clear that we have attached class labels to the patterns, which is predicated on our understanding of "letter" and "word".

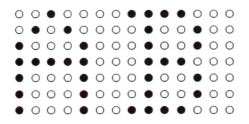

Figure 8.8 Letters used in competitive training example.

Another set of experiments used the letter pairs AA, AB, AC, AD, BA, BB, BC, BD. When a net with only two units was used, one unit learned to recognize the pairs that started with A, while the other learned to respond to those that began with B. When four units were used each unit learned to recognize the pairs that ended in one of the four different letters A, B, C, D. This again represents the two natural ways of clustering the training set, although both are examples of "letter" detection.

8.3   Kohonen's self-organizing feature maps

In addition to identifying clusters in training data, there is an additional level of organization that a competitive network can develop. This occurs when nodes that are physically adjacent in the network encode patterns that are "adjacent", in some sense, in the pattern space of the input. The concept of proximity leads to the idea of a *topography* or *map* defined over a neural layer in which these maps represent some feature of the input space. This property is one that is enjoyed by many areas of cortex in animal brains, which makes their description a natural starting point.

8.3.1 Topographic maps in the visual cortex

The mammalian cortex is the externally visible sheet of neural tissue that is folded and then wrapped to enclose more central areas of the brain. Among other things, it is responsible for processing sensory information such as sound and vision. Here we focus on the visual cortex, which is a rich source of topographic maps.

The simplest example occurs when the measure, or *metric*, for map proximity is just the spatial separation of luminance within the visual field. Thus, in the primary visual cortex (area V1), patches of light that are physically close to each other will stimulate areas of cortex that are also in close proximity. This is a so-called *retinotopic map* since it relates cortical location to position on the retina of the eye. Connolly & Van Essen (1984) have demonstrated this for the Macaque monkey V1 as shown in Figure 8.9. Part (a) shows the visual field for one eye expressed in a co-ordinate system with circular symmetry that is labelled according to the visual eccentricity (in degrees) from the centre of gaze. The bold line delimits the extent of the field of view. Part (b) is the representation in V1 of this field, where the locations of cortex responding to the dark squares in (a) have been shown to facilitate comparison. Two points need to be emphasized. First, adjacent areas in the field of view are processed by adjacent areas of cortex and, secondly, more cortex is devoted to the immediate area surrounding the centre of gaze (the *fovea*). The first 5° of foveal vision are mapped into a region that represents about 40 per cent of the cortex (shown by the shaded area in the diagram). This is quite general in topographic maps; although the proximity relation *between* areas (or *topology*) of the input is preserved, the relative size *within* regions of the input space may not be.

Another example occurs in V1 by virtue of the fact that many of its cells are "tuned" to oriented features of the stimulus. Thus, if a grid or grating of alternating light and dark lines is presented to the animal, the cell will respond most strongly when the lines are oriented at a particular angle and the response will fall off as the grating is rotated either way from this preferred orientation. This was established in the classic work of Hubel & Wiesel (1962) using microelectrode

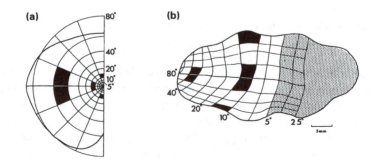

Figure 8.9 Retinotopic maps.

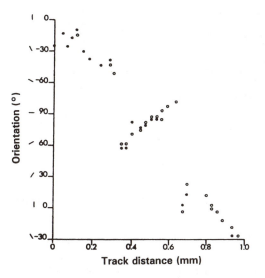

Figure 8.10 Orientation tuning of cat visual cortex.

studies with cats. Two grating stimuli are now "close together" if their orientations are similar, which defines the input space metric. In a later study Hubel & Wiesel (1974) made recordings from an electrode inserted almost tangentially to the cortex and plotted the optimal orientation tuning of the cells encountered against the distance of electrode penetration. Two sets of data are shown in Figure 8.10 (the open and filled symbols refer to which eye is dominant for that cell and their distinction can be ignored here). In the graph on the left hand side the orientation varies smoothly with electrode track distance. That on the right shows several smooth segments interrupted by discontinuities. This pattern is typical and has been demonstrated more graphically for cat visual cortex using a direct optical imaging technique (Bonhoeffer & Grinvald 1991), which makes use of the small changes in reflectivity of the surface of the exposed cortex when it is in metabolic demand due to neural activity. By presenting stimuli at different orientations, it is possible to map *simultaneously* the orientation preference of cells in an entire region of cortex. Apart from reinforcing the results of Hubel and Wiesel, this new data showed that there were point discontinuities around which the orientation tuning changed gradually, resulting in what the authors refer to as "pinwheel" structures. Bonhoeffer and Grinvald displayed their maps using artificial colour codes for orientation preference. We have reproduced a typical pinwheel structure in Figure 8.11 by using small bars oriented in alignment with the optimal tuning for that region. The orientation centre has been marked with a shaded disc. Note that orientation is defined over the range 0–180° and that no directions are implied so that orientations differing by 180° are identified as the same.

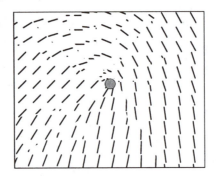

Figure 8.11 Pinwheel structures for orientation tuning.

8.3.2 Developing topographic maps

The first attempt to train a map of this kind was that of von der Malsburg (1973). A network of units arranged on a two-dimensional hexagonal grid learned orientation tuning from a "retina" of 19 nodes also arranged hexagonally (see Fig. 8.13). The training set consisted of Boolean patterns of light bars ("on" units) against a dark background ("off" units) at nine different orientations. The model was biologically motivated so that, rather than there being a single self-excitatory connection per node, the lateral excitatory region included a unit's nearest neighbours, and lateral inhibition was mediated via a separate set of neurons. Further, the resulting inhibitory region did not then extend to the rest of the net but was restricted only to units that were at most three nodes distant. At each pattern presentation, the competitive dynamics were allowed to run so that an equilibrium output profile was established. At equilibrium a Hebb rule was applied, followed by an explicit renormalization of the weights.

This model worked well and the net learned a *local* map, in which several parts of the net responded well to a given orientation. To understand how this emerges, consider a typical equilibrium output profile in the latter stages of training, as shown schematically in 1D in Figure 8.12. There are two points to note here. First, there is more than one region of significant activity which occurs because the lateral inhibition does not operate globally over the entire net. This allows parts of the net that are sufficiently well separated to act independently and develop their own local maxima. Secondly, the activity within each region is spread across several units with there being no single "winning node". This is a result of the excitation extending over a small region of the net and not being restricted to a single self-excitatory connection per node. Now consider what happens under the Hebb rule. Connections from the "on" units in the input retina will have their strengths increased to those units that are active, and this increase will be in proportion to the unit's output. Thus, nodes in active network regions will learn to respond more strongly to the current pattern. In this way neighbouring nodes

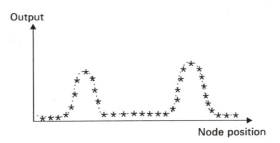

Figure 8.12 Output profiles in orientation map.

tend to develop similar weight vectors and so the network topography has its origins in the extended regions of activity prior to training.

Although this example worked well, there are aspects of the model that are potential causes of difficulty. The use of competitive dynamics *per se* leads to a problem concerning the parametrization of the lateral weights. What is the best radius of excitation and the best ratio of inhibition to excitation? Although not crucial in the orientation net, it should be borne in mind that the input space had only a single feature or dimension to be encoded (i.e. orientation) and in most problems there are several metric dimensions to the input (discussed further in Sect. 8.3.5). This can serve to make the learning more sensitive to the activity profiles at equilibrium. Secondly, the iterative solution of the net dynamics can be very computationally intensive and, if a global rather than local solution were sought (requiring full lateral interconnectivity), this could be prohibitive.

Kohonen (1982) re-examined the problem of topographic map formation from an engineering perspective and extracted the essential computational principles. Most work in this area now makes use of the algorithm he developed for self-organizing feature maps (SOFMs or simply SOMs). He has described the principles and further developments in a subsequent book (Kohonen 1984) and review paper (Kohonen 1990).

8.3.3 The SOM algorithm

The network architecture still consists of a set of inputs that are fully connected to the self-organizing layer, but now there are no lateral connections. It is clear, from the analysis of the orientation map in the last section, that the key principle for map formation is that training should take place over an extended region of the network centred on the maximally active node. All that is required is that the concept of "neighbourhood" be defined for the net. This may be fixed by the spatial relation between nodes within the self-organizing layer, as shown in Figure 8.13. Three neighbourhood schemes are shown based on a linear array of nodes and two two-dimensional arrays in the form of rectangular and hexagonal grids. In all cases, three neighbourhoods are shown delimited with respect to a shaded unit at distances of 1, 2 and 3 away from this node. Thus, the linear, rectangular and hexagonal arrays have 5, 25 and 19 nodes respectively in their distance-2 neighbourhoods (including the central nodes). Although three-dimensional arrays of nodes are conceivable, they tend not to get used in practice owing to their complexity. We now give details of the algorithm, followed by a discussion of each step.

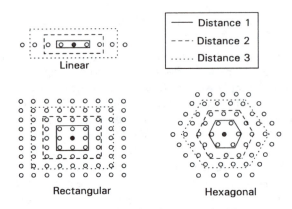

Figure 8.13 Neighbourhood schemes for SOMs.

The weights are initialized to small random values and the neighbourhood distance d_N set to cover over half the net. Vectors are drawn randomly from the training set and the following series of operations performed at each selection.

1. Find the best matching or "winning" node k whose weight vector $\mathbf{w}_k$ is closest to the current input vector $\mathbf{x}$ using the vector difference as criterion:

$$\|\mathbf{w}_k - \mathbf{x}\| = \min_i\{\|\mathbf{w}_i - \mathbf{x}\|\} \tag{8.11}$$

2. Train node k and all nodes in the neighbourhood N_k of k using a rule similar to that in (8.4)

$$\Delta\mathbf{w}_j = \begin{cases} \alpha(\mathbf{x} - \mathbf{w}_j) & : \text{ if } j \text{ is in } N_k \\ 0 & : \text{ if } j \text{ is not in } N_k \end{cases} \tag{8.12}$$

3. Decrease the learning rate α slightly.

4. After a certain number M of cycles, decrease the size of the neighbourhood d_N.

Concerning the definition of best matching node (point 1) the weight–pattern inner product or node activation has been abandoned in favour of the distance between the weight and pattern vectors. This uses both angular and length information from $\mathbf{w}$ and $\mathbf{x}$, and so does not suffer from the difficulties that require vector normalization. If the vectors *are* normalized, then the two schemes are equivalent. To show this formally we use (3.10) to show that, for any $\mathbf{w}$ and $\mathbf{x}$,

$$
\begin{aligned}
\|\mathbf{w} - \mathbf{x}\|^2 &= (\mathbf{w} - \mathbf{x}) \cdot (\mathbf{w} - \mathbf{x}) \\
&= \|\mathbf{w}\|^2 + \|\mathbf{x}\|^2 - 2\mathbf{w} \cdot \mathbf{x} \\
&= 2(1 - \mathbf{w} \cdot \mathbf{x})
\end{aligned}
\tag{8.13}
$$

Thus, a decrease in the distance $\|\mathbf{w} - \mathbf{x}\|$ implies an increase in the dot product $\mathbf{w} \cdot \mathbf{x}$ and vice versa.

Secondly, the winning node is found using a straightforward search rather than by the internal dynamics of the net, which therefore obviates the overhead associated with this task. Both these features make for computational ease and efficiency but are biologically unrealistic. It *is* possible to train using the inner product measure but this then requires normalization at each training step. Alternatively, if the training set has only positive components, we can use the simple, linear normalization method described in Section 8.2 and rely on the auto-renormalization implied (8.9). If we adopt the vector difference criterion, the response of the net when used after training is given by supposing that the winning node is "on" while all others are "off". The advantage of the inner product measure is that it leads to a more natural network response in which each node computes an activation $a = \mathbf{w} \cdot \mathbf{x}$. We can then either pass this through a sigmoid output function or simply interpret it directly as the output so that $y = a$.

The learning rule (point 2) is identical to that used in competitive learning if we suppose that the nodes in the current neighbourhood are active with output equal to 1, and the rest of the net is quiescent with output 0. However, learning now takes place over an extended neighbourhood and, as noted previously, it is this regional training that induces map formation. By starting with a large neighbourhood we guarantee that a global ordering takes place, otherwise there may be more than one region of the net encoding a given part of the input space. The best strategy is to let d_N decline to zero over a first phase of training, during which the map topography is formed, and then continue to train only the best-match nodes to make small adjustments and pick up the finer detail of the input space. If the learning rate is kept constant, it is possible for weight vectors to oscillate back and forth between two nearby positions in the later stages of training. Lowering α ensures that this does not occur and the network is stable.

8.3.4 A graphic example

It is possible to illustrate the self-organization of a Kohonen net graphically using a net where the input space has just two dimensions. Consider a net with six nodes on a rectangular grid, as shown in Figure 8.14. Because each node has only

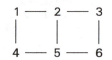

Figure 8.14 Six-node network with node labels.

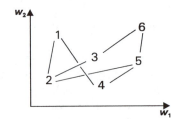

Figure 8.15 Untrained net in weight space.

two inputs, it is possible to visualize the representation of this net in *weight space* (Fig. 8.15) in which a marker is placed at the position corresponding to each node's weight vector (as drawn from the co-ordinate origin). The weights are assumed to start with positive random values, and lines have been drawn connecting markers for nodes that are physically adjacent in the net. For example, nodes 2 and 5 have small and large weight vectors respectively and are therefore widely separated in weight space. They are, however, nearest neighbours in the network and so are linked by a line in the diagram.

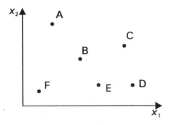

Figure 8.16 Training set in pattern space.

Suppose now that there are six training vectors A, B, C, D, E, F, as shown in the pattern space diagram in Figure 8.16. Since there are six units in the network and six training patterns we should expect that, in a well-trained net, each unit is assigned a unique training pattern so that its weight vector matches the corresponding input vector. This is the result of the competitive learning but, under the Kohonen algorithm, we also expect a topographic map to emerge. The implication of this is that neighbouring nodes will become associated with neighbouring patterns so that the weight space of the trained net looks like that of Figure 8.17.

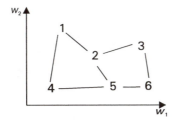

Figure 8.17 Trained net in weight space.

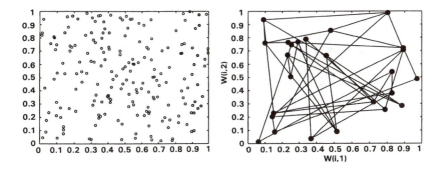

Figure 8.18 A 25-node net: training set and initial weight space.

The intermediate stage between the initial and final weight space diagrams is better illustrated using a slightly larger net. In this example, 200 vectors have been chosen at random from the unit square in pattern space and used to train a net of 25 nodes on a 5 by 5 rectangular grid. The vectors and the initial weight space are shown on the left and right hand sides respectively of Figure 8.18. Subsequent "snapshots" of weight space are shown in Figure 8.19, where the numbers refer to how many patterns have been used to train up to that point. After only 60 iterations, all nodes have weights that are close to the centre of the diagram[1], which indicates that they are near the average values of the training set. This is a result of using a large initial neighbourhood so that nearly all nodes get trained at every step. As the neighbourhood shrinks, the weight space representation starts to "unravel" as distinct parts of the pattern space can start to be encoded by different regions of the net. After 600 training steps, the net has become ordered with the correct topology, which is apparent as there are no internode connection lines crossing each other. Further training does not alter the ordering of the map but makes fine adjustments to the weight vectors so that the entire input space is represented equally. Since the training patterns cover the square uniformly, the final map reflects this by being almost regular in shape.

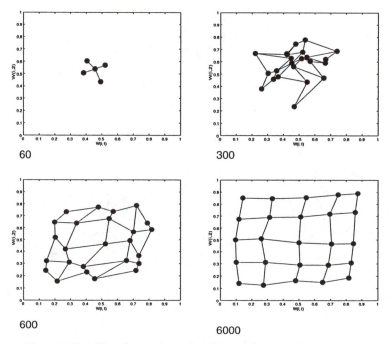

Figure 8.19 A 25-node net: "snapshots" in weight space during training.

8.3.5 Maps, distributions and dimensionality

In another example, the training set is not uniformly distributed in pattern space but is drawn from a semicircular arc of width 0.2; the initial weight space and patterns are shown in Figure 8.20. A net of 100 nodes on a 10 by 10 grid was trained using these patterns and some snapshots of weight space are shown in Figure 8.21. Once again, ordered map formation takes place and the node weights occupy the same region in pattern space as the training set. However, this time

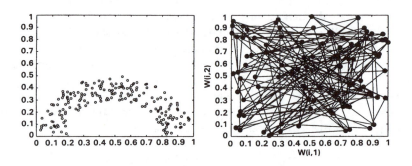

Figure 8.20 Vectors constrained to a 2D arc: training set and initial weight space.

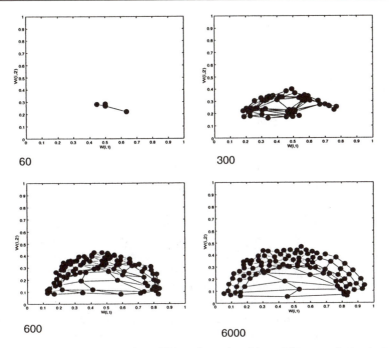

Figure 8.21 Vectors constrained to a 2D arc: "snapshots" in weight space during training.

the pattern space representation on the net has to be contorted to enable the map to exist. In this process there are a few nodes that have developed weight vectors which do not represent any members of the training set and which have become "stranded", as it were, in a pattern-free zone. This is almost inevitable, and another example of this phenomenon is provided by Kohonen (1984) in his book.

The situation becomes even more complex when the input space has more than two dimensions. Now, the higher dimensions must be "squashed" onto the two-dimensional grid but this will be done in such a way as to preserve the most important variations in the input data. To see what is meant by "important variation" here, consider the example illustrated in Figure 8.22. Here, patterns that are specified by their two (x and y) co-ordinates in the plane have been sampled from an arc of a circle. However, any pattern in this set is uniquely specified by a single number – for example, the angle θ around the arc from one of its end points. Its *underlying* dimensionality is therefore 1, and provides us with a simple example of a low-dimensional space (a line) embedded in a higher dimensional one (the plane). It is therefore possible to train a set of two-input units arranged in line (rather than a two-dimensional array) to map accurately the input set shown in the figure. Then, nodes get assigned according to the density of vectors along the line in pattern space, so that more nodes would be assigned to the ends of the arc than the middle. The data nominally in 2D have been mapped into the 1D of the linear neural net array, which has therefore effected a *dimension reduction* of the data.

133

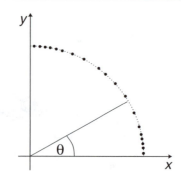

Figure 8.22 Two-dimensional data with underlying dimensionality 1.

Oriented patterns on a simple, circular array provide another example as shown in Figure 8.23. Each pattern is Boolean and is set on an array of 32 elements so that its nominal vector dimensionality is also 32. However, each one has the same shape and the only difference between them is their orientation. A single parameter – the angle of orientation – may then be used to specify the pattern uniquely so the underlying dimensionality is, once again, 1. In general, the underlying dimensionality of the training set is greater than 2 and so, even after dimension reduction, the input space has to be deformed to be mapped onto a two-dimensional neural layer. Further, the representation of the data in the lower dimensional space is usually not perfect in a real-world, non-idealized situation. For example, the "linear" dataset in Figure 8.22 would realistically occupy a finite width in the plane rather than being strictly confined to the line, and the orientation set would not be exactly the same shape. In spite of this, the net can still develop good maps for these sets along their primary parameter dimension.

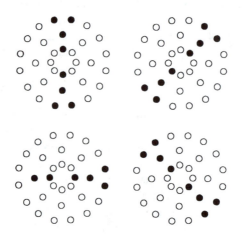

Figure 8.23 Oriented patterns on a grid.

8.3.6 SOMs and classification: LVQ

Our emphasis in discussing self-organization has been on encoding clusters in the training set. Class labels may be attached to nodes if we have already assigned labels to patterns in some way. This was the case, for example, in the examples provided by Rumelhart and Zipser (in Sect. 8.2.1). In general, nodes may become classifiers by repeatedly presenting patterns to the net, finding the maximally responding node and labelling it according to the class of that pattern. The problem with this simple-minded approach is that, in general, a node may respond maximally to more than one class of pattern. Therefore, we have to base the node's class label on a majority vote to find the class to which it most frequently responds.

The relation between clusters and classes may be discussed further using the patterns in Figure 8.1. To facilitate this, let the two smaller clusters on the left be designated L_1 and L_2 and the loosely bound cluster on the right, R. If a net with three units is trained on these patterns then each unit would be assigned to one of L_1, L_2 and R. Now, how these are interpreted in terms of class labels is entirely dependent on the context of these patterns in relation to the problem domain in which they originated. Thus, it may be that each of the three clusters does indeed represent a separate class and it is comparatively straightforward to make node assignments. Alternatively, L_1 and L_2 may be from the same class, which may then be thought of as containing two subcategories – perhaps upper and lower case versions of the same letter in a character recognition task – and then two nodes will be used for one of the classes. Another possibility is that one of the three visually apparent clusters we have identified is, in fact, a result of two adjacent or overlapping subclusters, each of which has a different class label. This gives rise to the problem alluded to above in which a node will appear to belong to more than one class. Now suppose the net has only two nodes. The most probable outcome is that L_1 and L_2 will be represented by one node while R is assigned to the other. If there is a one-to-one mapping between clusters and classes we will then necessarily fail to distinguish between two of them. On the other hand, if we have more than three nodes, several nodes will be assigned to a single class.

Having made the initial class–node assignment, is it possible to improve the network's performance in classification? Kohonen has shown (Kohonen 1988a, Kohonen 1990) that it is possible to fine-tune the class boundaries of an SOM in a *supervised* way and has developed several methods for doing this. They are all variants of what he calls *linear vector quantization* (LVQ). Vector quantization is a standard statistical clustering technique (Gray 1984), which seeks to divide the input space into areas that are assigned typical representatives or "code-book" vectors. The problem, of course, is to discover what is meant by "typical" and to cover the input space in an efficient manner. These ideas are, of course, at the heart of the SOM algorithm. The weight vector of each node may be thought of as a stereotypical example of the class assigned to that node since, by the nature of the training, it is necessarily close to vectors in that class. The weights are therefore code-book vectors and the SOM algorithm a kind of vector quantization.

In order to understand the LVQ techniques it should be borne in mind that the closest weight vector $\mathbf{w}_k$ to a pattern $\mathbf{x}$ may be associated with a node k that has the wrong class label for $\mathbf{x}$. This follows because the initial node labels are based only on their most frequent class use and are therefore not always reliable. In the first variant, LVQ1, the procedure for updating $\mathbf{w}_k$ is as follows:

$$\Delta\mathbf{w}_k = \left\{ \begin{array}{ll} \alpha(\mathbf{x} - \mathbf{w}_j) & : \text{ if } \mathbf{x} \text{ is classified correctly} \\ -\alpha(\mathbf{x} - \mathbf{w}_j) & : \text{ if } \mathbf{x} \text{ is classified incorrectly} \end{array} \right. \tag{8.14}$$

The negative sign in the misclassification case makes the weight vector move *away* from the cluster containing $\mathbf{x}$, which, on average, tends to make weight vectors draw away from class boundaries.

Two variant techniques (LVQ2 and LVQ3) have also been described by Kohonen (1990). These are more complex than LVQ1 but allow for improved performance in classification.

8.3.7 The role of SOMs

Biological purpose

What purpose do topographic maps serve in cortical networks? In artificial neural nets it is sufficient for a single node to encode a cluster or region of the input space. This was the case when the competitive dynamics sharpened the output profile in an extreme way in the winner-takes-all net. In biological nets, however, structural and signal noise require considerable redundancy if a network is to represent an input feature in a robust way. It is therefore better to use a *distributed* code at dynamic equilibrium in which several nodes respond to some extent when presented with a given input. This was the case in the orientation maps of von der Malsburg (1973) whose equilibrium activity was shown in Figure 8.12. The other side of this coin is that even though each node responds optimally to a particular input pattern it also gives significant output to nearby patterns in the input space. That is, nodes have a broad tuning with respect to the dimensions encoded in the net so that in the orientation maps, for example, each node responds somewhat to a range of orientations. This is shown in Figure 8.24, which contrasts it with the point-like tuning in a winner-takes-all net.

Recall that, in order for distributed profiles to emerge, there had to be an extensive excitatory region around each node. Now imagine that, instead of the excitatory links being local, they are spread randomly throughout the net. Under competitive learning, the same distributed encoding would emerge, albeit in a non-topographic way and leading to apparently random output profiles. However, the average length of axonic projections would be longer since there is now no predisposition to local connections. Turning the argument around, since we know that local connectivity leads to topographic maps, it is possible that maps appear in the cortex through the requirement of minimizing "wiring"

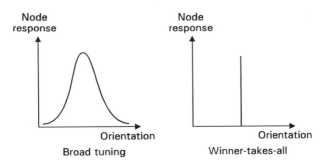

Figure 8.24 Node tuning to pattern features in competitive nets.

length or, equivalently, of ensuring that intra-cortical computation is carried out locally. This hypothesis has been tested in simulation by Durbin & Mitchison (1990), who showed that the criterion of minimizing the cortical wiring led to the kind of dimension-reducing topographic maps observed in the cortex.

Understanding cortical maps

Self-organizing topographic maps were introduced from the biological perspective and one of the objectives in using them is to explore the computational principles that may be at work in their generation in real cortical tissue. Willshaw & von der Malsburg (1976) gave an account of the emergence of retinotopic maps; Obermayer et al. (1990) showed how retinotopy and orientation maps can develop concurrently; Goodhill (1993) has discussed the generation of ocular dominance maps in which areas of cortex become associated with processing input from each eye when initially driven binocularly. Gurney & Wright (1992b) showed how a self-organizing network can develop topographic maps of image velocity in which the dimensions encoded are the speed and direction of a rigidly moving body. One of the direction maps that was learned is shown in Figure 8.25. Compare this with the orientation pinwheels discovered by Bonhoeffer and Grinvald (Fig. 8.11). There is the same basic swirling pattern but, because we are dealing with direction rather than orientation, the encoding covers the entire range of angles between 0° and 360°. Notice also the discontinuity or "fracture" in the map in the left hand upper region, which was a characteristic of the data of Hubel and Wiesel (Fig. 8.10).

Visualizing the input space

In artificial neural nets, the dimension reduction framework provides a basis for understanding the nature of the training set in that it may be useful to be able to visualize metric relations in the input space. This is apparent in the work of Kohonen et al. (Kohonen et al. 1984, Kohonen 1988b) in which a map

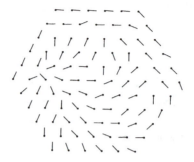

Figure 8.25 Direction tuning in velocity-encoding net.

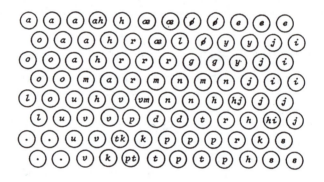

Figure 8.26 Phonemic map.

of the *phonemes* in the Finnish language was developed from natural speech samples. Phonemes are the smallest units of sound that characterize speech – they are usually smaller than syllables and consist of the primitive utterances that constitute speech in a given language. One of the phonotopic maps that Kohonen developed is shown in Figure 8.26. Although a full appreciation of this map requires knowledge of the phonemic notation used and its Finnish speech equivalent, it is apparent that vowel-like sounds occur in the top right hand part of the map and grade into consonant-like sounds over the rest of the net. Clearly, the true dimensionality of "phoneme space" is not known a priori, but the final two-dimensional representation gives us some insight into the metric relations between phonemes. The net also works as a phoneme classifier first stage in an automatic speech to text translation device in which phonemes are subsequently transcribed into the corresponding textual symbols.

One of the problems in speech recognition is that each time a phoneme is uttered it is slightly different. This is most severe between different speakers but is also apparent within the speech of a single person. The neural network is ideally suited to overcoming these types of noisy data. However, there are more fundamental problems to be overcome. Continuous speech does not come ready parcelled in phonemic segments, leading to so-called *co-articulation effects* in which the exact sound of a phoneme can vary according to its context within a word. These difficulties are addressed by Kohonen but with methods that do not use neural networks. For example, context sensitivity is dealt with using a conventional rule-based system. This is an example, therefore, of a hybrid approach, which is often the most pragmatic in engineering a problem solution (see Sect. 11.4.4).

Another example concerns the representation of animal categories given an input vector of animal properties (Ritter & Kohonen 1989). The input patterns consist of Boolean vectors, each describing a particular animal, and with components signalling the presence or absence of properties such as "is small", "is big", "has two legs", "has four legs", "likes to fly", "likes to run", etc. When an SOM is trained on these descriptors, each animal gets assigned to a distinct part of the net so that the net becomes partitioned into regions representing the three types of animal: birds, hunter–carnivores and herbivores. In the original work of Ritter & Kohonen, the input vectors were augmented with preassigned classification information. However, there are several unsatisfactory aspects to this, as noted by Bezdek & Pal (1995), who go on to show that this extra information is unnecessary for good class ordering on the SOM.

Combining SOMs and MLPs

Huang & Kuh (1992) used a combination of a single-layer perceptron, an SOM and a multilayer perceptron to solve the problem of isolated word speech recognition on a database of 20 words consisting of numbers (0 through to 9) and ten so-called "control" words. The latter were drawn from the kind of commands required to interact with a computer program, such as "go", "help", "yes", "no", etc. This problem is considerably simpler than the recognition of continuous speech discussed above, since the vocabulary is small and the words are supposed to be spoken separately with distinct interword silence. Nevertheless, there will still be inter- and intra-speaker variations in the input, and true silence has to be distinguished from background noise.

The raw input was split into samples of 16 ms duration. Each sample was then processed to give information about 15 frequency channels and three other parameters that were used in a simple perceptron to distinguish speech from noise. If a sample was classified as speech then it was fed into a rectangular-array SOM, which was used to learn an *acoustic map* of the words in the training set. This is similar to the phonotopic map shown in Figure 8.26 but this time there is no attempt to distinguish phonemes *per se* and each 16 ms segment is treated as a valid input. When a complete word is input to the net, a temporal sequence of sound segments is generated and, by recording all those units that responded to a word, a pattern of excitation is built up which is characteristic of that word. These characteristic word signatures produced by the SOM are then used as input vectors to an MLP, which is trained to recognize them using backpropagation. In this way, the SOM is being used as a preprocessor for the MLP and it is in this way that SOMs often find practical application.

Several further points are worth mentioning. First, the SOM was trained using Kohonen's self-organizing algorithm but was fine-tuned using a kind of vector quantization known as *K-means clustering*. Secondly, the topographic nature of the acoustic map was used to good effect in searching for best-matching units. Thus, adjacent segments in an acoustic word sequence are often not too different because of physical constraints on the vocalization of sounds. The result is that they tend to excite nodes that are close to each other (although not necessarily adjacent) on the network array. Having located the first best match in a word sequence, the next one is likely to be found in its near vicinity, the subsequent match close to this and so forth. Finally, the combined network was very successful, with the best recognition rates approaching 99.5 per cent.

8.4 Principal component analysis

We have seen that one way of viewing SOM learning is that it accomplishes a dimension reduction. There is another way of performing this, which we first examine in pattern space before seeing its implementation in a network.

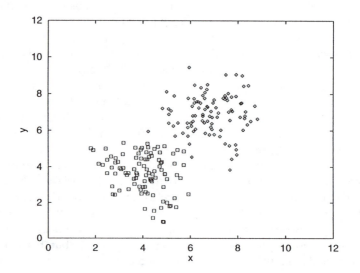

Figure 8.27 Clusters for PCA.

Consider the two clusters of two-dimensional patterns shown in Figure 8.27. It is clear in this graphical representation that there are two clusters; this is apparent because we can apprehend the geometry and the two sets have been identified with different marker symbols. However, suppose that we did not have access to this geometric privilege, and that we had to analyze the data on the basis of their (x, y) co-ordinate description alone. One way of detecting structure in the data might be to examine the histograms with respect to each co-ordinate – the number of points lying in a series of groups or bins along the co-ordinate axes – as shown in the top half of Figure 8.28. There is a hint that the histograms are bimodal (have two "humps"), which would indicate two clusters, but this is not really convincing. Further, both histograms have approximately the same width and shape. In order to describe the data more effectively we can take advantage of the fact that the clusters were generated so that their centres lie on a line through the origin at 45° to the x axis.

Now consider a description of the data in another co-ordinate system x', y' obtained from the first by a rotation of the co-ordinate axes through 45°. This is shown schematically in Figure 8.29. The new x' axis lies along the line through the cluster centres, which gives rise to a distinct bimodality in its histogram, as shown in the bottom left of Figure 8.28. Additionally, the new y' histogram is more sharply peaked and is quite distinct from its x' counterpart. We conclude that the structure in the data is now reflected in a more efficient co-ordinate representation.

In a real situation, of course, we are not privy to the way in which the clusters were produced, so that the required angle of rotation is not known. However, there is a simple property of the data in the new co-ordinate system that allows us to find the optimal transformation out of all possible candidates; that the variance along one of the new axes is a maximum. In the example this is, of course, the x' axis. A corollary of this is that the variance along the remaining y' axis is reduced. With more dimensions, a "rotation" of the co-ordinate axes is sought such that the bulk of the variance in the data is compressed into as few vector components as possible. Thus, if the axes are labelled in order of decreasing data variability, x_1 contains the largest data variance commensurate with a co-ordinate rotation; x_2 contains the largest part of the remaining variance; and so forth. The first few vector components in the transformed co-ordinate system are the *principal components* and the required transformation is obtained by *principal component analysis* or PCA. This is a standard technique in statistical analysis and details of its operation may be found in any text on multivariate analysis – see, for example, Kendall (1975).

To the extent that the essential information about the dataset is contained in the first few principal components, we have effected a dimension reduction. Thus, in our simple two-dimensional example, the class membership is related directly to the distance along the x' axis. Then, although each point still needs two co-ordinates, the most important feature is contained in the single dimension – x'. The situation is reminiscent of the dimension reduction discussed for SOMs. However, the transformation under PCA is linear (since co-ordinate rotation is a

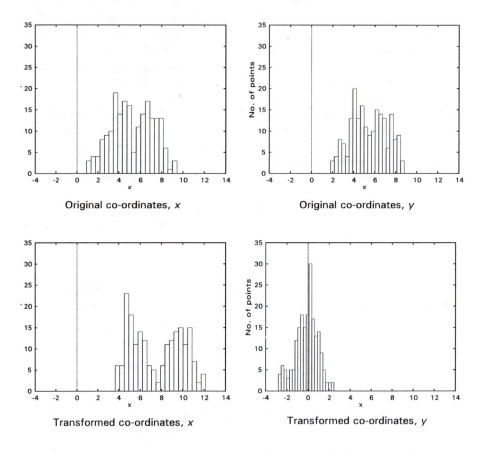

Figure 8.28 Histograms for PCA data.

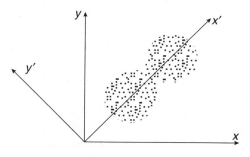

Figure 8.29 Rotated co-ordinate axes.

linear transformation) whereas dimension reduction on an SOM is not necessarily so. For example, the embedding of the arc in the plane (Fig. 8.22) requires a nonlinear transform to extract the angle θ around the arc (e.g. $\theta = \tan^{-1} y/x$).

We now attempt to place PCA in a connectionist setting. Figure 8.30 shows a single pattern vector $\mathbf{v}$ taken in the context of the two-dimensional example used above. Also shown is the expression $\|\mathbf{v}\| \cos \theta$ for its first principal component $v_{x'}$ along the x' axis, in terms of the angle θ between $\mathbf{x}$ and this axis. Consider now a node whose weight vector $\mathbf{w}$ has unit length and is directed along the x' axis. The following now holds for the activation: $a = \mathbf{w} \cdot \mathbf{v} = \|\mathbf{w}\|\|\mathbf{v}\| \cos \theta = \|\mathbf{v}\| \cos \theta$, since $\|\mathbf{w}\| = 1$. But $\|\mathbf{v}\| \cos \theta = v_{x'}$ so that $a = v_{x'}$. That is, the activation is just the first principal component of the input vector. Thus, if we use a linear node in which the output equals the activation, then the node picks up the most important variation in its input. Further, we may obtain an approximation of $\mathbf{v}$ according to

$$\mathbf{v} \approx v_{x'} \mathbf{w} \tag{8.15}$$

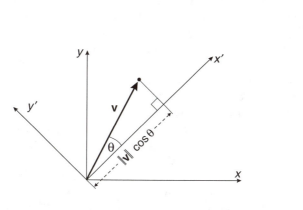

Figure 8.30 Vectors and PCA.

This property only becomes useful, however, if we can develop the required weight vector in a neural training regime. This was done by Oja (1982), who showed that it occurs under self-organization with a Hebb-like learning rule

$$\Delta \mathbf{w} = \alpha(\mathbf{x} - y\mathbf{w})y \tag{8.16}$$

This is similar to (8.5) except that the decay term is $y^2\mathbf{w}$ instead of $y\mathbf{w}$. Of course, it is more useful if we can extract principal components other than just the first, and Sanger (1989) has shown how to do this using a single layer of linear units, each one learning one of the component directions as its weight vector. Sanger also gave an application from image compression in which the first eight principal component directions were extracted from image patches of natural scenes. Let the resulting weight vectors be $\mathbf{w}_1 \ldots \mathbf{w}_8$ and their outputs in response to an image patch be $y_1 \ldots y_8$. These outputs are just the principal components and so, under a generalization of (8.15), the original patch may be reconstructed by forming the vector $y_1\mathbf{w}_1 + y_2\mathbf{w}_2 + \cdots + y_8\mathbf{w}_8$. Sanger showed how the components y_i can be efficiently quantized for each patch, without significant loss of image information, so that the number of bits used to store them for the entire image was approximately 4.5 per cent that of the original image pixels.

Finally, we note that it is possible to extend PCA in a neural setting from a linear to a nonlinear process – see, for example, Karhunan & Joutsensalo (1995).

8.5   Further remarks

We have seen how self-organization has connections with clustering, vector quantization and PCA. It also has connections with a branch of the theory of communication known as *information theory*. This deals with the structure and relations between signals treated in the abstract. There is not room to develop these ideas here but the interested reader may find a suitable introduction in Jones (1979). Linsker was one of the first to explore these connections in a series of papers (Linsker 1986), which are summarized in Linsker (1988). Linsker showed how a layer of linear neurons can, using a type of Hebb rule under self-organization, learn to extract features from its input simply by virtue of there being a local receptive field structure in the input connections. By training a set of hierarchical layers one at a time, it was possible for the net to learn a set of progressively more complex features. Further, he went on to demonstrate how the Hebb-like rule was equivalent to a learning principle that tried to optimize the preservation of information through the net. Plumbley (1993) has shown similar principles at work with so-called *anti-Hebbian* learning in which weight values are *decreased* in response to input–output correlation. This type of learning has the effect of decorrelating the outputs of a net so they respond to different patterns.

Self-organizing multilayer nets with local receptive fields have also been studied by Fukushima in a network known as the *neocognitron* (Fukushima 1980, Fukushima 1988, Fukushima 1989). It is a complex structure with three cell or node types and its overall connection scheme is similar in broad outline to the animal visual system in that each successive layer sees a local patch (receptive field) of its input. The neocognitron is therefore best suited to visual pattern recognition problems and is able to generalize to scaled, translated, rotated and highly distorted versions of the training exemplars, just as humans are able to do when reading handwritten characters. Fukushima reports simulations with the numerals 0–9, and Kim & Lee (1991) have demonstrated the ability of a neocognitron to recognize Hanguls (Korean) syllabic characters.

8.6   Summary

Lateral on-centre, off-surround connections in a layer of neurons enable the activity profile of the layer to be contrast enhanced. Thus, nodes being supplied with the strongest external input become very active at the expense of nodes that are being weakly driven. With suitable lateral weights this can result in the extreme case of "winner-takes-all" dynamics in which the node with the largest external input reaches its maximum activity strength while all others have their activities reduced to a minimum. This mechanism is used in competitive learning where nodes become associated with pattern clusters by aligning their weight vectors with cluster centres. For any given pattern $\mathbf{x}$, the node whose weight vector $\mathbf{w}$ is best aligned with $\mathbf{x}$ is adapted so that $\mathbf{w}$ moves even closer to $\mathbf{x}$. The degree of weight–pattern alignment is determined by node activity since this is proportional to the dot product $\mathbf{w} \cdot \mathbf{x}$ of the two vectors (under a scheme in which these two sets of vectors are normalized). The most active node is therefore the one whose weight vector should be adapted and may be found using the competitive (winner-takes-all) dynamics. In an ideal case each cluster is encoded by (gives maximal response with) at least one node although what constitutes a cluster is determined by the network. The learning rule used in weight adaptation may be written as the sum of a Hebb rule and a decay term. This type of learning is called unsupervised – equivalently the net is said to undergo a process of self-organization – because there are no target outputs.

In a topographic feature map, not only are nodes responsive to clusters but also they are arranged in the net so that adjacent nodes encode clusters that are "close" to each other. The concept of proximity here is based on the idea that the pattern space has an underlying dimensionality significantly smaller than the nominal dimensionality of each vector. If this is the case then the feature map will vary smoothly along each of these main dimensions although singularities or fractures may also be found. Topographic feature maps are found extensively in animal cortex where they encode sensory and motor information. They may be developed in artificial nets under self-organization using a learning rule similar to that used in competitive learning but now, not only is the "winning" node trained, but also nodes within a surrounding neighbourhood. To ensure well-ordered maps with good resolution of pattern space detail, both the neighbourhood size and learning rate must be gradually reduced as training progresses. After training a self-organizing map (SOM) in the manner outlined above, its class boundaries (if these are known) may be improved using linear vector quantization (LVQ).

The purpose of feature maps in the biological setting may be related to a need to conserve "wire length". The SOM algorithm sheds light on possible developmental processes in the brain and feature maps allow visualization of fundamental relations in the pattern space of the training set. SOMs may be thought of in terms of a dimension reduction of the input space; an alternative, linear statistical method that attempts to do this is principal component analysis (PCA), which has a neural network implementation.

8.7 Notes

1. All the weights are slightly different although only five points are shown; the graphic resolution is not able to make these fine differences apparent.

Chapter Nine

Adaptive resonance theory: ART

Adaptive resonance theory, or ART, refers to a class of self-organizing neural architectures that cluster the pattern space and produce archetypal weight vector templates. As such they have many features in common with the networks described in Chapter 8. However, ART networks are substantially richer architecturally and dynamically since they attempt to fulfil a much broader programme of objectives.

9.1 ART's objectives

9.1.1 Stability

One of the problems noted in connection with simple competitive nets was that, under certain circumstances, the assignment of best-matching nodes to patterns can continually be in a state of flux so that no stable coding is reached. Grossberg (1976a,b) gives specific examples of this phenomenon and has examined the general conditions under which it is likely to happen. In particular, he notes that an attempt to use too few nodes may well lead to instability and shows how the order of vector presentation may be crucial in this respect. Carpenter & Grossberg (1987b) refer to this problem as the *plasticity–stability dilemma*: how can a network remain open to new learning (remain plastic) while not washing away previously learned codes? In the SOMs developed under Kohonen's algorithm this was overcome by gradually reducing the learning rate. However, this is a rather *ad hoc* solution that simply limits the plastic period of the net. One of the main claims made for ART is that it overcomes the plasticity–stability dilemma in a natural way, so that the net is continually immersed in a training environment where there are no separate learning and testing phases.

9.1.2   Control over detail of encoded features

A further problem is to know a priori how many nodes are required to cluster the pattern space. Clearly, if we provide a large number then we shall obtain an extremely finely graded classification, while too few and the clusters will be too large. It would, therefore, be more satisfactory if we could allow the net to decide for itself how many templates or clusters to provide according to the setting of a single parameter that determines the net's "attention to detail".

9.1.3   Biological plausibility

Several aspects of the SOM algorithm were clearly not biologically plausible. Indeed, its motivation was to extract the required computational principles and then discard their biological basis. The gradient descent algorithms like back-propagation used with MLPs do not even attempt to provide any biological support. It is therefore a significant challenge to ensure that each mechanism and component of a network can be identified (at least in principle) with a neurobiological counterpart.

9.1.4   System integration

The learning rules and training algorithms we have dealt with so far imply that there is an external controller which supervises the sequencing of many of the steps during learning. For example, weight adjustment is initiated at specific times at the end of a pattern presentation cycle, an error signal is accumulated at the output layer of an MLP, or a neighbourhood size parameter is reduced in an SOM. Is it possible, at the neural level, to integrate a large part of this system control into the fabric of the network itself or, at a higher level, to make each part manifest and exhibit it as a seamless part of the whole system?

9.1.5   Mathematical foundation

One requirement when developing a network algorithm is to ensure that properties of the net such as convergence, stability, the nature of internal representation, etc., should be mathematically provable. With some of the algorithms described so far, attempts to characterize their behaviour have often been carried out well after their initial use, which was largely empirically driven; they worked and the results appeared to justify the means. It is therefore desirable that a mathematically proven foundation of the network properties be developed as early as possible so that empirical simulation work is avoided which may be directed at trying to achieve the impossible.

9.1.6   The way forward

The construction of a self-organizing network that addresses all these issues is an extremely ambitious programme to fulfil. Nevertheless, Grossberg and Carpenter attempted to do just this with the ART1 architecture and learning scheme. This paper is the culmination of a long development effort initiated by Grossberg (1973), who had started by characterizing the behaviour of the competitive dynamics that would be an essential component of the network. The elements of the learning theory were laid in Grossberg (1976b) and refined in Grossberg (1980). The final form of ART1 is presented by Carpenter & Grossberg (1987b). ART1 is restricted to dealing with Boolean input patterns but further enhancements and revisions have extended the scope of the ART family of architectures. We shall, however, restrict our main focus of attention to ART1, only briefly describing subsequent developments in Section 9.4. Reviews of ART may be found in Grossberg (1987) and Carpenter & Grossberg (1988, 1992), and Grossberg (1988) includes a review of Grossberg's work on competitive dynamics.

The literature on ART sometimes has the appearance of being rather impenetrable and Byzantine. This is partly because it *is* a complex system and partly because the programme is so all embracing, attempting to make connection with neurobiology at both the cellular and anatomical levels, and with psychological theories of learning. All of this is then interwoven with a rich mathematical description. The connection with biology often results in many of the familiar network features we have described being referred to by unfamiliar names. The mathematics also makes occasional use of notation that is not intuitive in a connectionist context.

Our purpose here is not to give an exhaustive description of every aspect of the ART paradigm; rather, we wish to give an overview that will (hopefully) make it more accessible. The key to our approach is not to try and tackle ART "head on" in all its complexity, but to try and disentangle a set of levels of analysis using a suitable hierarchical approach. This perspective is of quite general applicability and so we will revisit some networks and algorithms described earlier, both to deepen our understanding of these systems and to illustrate how it may be applied to ART.

9.2   A hierarchical description of networks

In his book *Vision*, David Marr (1982) described a hierarchical framework for discussing the nature of computational processes. The motivation for this was an understanding of the nature of computation in the visual system. However, Marr's approach is of quite general applicability and we shall use a modified version of it to describe the process of training a neural network (in particular the ART1 net).

The top level of the hierarchy is the *computational* level. This attempts to answer the questions – what is being computed and why? The next level is the *algorithmic*, which describes how the computation is being carried out, and, finally, there is the *implementation level*, which gives a detailed "nuts-and-bolts" description of what facilities the algorithm makes use of. In applying this scheme, the clear distinctions that are hypothesized may not be so easy to make in practice, and how system features get allocated to levels may be, to some extent, a matter for debate. However, Marr's original example helps illustrate the meaning intended. It examines the computation of the bill in a supermarket with a cash register. In answer to the top-level question of "what" is being computed, it is the arithmetical operation of addition. As to "why" this is being done, it is simply that the laws of addition reflect or model the way we should accumulate prices together from piles of goods in a trolley; it is incorrect, for example, to multiply the prices together. Next we wish to know how we do this arithmetic and the answer is that it is done by the normal procedure taught at school where we add individual digits in columns and carry to the next column if required. This will be done in the usual decimal representation rather than binary (normally encountered in machine arithmetic) because of the possibility of incurring rounding errors when converting to and from binary. As for the implementation, this occurs using logic gates made out of silicon, silicon oxide and metal. Notice that, in principle, the three levels are independent. In particular the type of implementation used is quite independent of the chosen algorithm (alternatives in the above example might make use of an older mechanical machine or pencil and paper). In addition, for any given computation, we may choose from a variety of algorithms to achieve the same final result.

In Marr's original hierarchy, the implementation level was associated with a particular set of hardware resources. Here we are not so concerned with this issue *per se* as much as supplying a more detailed account of the network operation. Further, we shall find it useful to divide the implementation level into two – a high or *system implementation* level and a low or *signal implementation* level. The system level includes processes and mechanisms that have yet to be articulated at the level of artificial neurons. For example, in backpropagation no specific neural mechanism is indicated for finding the error. This may be possible in principle but its instantiation would reside at the signal level. This distinction will become clearer as we proceed with the explanation of ART1, and further examples of this approach may be found in Chapter 11.

9.3 ART1

Historically the first (and simplest) member of the ART family is ART1. It is a two-layer network that discovers pattern cluster templates in arbitrary Boolean pattern sets.

9.3.1 Computational level

The computational level has the same goal of finding cluster templates as simple competitive learning. However, the number of templates is not fixed *ab initio* but is determined by the requirement that each pattern should be sufficiently similar to its associated template. Further, the template set and the mapping between patterns and templates should be stable so that, after a finite time, these do not change.

In order to make this more concrete, first recall that ART1 deals with Boolean patterns. It also uses Boolean templates and each "1" in a template or pattern is referred to as a *feature*. Now let d be the number of features common to the template and pattern, divided by the number of features in the pattern. In other words, d is that fraction of the features in a pattern that are held in common with the template, and $0 \leq d \leq 1$. Notice that large values of d imply that the pattern is close to the template, so d is a measure of proximity rather than distance.

The computational requirement is now that each pattern should be assigned a template such that the pattern–template similarity d is greater than some prescribed value ρ. The object of this is to overcome the problem outlined above concerning the level of detail in encoding features. For, if ρ is small then the similarity criterion is loose, comparatively few templates will be required and a few coarse clusters will be found. If, on the other hand, ρ is large then the similarity criterion is demanding, and many templates may be used in encoding a large number of smaller clusters, many of whose templates may be similar to each other. In the terminology of ART, ρ is known as the *vigilance* since it informs the net of how closely it should examine new patterns to see if they are similar to existing stored templates.

9.3.2 Network architecture

The intimate relation between the algorithm and the ART network makes it profitable to describe the neural network architecture at this stage (the relation between algorithms and networks is explored further in Sect. 11.2). The network (Fig. 9.1) has two layers of leaky-integrator-type neurons. Although the dynamics of each are somewhat more complex than those described by equation (2.6) this is not a problem as we will be concerned primarily with their equilibrium properties.

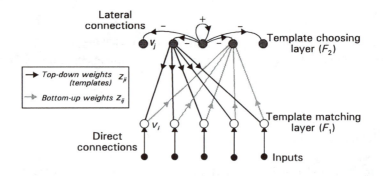

Figure 9.1 ART1 network architecture.

The first layer (labelled F_1 in the ART notation) receives input from the external environment and from the second layer labelled F_2. Quantities relating to layers F_1, F_2 are indexed by i, j respectively and individual nodes denoted by v_i and v_j. Layers F_1 and F_2 contain M and N nodes respectively. The input to F_1 from F_2 is mediated by a set of *top-down* weights z_{ji}, which constitute the stored templates. Layer F_2 is subject to competitive, winner-takes-all dynamics and receives input from F_1 via a set of *bottom-up* weights z_{ij} (notice that the ordering of the i, j indices indicates bottom up or top down). In contrast with simple competitive learning, these weights do not store templates as such, although, as will be shown later, they are closely related. Note that, in some versions of ART1, layer F_1 is also equipped with lateral on-centre, off-surround connections. Only one set of each type of connections has been shown for simplicity.

9.3.3 Algorithmic level

We proceed by first describing the algorithm informally. Next it is formalized in some pseudo-code and detailed points are subsequently discussed.

At the algorithmic level, each pattern presentation initiates a search for a closely matching template. If the template–pattern match is within the vigilance criterion, then the template is adjusted to incorporate information provided by the new pattern by losing any features that are not shared with it. If no sufficiently well-matched template can be found, a new template is created that is set equal to the current pattern.

The success of ART lies in the subtlety with which the templates are searched, as it is not necessarily the case that the closest template is chosen first. Rather, the bottom-up weights z_{ij} determine the order of search by specifying the F_2 node that has the largest response to the input out of a set **J** of nodes which are currently eligible for template match. By "largest response" here is meant the weighted (by w_{ij}) sum of inputs from F_1. If a node selected in this way does not match its template well with the pattern then it is deleted from the list **J**, which initially contains all N nodes in F_2.

Thus, there is a sequence of selection–match trials in which F_2 selects the most active node (in response to the current input pattern) from its remaining pool of untried nodes, and then tests its template against the input. If there is a match (under the vigilance criterion) *resonance* is said to occur between the template and the pattern, and the weights are updated. If there is no match then the currently active F_2 node is deleted from **J** and the search continued. The search will terminate if either there is a previously trained template that matches well, or an untrained node in F_2 is selected. The initialization conditions ensure that such a node resonates with any input since it is non-specific and provides strong inputs to the whole of F_1. Of course, in limiting cases, all nodes are trained and there are no free ones to take new templates. In this case the net cannot learn the entire training set.

At resonance, all top-down weights that correspond to template–pattern feature matches are set to 1, while the rest are set to 0. All bottom-up weights are set to 0 or the same positive value, which is determined by the number of matching features between pattern and template. Larger numbers of matches cause smaller positive weights and vice versa so that, as discussed later, there is some kind of normalization at work. Finally, if z_{ij} is set to 0 then so too is z_{ji} so that the bottom-up weight vector to any F_2 node is like a normalized version of that node's top-down template.

In order to develop this more formally we introduce some new notation in keeping with that due to Carpenter and Grossberg. Vectors are written in upper case italic and, for any vector V, let **V** be the set of component indices in V that are greater than zero. For example, $V = (1, 0, 0.7, 0, 0.5)$ has positive elements at the first, third, and fifth positions so **V** = $\{1, 3, 5\}$. If V is a Boolean vector then, in the terminology of ART, the 1s are features so that **V** is a feature-index set. Further, let $|\mathbf{V}|$ be the number of elements in **V**, which, for a Boolean vector, is just the number of features in V. The top-down template vector will be denoted by $Z^{(j)1}$ so that $Z^{(j)}$ has components z_{ji}. Then, if I is the input pattern, use will be made of the set **X**, which is the set intersection, $\mathbf{I} \cap \mathbf{Z}^{(j)}$. That is, **X** is just the index set for the features that the input and the template have in common.

The ART1 algorithm may now be expressed as follows. Comments are bracketed by the symbols /* */ and use has been made of the set notation $x \in Y$ to mean "x is a member of set Y".

/* Initialization – top-down weights */
put all $z_{ji} = 1$

/* Initialization – bottom-up weights */
Choose constant $L > 1$
Choose random values for z_{ij} ensuring all $z_{ij} < L/(L - 1 + M)$

repeat
>   Apply input I

>   /* Initialize eligibility set to include all F_2 nodes */
>   Put $\mathbf{J} = \{v_1, \ldots, v_j, \ldots v_N\}$

>   Resonance = FALSE
>   repeat /* search for match */
>>   find v_j in F_2 with largest value of $I \cdot Z^{(k)}$, where $k \in J$
>>   /* $I \cdot Z^{(k)}$ is what we call the activation */
>>   compute $\mathbf{X} = \mathbf{I} \cap \mathbf{Z}^{(j)}$
>>   if $|\mathbf{X}|/|\mathbf{I}| > \rho$ /* template matches pattern */
>>>   Resonance = TRUE
>>   else
>>>   delete v_j from $\mathbf{J}$
>>>   /* v_j no longer eligible for template searched */
>>   endif
>   until Resonance or $\mathbf{J}$ is empty
>   if Resonance then /* weight update */

$$z_{ji} = \left\{ \begin{array}{lcl} 1 & : & i \in \mathbf{X} \\ 0 & : & \text{otherwise} \end{array} \right.$$

$$z_{ij} = \left\{ \begin{array}{lcl} L/(L-1+|\mathbf{X}|) & : & i \in \mathbf{X} \\ 0 & : & \text{otherwise} \end{array} \right.$$

>   endif
until. . .

We now comment on some of these steps by way of explanation and to help show their interrelation.

- The condition $|\mathbf{X}|/|\mathbf{I}| > \rho$ is the symbolic representation of the matching criterion; that is, the fraction of input features that are also common to the template must be greater than the vigilance. One corollary of this definition is that inputs with a large number of features require more feature mismatches to fail the vigilance test than do inputs with only a few features. For example, suppose I_1 and I_2 have 10 and 100 features respectively and that they match against templates with 7 and 81 features respectively. For I_1 the test ratio is $7/10 = 0.7$ while for I_2 it is $81/100 = 0.81$. Thus, if $\rho = 0.8$, I_1 would fail a vigilance test against a template with only three mismatching features, while I_2 would pass with 19 mismatches. Carpenter and Grossberg call this the *self-scaling property*, pointing out that, for a pattern like I_1, each feature contains useful information about the pattern because there are so few of them. However, for a pattern like I_2 a few missing features may be due to noise rather than true informational content.

- The prescriptions given for weight update constitute a pair of learning rules for bottom-up and top-down weights.

- The search sequence is such that trained nodes are always tested first before an untrained node is used to establish resonance. However, if a search ends in this way, it must be guaranteed that resonance occurs. This is done by virtue of the initialization that sets all the top-down weights to 1. This template matches any input and then $X = I$ so that a fresh template simply encodes the current pattern. Subsequent matches with this new template are always partial so that templates always lose features and can never gain them.

- Although $L > 1$ (Carpenter & Grossberg 1987b) it is of interest to see what happens in the limiting case when $L = 1$. Then the initial values of z_{ij} are all $1/M$ so that the sum of the weights is 1 and the bottom-up weight vector is normalized according to the criterion in (8.8). Then, the bottom-up learning rule becomes $z_{ij} = 1/|X|$ for those i in X and 0 otherwise. Again $\sum_i z_{ij} = 1$ so that the weights remain normalized. In general $L \neq 1$ so that normalization is not obtained in the sense we have used. Carpenter and Grossberg refer to the quasi-normalization condition occurring for arbitrary L as the *Weber law rule*. We have seen that this class of process is essential for self-organized learning.

- Although $L > 1$ is required for correct operation, L should not be chosen too large or new templates will be chosen at the expense of adapting previously learned ones, even though ρ may be small (Carpenter & Grossberg 1987b).

- In later variants of the architecture, F_1 is equipped with competitive dynamics and can normalize the input prior to sending it on to F_2. This allows for a simpler bottom-up learning rule that puts $z_{ij} = 1$ for those i in X and 0 otherwise.

- If resonance does not occur then all nodes in F_2 have been searched for match without success (J is empty). In this case, the net cannot classify all the patterns at the required level of vigilance. Lowering ρ sufficiently will allow full classification since this decreases the number of clusters required. This is emphasized by the extreme cases of $\rho = 0$, for which all patterns are assigned the same template, and $\rho = 1$, for which all patterns are assigned their own template.

- It can be shown (Carpenter & Grossberg 1987b) that after a finite number of presentations of the training set, the learned templates stabilize so that applying the learning rules at resonance does not alter the weight sets. At

155

this point, each pattern *directly accesses* a learned template. That is, the first template to be chosen on presentation of a pattern is the one that causes resonance. This allows us to avoid having to supply a terminating condition to the outer loop (it has been written – *until...*). The implication of this is that the whole process carries on indefinitely and there is no separate learning and testing phase with ART (as is the case with most architectures) although, in a real application, we would stop presenting patterns after template stabilization. If, on the other hand, the training environment were changed and new vectors were suddenly to be presented, then learning would start again as new templates are assigned and old ones updated.

– Georgiopoulous et al. (1991) have shown that, although the learned templates are always stable, their form depends on the order of pattern presentation. They also showed that it is possible for a learned template to exist that is not directly accessed by any training pattern. These are therefore spurious templates with the same status as the spurious stable states in the Hopfield nets. However, several computer simulations exhibited by Carpenter & Grossberg (1987b) have shown an absence of such templates and so it appears that these may be the exception rather than the rule.

– In another result, Georgiopoulous et al. (1991) showed that the number of epochs (complete presentations of the training set) is limited by the number of different pattern sizes. The *size* of a pattern is just its number of features and, if there are m pattern sizes, then the net will stabilize in at most m epochs. This occurs irrespective of any possible reordering of the training set at each epoch.

9.3.4 An example

The principles outlined above are now applied to a simple example, which is shown in Figure 9.2. The four patterns A, B, C, D are presented to a net with at least three F_2 nodes and the vigilance is set at 0.8. Eventually, three templates will be assigned after a single pass through the training set, after which stability has been reached. Initially the three templates are unassigned, having all $z_{ji} = 1$, indicated by the grid squares being filled in the topmost row of the figure. Subsequent rows show the development of the templates after each of the patterns (shown on the right) has reached resonance and learning taken place. Thus, the second row shows the net after training with pattern A, during which it attains resonance with the first unassigned template. The common feature set, or template match, is just the pattern itself and so the first template becomes equal to A. When B is presented, it first searches against template 1. There are 11 features in pattern B and, of these, B shares eight in common so that, at resonance, $|\mathbf{I}| = 11$ and $|\mathbf{X}| = 8$. In this case, then, $|\mathbf{X}|/|\mathbf{I}| < \rho$ since $8/11 = 0.73 < 0.8$. The node with

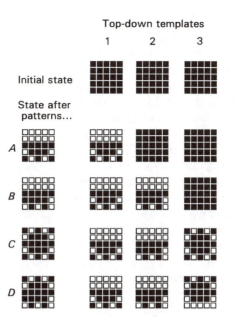

Figure 9.2 Simple ART training example.

template 1 is therefore taken out of the eligibility set **J** and B is forced to resonance with the next unassigned template.

Patterns C and D consist of a common upper region of ten elements overlaid on A and B respectively so that they differ in the same group of elements as A and B. C is quite different from templates 1 and 2 and so, after searching them, reaches resonance with template 3. On presentation of D, it also fails to reach resonance with templates 1 and 2. On comparison with template 3, we have $|\mathbf{I}| = 17$ and $|\mathbf{X}| = 14$. The difference $|\mathbf{I}| - |\mathbf{X}| = 3$ is the same as it was in comparing templates for A and B since the third template is the same as C, and D differs from C by the same group of elements that distinguish A and B. Now, however, $|\mathbf{X}|/|\mathbf{I}| > \rho$ since $14/17 = 0.82 > 0.8$. Resonance occurs and template 3 is set to the common features between its original form (C) and pattern D. Here we have an example of the self-scaling property for, although the same group of features distinguish the pairs A, B and C, D, they give rise to different learning strategies depending on their context. In the case of A, B they are regarded as true pattern features and are retained in separate templates. In the case of C, D, however, they are regarded as noise since they represent a smaller fraction of the total feature set. Separate templates are therefore not required and the existing one is modified to discard the feature difference set.

9.3.5   A system-level implementation

In our development of the implementation, we attempt to adhere to the ART terminology in order to accustom the reader to what can be expected in the literature. Two terms are usefully dealt with right away.

The *short-term memory* (STM) is the pattern of neural activity or activation profile in the network as a result of stimulation by an input pattern. In his work on competitive dynamics, Grossberg (1973) showed how it is possible (with the right dynamics and weight structure) for the activation profile to continue after the input has been withdrawn. In this way, the net "remembers" its previous input although this is truly "short term" since, if the activity is destroyed by further input, this memory trace is lost. The *long-term memory* (LTM) traces, in contrast, are the sets of network weights (either top down or bottom up).

At the system level, the network in Figure 9.1 is now supplemented by some extra control structures as shown in Figure 9.3. The individual units or neurons are no longer shown, and each layer is now represented by an unfilled rectangle. The two layers together are known as the *attentional subsystem*. The weights (LTM traces) have also been lumped graphically into single open arrow symbols. The filled arrows represent control signals that may be thought of as formed by summing the outputs from one of the neural layers, or by combining other control signals. The signs over the arrows indicate whether the signals contribute additively or subtractively from their destination. Where a control signal meets a neural layer it is supposed to affect all nodes in that layer. Note that the control signals here are not resolved at the neural level (in accordance with the definition of the system level), and specific mechanisms for affecting each node are not specified.

Much of this control mechanism is devoted to orchestrating the search for template matches and to determining what constitutes a template mismatch. As indicated in Figure 9.1, the template matching is accomplished in F_1 and the winner-takes-all dynamics of F_2 ensure that only one template is chosen at any one time.

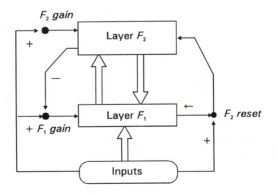

Figure 9.3 ART1 – system level.

We now examine the sequence of events that occurs for each pattern presentation with short summaries posted before each main point.

Summary The F_2 node that responds most strongly to the input I is active while all others are inactive.

The input I produces an STM trace X in layer F_1 (vector of activations) which, in turn, results in a set of F_1 outputs, S. The latter is related to X via a squashing function of some kind (although its exact form is not often specified in many descriptions of ART). Each F_2 node v_j then multiplies or *gates* S by its bottom-up LTM traces z_{ij} to form an input signal T_j; that is, each node forms the weighted sum of its inputs from F_1 (the summation component is also referred to as an *adaptive filter*). The competitive dynamics contrast-enhance the activity to give a pattern of STM Y at F_2 and a final pattern of output U related to Y by another squashing function. U is such that it specifies a single node with output 1, corresponding to the node with largest input T_j, while the rest have output 0. Thus, F_2 executes the normal winner-takes-all choice.

Summary The F_1 gain control allows the input to be transmitted to F_2 under the 2/3 rule. The orienting subsystem is not active.

The above choice at F_2 is made possible by the correct values of the control signals. Until F_2 has chosen an optimally responding node, all its outputs are weak and it provides no signal input to inhibit the F_1 gain control. This is, however, being excited by the input I so that it provides input to F_1. Now, one of the criteria for an F_1 node to be active is that it should have at least two out of three of its inputs active; this is the so-called 2/3 *rule*. All nodes in F_1 receive input from the gain control but only those nodes that *also* receive input from I are able to become significantly active[2] and transmit the input to F_2 (the reason for this mechanism will become clear in the next step). A similar role is played by the F_2 gain control, which allows this layer to become active only while input is being applied.

Additionally, before F_1 has had a chance to process its input from F_2, it sends a signal to the F_2 reset mechanism, which is the same as that from the input at this time, since the pattern in X is governed directly by I. This mechanism is also known as the *orienting subsystem* since it helps control the search for templates. The two signals providing input into the orienting subsystem therefore cancel and no signal is sent to F_2, which continues to operate in the normal way.

Summary If a match occurs then resonance takes place, otherwise F_2 is reset and a new template is read out.

The output pattern U now contributes to the STM trace at F_1 via the top-down LTM-gated signals V. That is, each node v_i in F_1 calculates the weighted sum of inputs V_i, from F_2. Since only one node v_j is active in F_2, the top-down template of LTM traces z_{ji} from v_j gets imposed on or "read out" to F_1 as shown in Figure 9.4. Note that Carpenter and Grossberg regard the signals V as the template (or *top-down expectation*) rather than the weights. However, since only

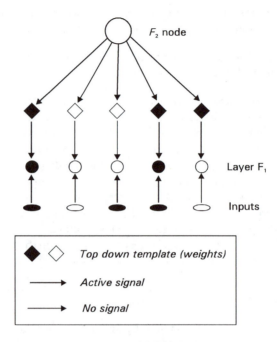

F_2 node

Layer F_1

Inputs

◆ ◇ Top down template (weights)

⟶ Active signal

⟶ No signal

Figure 9.4 Reading out top-down templates.

one node at F_2 is stimulating V, its components are identical to the z_{ji} and the two terms are functionally equivalent (at least in ART1).

Now, only those nodes in F_1 that have input from both external pattern and top-down template features are active in the new STM trace X^*. This follows because, when F_2 chooses a winning node, it is able to send an inhibitory signal to the gain control. The 2/3 rule now requires both external input and template signals for node activity; those for which the template and pattern input differ will be turned off. Note that the template match index set $\mathbf{X}$ (defined in the algorithm) is consistent with the use of the symbol X to denote F_1 STM. If X^* and X are sufficiently different, the inhibitory signal from F_1 to the orienting subsystem will be diminished to the extent that this now becomes active and sends an *arousal burst* to F_2. This excites all cells equally and results in the currently active node being *reset* to an inactive state in a long-lasting way. That a node can be inhibited in this way by an excitatory signal may appear paradoxical at first but possible neural mechanisms for its instantiation are discussed in the next section.

As soon as F_2 has been reset, the original input pattern I can be reinstated in STM at F_1 since F_2 is no longer able to inhibit the gain control. F_1 excites F_2 again but this time the maximally responding node (largest T_j) is not able to take part in the development of STM Y in F_2. The node with the next largest response now gives rise to the peak in STM under competitive dynamics, and therefore becomes the new active node in F_2.

The process of match and possible reset is continued in this way until a match is found that allows F_1 to continue inhibiting the orientation subsystem. The degree of inhibition required is, of course, governed by the vigilance ρ. When this is done, the two layers are supporting each other or *resonating* and learning takes place according to the rules given in the algorithm. The LTM traces are, in fact, supposed to be plastic at all times but the template search period is supposed to be very rapid in comparison to the duration of resonance, and so significant changes only take place at this time.

The training of the bottom-up z_{ij} is sometimes referred to as *in-star* learning since it trains LTM traces that are inbound to an F_2 node. This is in contrast to the *out-star* learning that takes place with the top-down z_{ji} since these modulate outbound signals from F_2.

On withdrawal of the input, the F_2 gain control becomes inactive and the STM at F_2 therefore collapses. The reset of any F_2 nodes is also discontinued so that all nodes are now eligible for template search.

9.3.6 The signal level: some neural mechanisms

It is not the intention here to give an exhaustive account of the neural-level signalling and processing mechanisms that (at least hypothetically) underpin ART1. Instead, we give brief descriptions to give a flavour of the approach taken and to help define some of the terms used in the literature.

As noted previously, all nodes in the network obey leaky-integrator-like dynamics. Grossberg also uses the term *membrane equation* to describe laws like this governing activation dynamics, because he thinks of the activation as analogous to the membrane potential in real neurons. However, unlike the simple model of (2.6), which incorporates the weighted sum of inputs s additively, the models used by Grossberg involve terms in which the activation is multiplied by the input. Neurophysiologically, multiplication of signals is sometimes referred to as a *shunting* operation so the ART neurons are shunting rather than additive. The advantage of this approach is that it enables input normalization using a type of on-centre, off-surround connection scheme that is feedforward (Fig. 9.5). In additive models this kind of process is only available with lateral competitive connections. For a review of these ideas see Grossberg (1988).

The control signals are established by providing neural inputs from the signal source. For example, the inhibition of the F_1 gain control by F_2 is implemented by a signal that is just the sum of all the F_2 outputs.

The reset mechanism at F_2 has been given a plausible basis in the so-called *on-centre, off-surround dipole* (Grossberg 1980). This is a small circuit of six neurons with recurrent connections and a pair of slowly adapting synapses that can have its output inhibited by an appropriately connected excitatory input signal. The long-lasting reset at F_2 is then mediated by the slowly responding synaptic links. Each node is now replaced by one of these dipoles and Grossberg's use of the

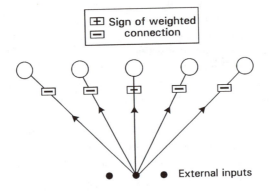

Figure 9.5 Feedforward, on-centre, off-surround architecture.

term *field* to mean an array of neurons leads to the term *dipole field* being used occasionally for layer F_2.

The LTM traces also obey equations governing their rate of change[3], which implies that they are, in general, continually plastic. However, as noted above, the search for resonance is supposed to take place on a much shorter timescale than resonance is maintained. Further, during this time, the LTM traces are supposed to be able to come to equilibrium in the so-called *fast-learning* regime. That is, LTM changes fast enough to allow its steady-state values to be reached at resonance but not so fast that they are substantially affected during search. The learning rules given in the algorithm are then the equilibrium values of LTM traces under fast learning. The assignment of zero to previously positive LTM traces occurs because the dynamics of LTM involve a decay component, leading to what is referred to as the *associative decay rule*.

9.4 The ART family

We have dealt here with the network known as ART1 but this is just one of a series of architectures rooted in the principles of adaptive resonance theory. ART2 (Carpenter & Grossberg 1987a, Carpenter et al. 1991b) extends ART1 to the classification and stable coding of analogue patterns. In ART2, the F_1 layer is replaced by a complex five-layer network, which is notionally split into a three-tier F_1 "layer" and a two-tier preprocessing "layer" F_0. The length of search involved here is a potential problem area, as it was with ART1, and has been addressed in a fast, algorithmic version of ART2 (Carpenter et al. 1991b).

A conceptually simpler analogue adaptation of ART1 is described in the so-called *fuzzy ART* system (Carpenter et al. 1991c). This is advertised as an algorithm rather than a network, although a neural implementation does exist (Carpenter et al. 1991d), and makes use of fuzzy set theory to generalize the notion of "feature". In ART1, a template location is either a member of the feature set or it is not. In fuzzy set theory (Zadeh 1965, Kosko 1992) an element can have a continuously graded membership between 0 and 1, with 0 and 1 implying "definitely not in" and "definitely in" the set respectively. By allowing template locations to take analogue values between 0 and 1 we can interpret them as fuzzy set membership values. The same applies to F_1 outputs and the template–pattern match is now made by the fuzzy equivalent of the set intersection $\mathbf{I} \cap \mathbf{X}$ at resonance; this reduces to finding the minimum of the pair (z_{ji}, x_i).

ARTMAP (Carpenter et al. 1991a) is a supervised system that learns input–output pairs $(\mathbf{x}, \mathbf{y})$. It consists of two ART1 modules linked by an intermediate layer or *map field*. Each ART module self-organizes in the normal way and is devoted to processing either the $\mathbf{x}$ or $\mathbf{y}$ patterns. The map field allows the learned templates of the ART module M_a on the input side to access the templates in the module M_b on the output side. In this way predictions from an input vector can be made and checked against the target output. The control system contains a facility to alter the vigilance of M_a so as to ensure that sufficient categories or templates are learned in M_a to reduce the discrepancy with the supervised output to a minimum. However, the vigilance is not increased unnecessarily and templates are kept as large as possible in order to promote generalization. The network is a hybrid, containing self-organizing elements in a supervisory environment, and has similarities with the algorithms that dynamically construct the hidden layer in MLPs (Sect. 6.10.4) if we think of F_2 templates in M_a as corresponding to hidden nodes. Remarkably successful results are reported by Carpenter et al. (1991a) for the classification of mushrooms on a database of over 8000 examples. Inevitably, the fuzzy extension of ART1 has been applied to ARTMAP to allow it to process analogue data (Carpenter & Grossberg 1992) giving rise to the *fuzzy ARTMAP* architecture. Carpenter & Grossberg (1992) contains a précis of the ARTMAP algorithm (albeit in its fuzzy guise), which is less theory bound than that in Carpenter et al. (1991a).

ART3 (Carpenter & Grossberg 1990) allows any number of ART2 modules to be concatenated into a processing hierarchy. In this way the F_2 nodes of one ART2 module send their output to the inputs of the next one. This paper also sees a return to the biological roots of ART in that a chemical transmitter mechanism is postulated for the F_2 reset mechanism.

9.5 Applications

Caudell et al. (1994) describe an application of ART1 to the classification of parts in the inventories of the aircraft industry. This was successfully used by Boeing in the early stages of the design process to avoid replication of effort and to make optimum use of existing parts. Each part was assigned a binary vector in a preprocessing stage that encoded shape, fastening hole locations and the number and type of metal bends. For two-dimensional parts like flat metal fasteners, the shape was encoded via its silhouette on a pixel grid, while three-dimensional parts were treated by describing polygons that were fitted to their surfaces. The resulting binary vectors were, in general, extremely long and, to avoid excessive storage, they were encoded by describing the run lengths of successive 0s and 1s. For example, 0000011110001111111 would map into 5437. The ART networks then used a modification of the standard algorithm that could work directly on the run-length encodings. The system consisted of a "hierarchical abstraction tree" of ART1 "macrocircuits", each of which contained a collection of ART modules (Fig. 9.6). Consider first a single macrocircuit as shown on the left of the figure. The run-length-encoded vectors are first divided into parts that describe shape, holes and bends. The partial vectors for shape are then applied to the first (bottom) ART1 network, which clusters or groups them accordingly. For each shape-based cluster learned in this way, the partial vectors for bends and holes are then separately applied to another pair of ART nets so that the cluster is further refined on the basis of these two criteria. Now consider the hierarchy of macrocircuits shown on the right of Figure 9.6. The bottom-most macrocircuit is trained with a comparatively low vigilance so that it carries out a coarse grouping of parts. Successively finer classification can be achieved by subsequently applying the pattern vector to macrocircuits further up the hierarchy, which will have higher levels of vigilance. Within each macrocircuit the design engineer can then specify a classification based on shape, shape and bends, shape and holes, or on all three aspects of the component part. The final system had over 5000 ART modules and dealt with a database of over 10 000 parts.

Carpenter et al. (1989) describe a system for recognizing images that uses an ART2 module to develop the categories. Much of this paper is, however, devoted to the image preprocessing that segments the region of interest and ensures a consistent size, orientation and contrast for input to the ART network.

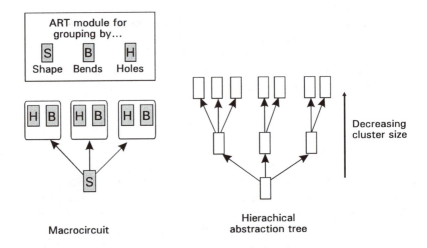

Figure 9.6 Aircraft part inventory system.

The results of several simulation studies for ARTMAP are reported in Carpenter & Grossberg (1992). In particular, they describe a letter recognition problem that attempts to classify a database of 20 000 noise-corrupted, black-and-white printed characters into one of 26 upper case letter categories. The training set was a subset of 16 000 patterns and the other 4000 were used for testing. Training took only one to five epochs (although note the comments below on training times) and there was a 90 to 94 per cent success rate on the test set.

ART was conceived with biological realism in mind and so one of its applications has been in the modelling of brain function. Thus, Banquet & Grossberg (1987) investigated EEG recordings under various conditions of human subject learning and compared them successfully with predictions made on the basis of ART. In connection with the primate visual system, Desimone (1992) identifies F_1 and F_2 with the prestriate and inferotemporal cortex respectively.

9.6   Further remarks

Although not proven here, ART1 does lead to stable learning under arbitrary Boolean training environments (Carpenter & Grossberg 1987b). However, as noted by Lippmann (1987), the templates that emerge under ART are not always the most useful. He uses an example (albeit a toy one) in the domain of character recognition in which, in order to obtain separate categories for two well-formed letters (C and E), it is necessary to allocate separate templates for two noisy versions of another letter (F). This may, however, be a problem with any clustering technique – our high-level intuitive understanding of what constitutes a class or template may not be that which is discovered by the algorithm or network. It is then necessary to assign many templates to each nominal category and to have a higher-level choice mechanism to associate templates logically with classes.

According to the result of Georgiopoulous et al. (1991), at most m epochs are needed for a training set with m different sizes. The implication of this is that training in ART is very fast. It should be realized, however, that, although the number of epochs needed may be small, the time to execute each one may be large if there are a large number of templates to be searched at each pattern presentation. To help overcome this difficulty, Hung & Lin (1995) have proposed an ART1-like network that can search its template space much faster than the original ART1 net.

Historically, ART was developed from the bottom up; that is, the design was initially based at the signal level and the systemic approach came later. However, the algorithm defines what occurs in many ART simulators and has similarities (as does simple competitive learning) with conventional clustering analysis. This comparison was noted by Lippmann (1987) and has been pursued by Cheng & Titterington (1994) and Burke (1991). Nevertheless it is the system-level implementation of the algorithm that distinguishes it as characteristically connectionist and the neural-signal-level analysis as biologically plausible.

165

9.7 Summary

ART describes a set of networks that undergo self-organization to learn a set of stable cluster categories or templates. However, in contrast to simple competitive self-organizing networks, ART systems allow the number of categories to be determined using a single vigilance parameter. This is achieved by controlling the degree of match between stored templates and new patterns, which is, in turn, implemented by a set of top-down weights from the second to the first layer. An explanation of the principles of ART is facilitated by describing the net at several levels in a hierarchy. At the signal level it consists of biologically plausible mechanisms and many aspects of system behaviour may be described in rigorous mathematical terms (although this has not been addressed here). ART nets represent one of the few attempts to incorporate all control mechanisms into the totality of the architecture (rather than leaving them to some extrinsic control software). It is necessary, however, to be aware that the learned templates may not match our intuitive expectations and that the theoretical bounds on the time to learn may obscure lengthy, single-epoch computation.

9.8 Notes

1. This is not a Carpenter–Grossberg form although it is in the spirit of their notation.
2. Carpenter & Grossberg refer to these as *supraliminally* – literally "above threshold" – active. This does not imply that there is a simple threshold output function but that the neuron dynamics are able to generate large outputs.
3. These are known as *differential equations* because they make use of differentials (derivatives or slopes).

Chapter Ten

Nodes, nets and algorithms: further alternatives

In this chapter we wish to disabuse the reader of some ideas that may have inadvertently been imparted: namely, that artificial neurons always look something like a semilinear node and that feedforward nets are always trained using backpropagation or its variants.

10.1 Synapses revisited

In everything we have seen so far the combination of input signals through a linear weighted sum has been a recurrent theme. This has been the case in spite of many variations in the way this is eventually used – semilinear nodes, TLUs, leaky integrators – as they all perform this basic operation as a first stage. It is now time to go back and review the validity of this assumption and, as with our first look at node functionality, our initial approach will be biologically motivated because we argue that real neurons have not developed their functional repertoire gratuitously but in response to computational needs. The stereotypical synapse shown in Figure 10.1 is the inspiration for the weighted connection in simple models of neural activation. It consists of an electrochemical connection between an axon and a dendrite; it is therefore known as an *axo-dendritic* synapse and its basic operation was discussed in Section 2.1.

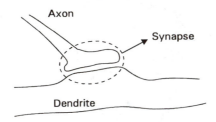

Figure 10.1 Single axo-dendritic synapse.

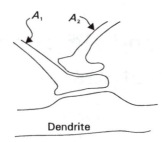

Figure 10.2 Presynaptic inhibitory synapse.

There are, however, a large variety of synapses that do not conform to this structure (Bullock et al. 1977). Of special importance for our discussion are the presynaptic inhibitory synapses shown in Figure 10.2. Here, one axon terminal A_2 impinges on another A_1 just as it, in turn, is making synaptic contact with a dendrite. A_2 can now modulate the efficiency of the synapse with A_1 by inhibiting its action; thus, signals at A_2 can "turn off" the (otherwise excitatory) effect of A_1. This structure is therefore of the *axo-axonic* type, it utilizes *presynaptic inhibition*, and it is supposed to be of crucial importance in detecting image motion in early visual processing (Koch et al. 1982).

Elaborations of this structure occur when several synapses are grouped together into so-called glomeruli (Steiger 1967) – see Figure 10.3. It is difficult to know exactly what kind of intersynaptic processing is going on here but it is almost certainly not linear. Even when regular axo-dendritic synapses occur in close proximity (Fig. 10.4) they are liable to interact in nonlinear ways. The basic unit of neural processing is starting to look like the synaptic cluster, an approach promoted by Shepherd (1978) in which he refers to these as neural *microcircuits*.

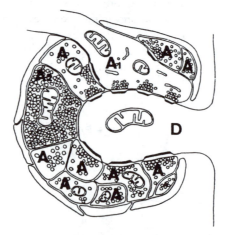

Figure 10.3 Glomerulus.

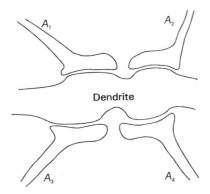

Figure 10.4 Synaptic cluster.

10.2 Sigma–pi units

How can we model these more complex situations? Consider, again, the double synapse in Figure 10.2 and let the signals arriving from A_1 and A_2 be x_1 and x_2 respectively. If A_1 existed in isolation we could write its contribution δa to the activity of the postsynaptic neuron as wx_1. However, A_2 modulates this by reducing its value as x_2 is increased. In order to express this mathematically it is useful to ensure that all values are normalized (lie in the range $0 \le x_i \le 1$). This can be done by letting the x_i denote the original signal value divided by its maximum; in any case, there will be no problem with artificial neurons that use the sigmoid output function since signals are normalized by default. There is now a simple way of expressing the inhibitory effect of A_2 and that is to multiply by $(1 - w^* x_2)$ where $w^* \le 1$, so that $\delta a = wx_1(1 - w^* x_2)$. When $x_2 = 0$ this expression reduces to wx_1 and so A_2 has no effect, but when $x_2 = 1$, $\delta a = wx_1(1 - w^*)$, which can be made as small as we please by making w^* close enough to 1. This does indeed, therefore, capture the interaction between A_1 and A_2.

Expanding the expression for δa we obtain $\delta a = wx_1 - ww^* x_1$. This may now be written in a way that allows generalization to other types of pairwise interaction. Thus, we put

$$\delta a = w_1 x_1 + w_2 x_2 + w_{12} x_1 x_2 \tag{10.1}$$

where, for the case of presynaptic inhibition, $w_1 = w$, $w_2 = 0$ and $w_{12} = -ww^*$. Notice that we have allowed the possibility that A_2 can influence the postsynaptic cell directly by including a term like $w_2 x_2$. This may be the case, for example, in expressing the effect of A_1 and A_2 in Figure 10.4. For a neuron with n inputs we have to include all possible pairwise interactions (bearing in mind that a term including $x_1 x_2$ is not different from one with $x_2 x_1$). This gives the following expression for the total contribution to the activation a:

$$
\begin{aligned}
a = \sum_{i}^{n} w_i x_i &+ w_{12} x_1 x_2 + w_{13} x_1 x_3 + w_{14} x_1 x_4 + \cdots + w_{1n} x_1 x_n \\
&+ w_{23} x_2 x_3 + w_{24} x_2 x_4 + \cdots + w_{2n} x_2 x_n \\
&+ w_{34} x_3 x_4 + \cdots + w_{3n} x_3 x_n \\
&+ \cdots + \\
&+ w_{(n-1)n} x_{n-1} x_n
\end{aligned}
\tag{10.2}
$$

This is unwieldy because we have a compact notation for the linear sum but no equivalent for the sum of product terms. What is required is a generic symbol for product, which is provided by the Greek upper case pi (written Π). Then, we may rewrite (10.2) as

$$
a = \sum_{i}^{n} w_i x_i + \prod_{i<j} w_{ij} x_i x_j
\tag{10.3}
$$

In general we may want to include products of more than two inputs to capture the possibility that there are contributions that come only via the interaction of all participants in this particular group of inputs. Thus, we need to incorporate terms like $x_{i_1} x_{i_2} \ldots x_{i_j} \ldots x_{i_m}$ where $i_1, i_2, \ldots, i_m$ are some set of indices and, of course, $m < n$. Rather than deal with the input indices directly, it is easier to deal with them as sets since we can enumerate these and write $\{i_1, i_2, \ldots, i_m\} = I_k$ where I_k is the kth index set. How many such sets are there? One way to construct them is to write the integers $1 \ldots n$ in sequence, run along from left to right, and either include or not include each integer in the set. This process gives n two-way choices with each particular combination yielding a different index set. Altogether then, there are 2^n sets giving this many product terms in the expansion. These also include terms like x_i on its own, where the index set contains one entry, and the "empty" term that contains no variables and is therefore associated with a constant or threshold w_0. We can now write the entire activation in this most general case as

$$
a = \sum_{k=1}^{2^n} w_k \prod_{i \in I_k} x_i
\tag{10.4}
$$

where the range $i \in I_k$ means that we include all i in the index set I_k when forming the product string from the variables x_i. To summarize: this is just a compact way of writing expressions like (10.2) where we have included terms like w_0, $w_i x_i$, $w_{12} x_1 x_2$, $w_{123} x_1 x_2 x_3$, etc., all the way up to the single term $w_{1 \ldots n} x_1 x_2 \ldots x_n$.

The activation is now in the form of a sum of products or, using the notation itself, in sigma–pi form – hence the name *sigma–pi unit* for one that uses (10.4) to define its activation. Alternatively, they are also known as *higher order units* since they contain products of pairs of inputs (second order or quadratic), products of three inputs (third order or cubic) and so on. However, any term contains each variable only in a linear way; that is, there are no expressions like x_i^2 or x_i^3 etc. The activation is therefore sometimes referred to as a *multilinear* form.

Sigma–pi units were introduced by Rumelhart et al. (1986d). Networks of units with second order terms have been used to solve the so-called "contiguity problem" (Maxwell et al. 1987) in which the task is to determine whether there are two or three "clumps" of 1s in Boolean pattern strings. (A clump is just a group of contiguous components of the same value so that, for example, 1100011100 and 1011100111 have two and three clumps of 1s respectively.) Heywood & Noakes (1995) have shown how backpropagation and weight-pruning techniques may be applied to nets of sigma–pi units to perform orientation-invariant classification of alphabetic characters.

10.3   Digital neural networks

In this section we deal with networks of nodes that lend themselves easily to being implemented in digital computer hardware.

10.3.1   Boolean functions as artificial neurons

Consider once again the lowly TLU, which, when used with Boolean input, may be represented by a population of 0s and 1s at the vertices of the n-dimensional hypercube or n-cube. Recall that each input vector (string of 0s and 1s) locates a cube vertex or site that has the corresponding TLU output associated with it. For TLUs these values are, of course, constrained so that the cube can be divided by a hyperplane reflecting the linear separability of TLU functionality. Normally we think of a TLU as being specified by its weights and the geometric, pattern space representation on the cube as secondary. However, it is possible to imagine defining TLUs by endowing the cube sites with 0s and 1s while ensuring that the resulting two populations may be separated by a hyperplane.

Suppose now we allow any distribution of 0/1 values on the hypercube without regard to linear separability. We can now implement any Boolean function of the (Boolean) input vector. An example is given in Figure 10.5, which shows a three-input function with its pattern space, three-cube representation, and as a table of input–output correspondences. If there are more than three dimensions, we cannot draw the n-cube but may represent the situation schematically as shown in Figure 10.6. Shown on the left is a cartoon diagram of an n-cube, which has been populated so it can be implemented by a TLU. The cube on the right has had its site values randomly assigned. The TLU function may be defined in alternative form by supplying a suitable weight vector whereas the other function can only be defined by specifying its table of input–output correspondences. The possible advantage in breaking out of the linearly separable regime is that the increased functionality will allow more compact nets that learn more efficiently.

A table of Boolean assignments of the form shown in Figure 10.5 is, however, exactly what a computer memory component known as a random access memory

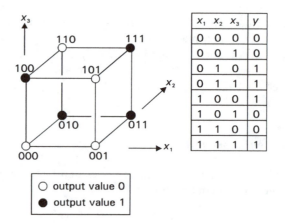

x_1	x_2	x_3	y
0	0	0	0
0	0	1	0
0	1	0	1
0	1	1	1
1	0	0	1
1	0	1	0
1	1	0	0
1	1	1	1

○ output value 0
● output value 1

Figure 10.5 Example of three-input Boolean function that is not linearly separable.

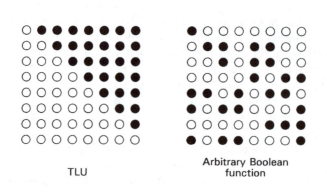

TLU

Arbitrary Boolean
function

Figure 10.6 Schematic representation of TLUs and general Boolean functions.

(RAM) performs (see Fig. 10.7). The input to a RAM is referred to as the *address* since it is used to select, via a decoder, one of a set of "pigeonholes" or cells in the memory store. Upon selection, the cell may then have its contents read out, or overwritten with a new value, depending on which mode (read or write) has been selected. In computer engineering parlance, each component of a Boolean vector (0 or 1) is a *bit* so that, if the address is n bits wide, then there are 2^n bits in the memory store. This follows because each address bit has two possible values so that there are $2 \times 2 \times \ldots \times 2$ (n times) different addresses. In the diagram, the address is 8 bits wide so that the memory store has 256 bits.

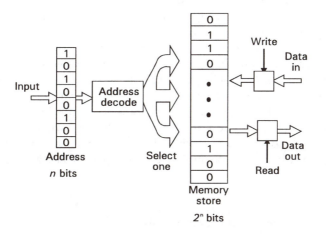

Figure 10.7 RAM as Boolean function.

It should now be clear that a RAM can be used to implement the table of input–output values for an arbitrary Boolean function. There are, therefore, three views of a Boolean function:

Lookup table It is a table of correspondences between Boolean vectors and scalar Boolean values. Such tables are sometimes called *truth tables* since the values 0 and 1 are able to represent "true" and "false" in the manipulation of statements in a logical algebra (not dealt with here).

Hypercube It is a population of Boolean values at the vertices or sites of the n-dimensional hypercube (n-cube). This is the geometric viewpoint and yields useful insights about generalization and learning – see Section 10.3.6.

RAM It is a random access memory component in which the memory store contains the values of the lookup table.

A further viewpoint on Boolean functionality will be articulated in Section 10.3.5 focusing on the development of a mathematical form for node function.

These different views give rise to their own terminologies, which, on occasion, are used interchangeably: truth-table locations are cube sites (or just "sites") and, in the RAM scheme, memory cells; the Boolean vector input is a RAM address or sometimes an n-tuple; truth-table values or site values are also RAM *bit* values. Note that the TLUs, when used with Boolean input, form a special subclass of Boolean function.

The development of the RAM implementation and its use in neural networks is largely attributable to Aleksander and co-workers. This can be traced from its beginnings with devices that used fusible links to store bit values (Aleksander 1965), through the use of "stored-logic adaptable microcircuits", or SLAMs (an early form of semiconductor memory) (Aleksander & Albrow 1968), to the use of what we now know today as RAMs (Aleksander et al. 1984).

The use of RAM technology as a means of implementation has led to the name *digital nodes* for these and a family of related node types, and their use in neural networks has largely been fostered by workers in the UK. Unfortunately a proliferation of acronyms has grown up, referring to essentially equivalent node structures, and this has not helped to popularize the area. One of the reasons for this is that many people were working on developing node structure at around the same time (late 1980s) and each variant was described under its own name. The term "digital node" appears the most neutral and will be adhered to as far as possible. An overview of much of this work is available in Gurney & Wright (1992a), which also serves to introduce several papers on digital nodes.

10.3.2 Using Boolean functions in nets

Recurrent nets

Several workers in the 1960s and 1970s became interested in what we might describe now as "Boolean Hopfield nets". That is, a set of interconnected units that are allowed to take arbitrary Boolean functionality and that have many feedback paths. However, since the size of the memory store, even in simulation, goes up exponentially with the size of the input, the nets were incompletely interconnected, often using units with only two or three inputs. Walker & Ashby (1966) examined the dynamics of nets composed of three-input functions in which one of the inputs is taken from the unit output and all functions are the same. They noted the appearance of stable states and multiple-state cycles as described in Chapter 7. However, the authors do not conceive of these systems as neural nets, there is no attempt to train and, surprisingly, no connection is made with associative memory. Kauffman (1969) investigated similar systems, but with variable functionality throughout the net, as models of genetic switching in DNA.

Aleksander & Mamdani (1968) are responsible for one of the first attempts to use a recurrent net of digital nodes as an associative memory. Training a state cycle in such a net is trivial. First, the desired pattern is clamped onto the net in its entirety; then, for each node, the memory cell addressed by the part of the clamp that forms its input is made to take on the value that the node currently

174

has as output. The clamp has then been made a stable state of the network. A desirable side effect (in incompletely connected nets) is that other state transitions are created which are associated with the confluent of the state cycle (Milligan 1988). Martland (1987) provides an example of using these nets in a character recognition task.

10.3.3 Feedforward nets

Consider the system shown in Figure 10.8. There is an input layer of Boolean values, which has been drawn as a two-dimensional array because we have image recognition in mind. An input pattern has been indicated that is supposed to be a character from the class of the letter "T". The input is randomly sampled by a collection of two-input Boolean functions, representatives of which have been shown by exhibiting their truth tables. These functions are all initialized to output 0 in response to any input. When a training pattern is presented, the locations addressed in each function are then changed to a 1. Thus, each function acts as a recorder of two-component features seen during training. In the figure, the truth tables are those that pertain after initialization and training with the single pattern shown at the input. Suppose now that a set of "T"s are presented whose members differ slightly from each other; then any feature that is present in this set will be recorded. However, if the patterns do not differ too much, many of their features will be the same and, in this case, only a few locations in each function will be altered to the value 1. Now suppose that another "T", not in the training set, is presented at the input and the function outputs are read out and summed together. Each feature that the new pattern has in common with all those seen during training will generate a 1, while any new features will produce a 0. If there are N Boolean functions and the pattern results in m previously seen features, then the response of the net may be defined as the fraction m/N. If the unseen pattern is quite different from anything seen during training, the response will be close to zero. If, on the other hand, it is close (in Hamming distance) then it will yield a response close to 1. In this example two-input Boolean functions were used but, in general, we may use functions with any number of inputs.

The system described so far is a single *discriminator* allowing the possibility of identifying a single class. Thus, in the example above we might hope to classify "T"s from non-"T"s. In general we require one discriminator per class and, during training, each discriminator adapts only to the class it is supposed to represent. In testing, the input is applied to all discriminators simultaneously and that which supplies the largest response is deemed to signify the pattern class.

Systems like this were first described by Bledsoe & Browning (1959), who referred to their technique as the *n*-tuple pattern recognition method. They used computer simulation in which the mapping of the algorithm onto the computer memory store was not suggestive of a hardware implementation. However, Aleksander and co-workers realized the possibility of using the newly developed

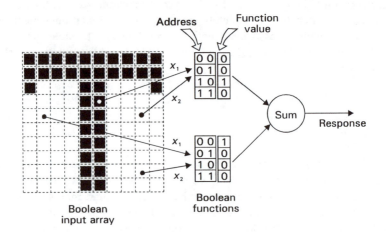

Figure 10.8 n-tuple recognition system.

semiconductor memory devices (later to be called RAMs) to build physical instantiations of n-tuple machines. Work initiated in the 1960s (Aleksander & Albrow 1968) was mature by 1979 (Aleksander & Stonham 1979) and culminated in the commercially available WISARD[1] pattern recognition machine (Aleksander et al. 1984). Aleksander was also responsible for casting the technique in the language of neural networks.

Suppose now that we have several WISARD discriminators whose pattern of connectivity to the input array is identical. Suppose further that there is a threshold θ such that, if the discriminator's response r is less than θ, then we regard it as signalling a 0 and if $r > \theta$, we consider it as outputting a 1. In this way we obtain a Boolean vector of outputs **y**. It is now possible to imagine training this discriminator array to associate patterns at the input with desired target vectors **t** at its output. To do this, those discriminators that are supposed to output 1 would be trained in the normal way by setting their addressed feature locations to 1, whereas those that are supposed to output 0 would leave their addressed locations at 0. This is the basis of the ADAM[2] architecture proposed by Austin (1987a). In addition, this also uses a two-stage process in which a large input image is first associated with a much smaller class code, which is associated, in turn, with the final (large) target output image. This two-stage process requires much less memory than a straightforward association between two large pattern vectors. The use of feedforward architectures for associative memory is discussed further in Section 11.1.1.

The learning scheme of writing 1s to a Boolean truth table can lead to several problems in training. The first is that there is substantial loss of information in only using two values $(0, 1)$ for each n-tuple feature – a feature that gets accessed once has the same effect in training as one that gets accessed many times. Bledsoe & Bisson (1962) noted this deficiency in their original n-tuple technique and proposed recording the frequency of feature occurrence at each location in the truth table. Secondly, if the size of each class is too big then the number of features recorded within each truth table will grow and eventually most of the table will be filled. This *saturation* effect may be avoided if we allow site values to decrease as well as increase so that, for the simple case of Boolean-valued sites, we allow transitions $1 \rightarrow 0$ as well as $0 \rightarrow 1$. This scheme is contingent, however, on developing more sophisticated learning rules. The development of such rules for semilinear nodes hinged on our ability to analyze them mathematically and evaluate things such as error gradients like $\partial E / \partial w$. We have avoided the machinations that actually deal with these calculations and chosen to focus on the conceptual basis for learning rules. However, their formal development requires that the node output be described by a smooth function of its input, which is not facilitated by any of the viewpoints (truth tables, hypercubes, RAMs) developed so far. In summary, two elements are required for progress in using digital-type nodes: an extension of the node structure to allow multiple-valued sites and a way of describing the node functionality in a mathematically closed form.

10.3.4 Extending digital node functionality

The frequency of occurrence scheme proposed by Bledsoe and Bisson is fine if we simply read out this value but is no good if the output must be Boolean, as it must be if it is to form part of the address of other nodes in a network. The first attempt to overcome this was made by Kan & Aleksander (1987) who used a function with three values in its truth table: 0, 1 and "u" or undecided. When "u" is addressed, a 1 is output with probability 0.5. These nodes were first used in recurrent Hopfield-like nets and dubbed probabilistic logic nodes or PLNs. The natural extension was to use more than three site values resulting in the multi-valued probabilistic logic node (MPLN) (Myers & Aleksander 1988). The probability of outputting a 1 is then related to the site value via a sigmoid function. Many people were experimenting independently with node structures of this type at around the same time, which is one of the reasons for the profusion of names in this field (my own term for the MPLN is a type-2 cubic node).

It is possible to formulate all classes of function dealt with so far in a unified framework that makes contact with the more normal weighted nodes. First consider the simple Boolean functions. We now suppose that cube sites store activation values +1 or −1 rather than Boolean values 1, 0 and that these are then passed as input to a threshold output function. For the purposes of subsequent development, it is useful to think of the function output y as defining the probability of the node emitting a 1 (of course, there is no distinction for a step function between this interpretation and that of a simple deterministic relation). This use of the threshold function in this way is shown in the top left of Figure 10.9. The three-valued PLN now has the interpretation shown in the top right of the figure, in which a piecewise linear function suffices. The MPLN has a finite set of activation values that have some maximum absolute value S_m. The value at site μ therefore lies in the range $-S_m \leq S_\mu \leq S_m$. The activation–output form is then shown at the bottom left[3]. Of course, any function f that obeys $f(-1) = 0$, $f(1) = 1$ would have served equally well for the Boolean function but the use of the step function fits well with the development shown here and allows contact to be made with the TLU. In another cube-based variant – the so-called probabilistic RAM or pRAM (Gorse & Taylor 1989) – output probabilities are stored directly at the site values and are allowed to vary continuously. This results in the simple activation–output interpretation shown on the bottom left of Figure 10.9.

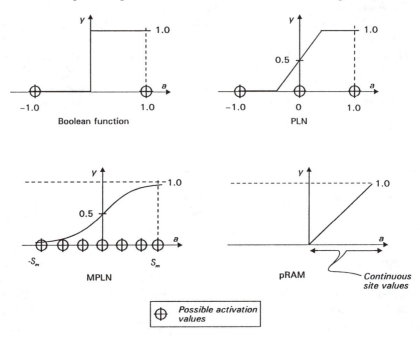

Figure 10.9 Digital node output functions.

10.3.5 Expressions for cube activation

The second requirement for progress with digital nodes was that it be possible to write the output y as a continuous function of the inputs. To achieve this we use a model in which the site values are continuous. Just as in the MPLN, the activation a is just the currently addressed site value S_μ, the output y is the sigmoid of a and is to be interpreted as a probability of outputting a 1. To reinstate the MPLN model (which has a RAM-based hardware implementation) we can later restrict the site value to a discrete set. This process of site quantization is not without repercussions, however, and introduces noise into the learning process (Gurney 1992b).

Our task now reduces to finding a form for a and, rather than exhibit a general expression, we focus on a two-input example in which the site values may be written $S_{00}, S_{01}, S_{10}, S_{11}$. The function of a node is effectively to *choose* the site value S_μ for which the site label μ is just the address string $x_1 x_2$. Therefore we require a "choosing function" $g(\mu, x_1, x_2)$ which is zero unless $\mu = x_1 x_2$, for then we may write

$$a = S_{00}g(00, x_1, x_2) + S_{01}g(01, x_1, x_2) + S_{10}g(10, x_1, x_2) + S_{11}g(11, x_1, x_2) \quad (10.5)$$

and only one term in the sum will survive because $x_1 x_2$ can only match one address.

To develop a form for g it is convenient to use the spin representation for Boolean values discussed in Section 7.5.1 in which we make the correspondence $0 \leftrightarrow -1, 1 \leftrightarrow 1$ so that $x_i = \pm 1$. Now let μ_i be the ith component of site address μ ($\mu_i = \pm 1$) and put

$$g(\mu, x_1, x_2) = \frac{(1 + \mu_1 x_1)}{2}\frac{(1 + \mu_2 x_2)}{2} \quad (10.6)$$

Then, if either $\mu_1 \neq x_1$ or $\mu_2 \neq x_2$, $g = 0$ since the corresponding product $\mu_i x_i$ is -1. The only way to avoid zero is if $\mu_1 = x_1$ and $\mu_2 = x_2$, in which case $g = 1$ as required. Substituting this in (10.5)

$$a = \; S_{00}\frac{(1 - x_1)}{2}\frac{(1 - x_2)}{2} + S_{01}\frac{(1 - x_1)}{2}\frac{(1 + x_2)}{2} + \\ S_{10}\frac{(1 + x_1)}{2}\frac{(1 - x_2)}{2} + S_{11}\frac{(1 + x_1)}{2}\frac{(1 + x_2)}{2} \quad (10.7)$$

The choosing function for n inputs involves n brackets multiplied together (one for each input) so, collecting all the factors of $1/2$ together, the general form of the activation may be written

$$a = \frac{1}{2^n} \sum_\mu S_\mu \prod_{i=1}^{n}(1 + \mu_i x_i) \quad (10.8)$$

This is reminiscent of (although not identical to) the activation of a sigma–pi node (10.4). However, after some rearrangement it is possible to show that (10.8) may indeed be expressed in sigma–pi form (Gurney 1989, Gurney 1992d) where the weights w_k are linear combinations of the site values. Digital nodes may therefore be thought of as an alternative parametrization of sigma–pi nodes so that any sigma–pi node has its digital node equivalent and vice versa. Although we have only dealt with Boolean values, it may be shown (Gurney 1989) that analogue values may be incorporated into this scheme using stochastic bit-streams of the type shown in Figure 2.8.

Equation (10.8) is the required relation between the activation, site values and inputs. It may now be used in a programme of training algorithm development for digital nodes (Gurney 1989, Gurney 1992a). Thus, it may be shown that a modification of backpropagation converges for nets of digital nodes. Further, two other algorithms discussed in Section 10.5 also apply; these are the reward–penalty scheme of Barto & Anandan (1985) and a new algorithm based on system identification in control theory.

10.3.6   Some problems and their solution

Generalization

Suppose a TLU has been trained to classify just two input vectors of different class. This fixes a hyperplane in pattern space and *every other* possible input pattern will now be classified according to its placement so that there is automatic generalization across the whole input space.

Consider now a cubic node (MPLN) which, in the untrained state, has all sites set to zero. The response to any vector is totally random with there being equal probability of a 1 or a 0. If this node is now trained on just two vectors, only the two sites addressed by these patterns will have their values altered; any other vector will produce a random output and there has been no generalization. We shall call sites addressed by the training set *centre sites* or *centres*. In order to promote Hamming distance generalization, sites close to the centres need to be trained to the same or similar value as the centres themselves. That is, there should be a clustering of site values around the centres. One way to do this is to "fracture" the hypercube according to a *Voronoi tessellation* in which each site is assigned the same value as its nearest centre (Gurney 1989, Gurney 1992c). Figure 10.10 shows this schematically for Boolean functions. Centre sites

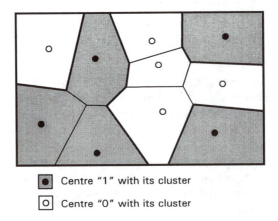

■ Centre "1" with its cluster

□ Centre "0" with its cluster

Figure 10.10 Voronoi tessellation

are shown as open or filled circles and clusters of 1s and 0s are indicated by shaded and plain filled regions respectively. Clusters associated with each centre can abut neighbouring clusters either of the same or different type. These have been indicated by thin and thick lines respectively and, in the example, there are five distinct regions produced from ten centres. This should be contrasted with the random assignment of site values shown on the right in Figure 10.6 where we would expect poor generalization. Notice that the linearly separable function shown in the same figure has excellent generalization but this has been obtained at the expense of functional generality.

The method of tessellation is an "off-line" technique in so far as it is carried out in a separate phase after the training set has been used to establish centre sites. An alternative, "on-line" method makes use of noisy copies of the training set, thereby visiting sites close to true centres, and is the basis of techniques developed by Milligan (1988) (the on-line, off-line distinction is explored further in Sect. 11.2). Noisy training patterns may be produced naturally using an enhancement of the node's architecture as described in Gurney (1992a).

Memory growth

Consider a digital node with n inputs. It has $N = 2^n$ sites and for $n = 8$, $N = 256$. For $n = 32$, $N = 2^{32} \approx 10^9$. Clearly there is an explosion in the number of sites as n grows, which is not only impractical from an implementation point of view, but also suspect from a theoretical viewpoint: do we really need to make use of all the functional possibilities available in such nodes? The answer is almost certainly "No" and one way of overcoming this is developed in the *multi-cube unit* or MCU (Gurney 1992a, Gurney 1992d) where several small subcubes sum their outputs to form the activation as shown in Figure 10.11. This also has a biological analogue in that the subcubes may be likened to the synaptic clusters described in Section 10.1, which are then supposed to sum their contributions

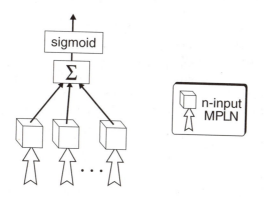

Figure 10.11 Multi-cube unit (MCU).

linearly. In terms of the sigma–pi form, we are limiting the order of terms that are used, so, for example, if all subcubes have four inputs, there can be terms of, at most, order 4. It is also possible to make a link with other network types via the perceptron. Recall that a perceptron has adaptive weights, predefined Boolean association units and a threshold output function. An MCU, on the other hand, has a superficially similar internal structure but has fixed unit weights, adaptive association units with multiple-site values, and a sigmoid output function.

Gurney (1995) has demonstrated several interesting properties of MCUs. Thus, it can be shown that they offer an intermediate degree of site clustering between that of linearly separable functions and randomly organized cubes. They therefore offer a natural approach to an optimal trade-off between functional variety and generalization. Further, it can be shown that they have the most "interesting" information theoretic profiles in terms of an array of conditional mutual information measures.

10.4   Radial basis functions

We now continue our description of alternative node structures with a type of unit that, like the semilinear node, makes use of a vector of parameters with the same dimension as the input.

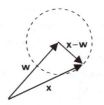

Figure 10.12 Vector difference as basis of node activation.

In Chapter 8 it was shown that, if the weight and input vectors **w** and **x** are normalized, then the activation term $\mathbf{w} \cdot \mathbf{x}$ gives an indication of the degree of alignment between the two vectors. In the language of pattern space, it says how well the input matches the feature template defined by the weights. If there is no normalization then it is better to use the difference $\|\mathbf{x} - \mathbf{w}\|$, a point that was discussed in connection with the SOM algorithm (Sect. 8.3.3). Therefore, if we require a pattern match without normalization, it makes sense to use units that incorporate the difference $\|\mathbf{w} - \mathbf{x}\|$ into their activation directly. The simplest way to do this is simply to put $a = \|\mathbf{x} - \mathbf{w}\|$ so that patterns at the same distance from **w** have the same activation. This is shown in 2D in Figure 10.12, which emphasizes the radial symmetry of the situation, since patterns at a constant distance from the weight vector lie on a circle with **w** as centre. We now require an output function $f(a)$ that falls off with increasing values of a. A suitable candidate is

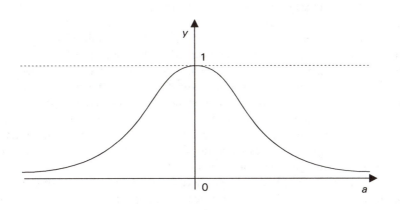

Figure 10.13 One-dimensional Gaussian.

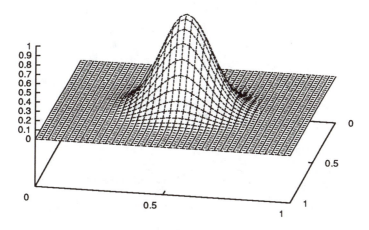

Figure 10.14 Radial basis function.

the Gaussian, a one-dimensional example of which is shown in Figure 10.13. The new unit is therefore defined according to

$$
\begin{aligned}
a &= \|\mathbf{x} - \mathbf{w}\| \\
y &= \exp\left(\frac{-a^2}{2\sigma^2}\right)
\end{aligned}
\tag{10.9}
$$

where $\exp(x) = e^x$. Notice that $\|\mathbf{x} - \mathbf{w}\| = \|\mathbf{w} - \mathbf{x}\|$ (because the length of a vector is independent of its sign or direction) so that both forms may be encountered. A plot of y against (x_1, x_2) for an example in 2D is shown in Figure 10.14 in which the output falls off in a circularly symmetrical way from a point $\mathbf{w} = (0.5, 0.5)$, and should be compared with the plots of functionality for TLUs and semilinear nodes given in Figure 6.10. This symmetry is responsible for the name *radial basis function* (RBF) and, since the components of **w** are no longer used in a multiplicative sense, we refer to **w** as a *centre* rather than a weight vector.

RBFs were introduced in a network context by Broomhead & Lowe (1988) although they had previously been studied in the context of function approximation and interpolation (Powell 1987). Poggio & Girosi (1990a, 1990b) have demonstrated the link between RBF networks and the theory of *regularization*, which deals with fitting functions to sample data, subject to a smoothness constraint. This is, of course, exactly the task of supervised learning, as Poggio & Girosi also emphasize, since, in the language of connectionism, we have to learn the training set (fit the function to the data) while simultaneously enforcing generalization (making a smooth functional fit).

RBFs are usually used in two-layer networks in which the first (hidden) layer is a series of RBFs and the second (output) layer is a set of linear units that can be thought of as computing a weighted sum of the evidence from each of the feature template RBF units. A typical example of such a net is shown in Figure 10.15. Notice that the node structure is quite different in the two layers (hidden and output).

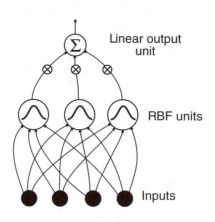

Figure 10.15 RBF network.

The function of such a net can be understood directly by examining the contributions of the RBF templates in pattern space. Each one contributes a Gaussian "hump" of the form shown in Figure 10.14 (albeit in n dimensions rather than in 2D), which is weighted before being blended with the others at the output. This is shown schematically on the left hand side of Figure 10.16 in which the individual RBF contributions are depicted as circles (plan view of two-dimensional cartoon of Gaussians) and their combined effect indicated by

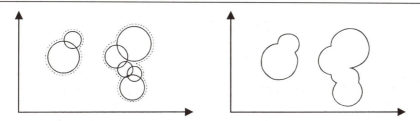

Figure 10.16 RBF net function in pattern space.

the dashed outline. This is the region of pattern space in which an input vector will produce significant output (assuming that there are no very small weights) and has been drawn again for clarity on the right hand side of the figure. It is disconnected and each part is non-convex. Thus, quite complex decision regions may be built up from comparatively few nodes. In the figure the most general situation has been shown in which the RBFs have different widths. In the simplest scheme, however, a set of functions with constant width is used, in which case it may take very many RBFs to cover the region of pattern space populated by the training data. It might be thought that this problem could be surmounted by using functions with a large width but there is then a risk that we will not be able to supply enough detail in the structure of the decision region.

The simplest scheme for training RBF networks is to take a series of centre values chosen randomly from the training, use fixed width functions, and train only the weights to the linear output units. This may be done in a single step by solving a set of linear equations for minimizing the sum of square errors between targets and net outputs (Broomhead & Lowe 1988). Alternatively it may be done iteratively according to the delta rule, in which case the RBF node outputs are used as the inputs in the algorithm. Further embellishments of training allow self-organization of fixed width centres (combined with supervised learning of output weights) and, in the most general case, learning of all network parameters including the width of each RBF.

10.5 Learning by exploring the environment

We now turn to look at alternative ways of training feedforward nets. The gradient descent algorithms like backpropagation rely on substantial intervention by the external "supervisor", which must calculate error signals for each output node. Further, the weight adjustments for hidden nodes are made only after extensive calculation to evaluate explicitly gradient information. In this section we look at learning paradigms that are conceptually simpler and are based on the idea that a network can learn by trial and error.

10.5.1 Associative reward–penalty training

Consider a single node (semilinear or digital) that has stochastic Boolean output. Suppose that there is a set of input–output pairs so that each input vector is associated with a 0 or 1. On applying a vector and noting the output, we compute a signal, which is "1" (reward) if the node classified the input correctly, and "0" (penalty) if it classified incorrectly. If the node is rewarded, it adjusts its internal parameters (weights or site values) so that the current output is *more* likely with the current input. If, on the other hand, the node is penalized, it adjusts its parameters so that the current output is less likely. Two things make this paradigm distinctive: first, the node is simply told whether it was "right" or "wrong" – no continuously graded error is calculated; secondly, in order to "discover" what the correct output should be, the node has to "experiment" with its two possible output options – it has to risk getting the wrong answer in order to find the right one – so that it does indeed use "trial and error".

To formalize this, let the ith input and output be x_i and y respectively ($x_i, y \in \{0,1\}$), let the reward signal be r, and α, λ be two positive constants, where $\alpha, \lambda < 1$. We now specialize to the case of semilinear nodes so that the weights w_i are the parameters to be adapted. The required action is taken using a learning rule of the form

$$\Delta w_i = \begin{cases} \alpha[y - \langle y|\mathbf{x}\rangle]x_i & \text{if} \quad r = 1 \\ \lambda\alpha[1 - y - \langle y|\mathbf{x}\rangle]x_i & \text{if} \quad r = 0 \end{cases} \tag{10.10}$$

where $\langle y|\mathbf{x}\rangle$ is the mean or *expected* value of the Boolean output y given the input vector $\mathbf{x}$. If a sigmoid output relation is assumed then $\langle y|\mathbf{x}\rangle = \sigma(a_\mathbf{x})$ where $a_\mathbf{x}$ is the activation induced by $\mathbf{x}$.

To see how this works, suppose $r = 1$. In general, $0 \leq \langle y|\mathbf{x}\rangle \leq 1$ but, for a sigmoid output function, strict inequality always holds so that, if $y = 1$, then $[y - \langle y|\mathbf{x}\rangle] > 0$. Thus, if $x_i = 1$, then w_i increases, tending to make the activation more positive and enhancing the likelihood of outputting a 1 (the correct response) next time $\mathbf{x}$ appears at the input. If, on the other hand, $y = 0$, then $[y - \langle y|\mathbf{x}\rangle] < 0$ and a positive x_i enforces a decrease in w_i, tending to make the activation more negative, thereby making it more likely to output a 0 (correctly) next time with $\mathbf{x}$. In either case, an input with $x_i = 0$ does not contribute to the activation and so it makes no sense to adjust its weight. If now $r = 0$ (node output is wrong) then the sense of the weight changes is reversed since the the rule for penalty learning is obtained from its reward counterpart by replacing y with $1 - y$ (the opposite Boolean value to y). Thus, $1 - y$ replaces y in having $\langle y|\mathbf{x}\rangle$ subtracted from it, and $1 - y$ is just the opposite Boolean value to y. This means that, on failure, the node learns to enhance the chances of the output opposite to the one it is currently producing.

The learning rule in (10.10) was developed by Barto and co-workers (Barto & Anandan 1985, Barto 1985) who call it the associative reward–penalty rule or A_{R-P}. In discussing the origins of their work, Barto et al. acknowledge its relation both to psychological theories of learning – in particular Thorndike's *law of effect*

(Thorndike 1911) – and the theory of stochastic *learning automata* (Narendra & Thathacar 1974).

In Thorndike's scheme, a neural connection is supposed to be built up between stimulus and response (input and output) when an animal is in a learning environment. The law of effect then says that this connection is likely to be strengthened if the response is followed by a satisfaction (reward) for the animal, whereas it will be diminished if the animal is made to undergo discomfort (penalized). In fact, Thorndike later modified this theory and denied the efficacy of administering discomfort. Interestingly, this seems to be in line with empirical simulation results, which show that small values of λ work best; that is, training when the net has been penalized takes place much more slowly than training when it has been rewarded.

By way of developing the connection with automata theory, a deterministic automaton is a machine that can exist in only a finite number of states and whose next state depends on its current state and input; additionally, each state is associated with a particular output. An example of such a machine is a Hopfield net running under synchronous dynamics. In this case there is no explicit input (although it is straightforward to allow external input to each node) and the output is just the state vector itself. A stochastic automaton is one in which the next state is related probabilistically to the current state and input (e.g. Hopfield net under asynchronous dynamics) and, if learning is allowed, it corresponds to altering the probabilities that govern each state transition. It is therefore a very general theory and is not tied to any particular model of computation, neural or otherwise. It has its roots in mathematical theories of animal learning, but was later developed as a branch of adaptive control theory (see Sect. 10.5.2). The connection with reward–penalty learning is that schemes very similar to it have been used to train stochastic automata.

There are some superficial similarities between the A_{R-P} rule and the delta rule, in so far as each uses a difference between two output quantities to determine a weight change. Barto et al. (1983) have also developed a reward–penalty-style rule, which is related more closely to the Hebb rule. This makes use of two components: an *adaptive search element* or ASE and an *adaptive critic element* or ACE. The ASE is the basic learning system while the ACE has the job of providing reward–penalty signals for the ACE that are based not only on the externally applied reward signal, but also on the current input. Further information on these methods may be found in Barto (1992).

Much of the early work on reward–penalty techniques considered single nodes or very simple nets. However, Barto & Jordan (1987) have reported simulation studies with multilayer networks of semilinear nodes, and network learning convergence for these nets has been demonstrated by Williams (1987). In his proof, Williams showed that the *effect* of the A_{R-P} rule was to perform a noisy or stochastic gradient ascent with respect to the mean value of the reward signal (trained nets will have high values of $\langle r \rangle$). However, this computation is implicit rather than explicit as it is with backpropagation. Further, the net can be trained using a single scalar signal (the reward) being fed back to the net, rather than a large array of delta values. In fact, Barto and Jordan trained the output layer of their nets using the delta rule and the hidden layer using A_{R-P}. This reduced training time considerably and is indicative of a general principle: the more information supplied to a node during training, the less time it takes to adapt successfully. Thus, a single scalar signal is less informative than a signal vector and so the output layer will take longer to develop useful weights under A_{R-P} than it will under the delta rule (in which each node has its own custom δ). However, the non-specific signal r is used to train the hidden layer, and the net does take longer to train than under backpropagation. In spite of this, the algorithm is much simpler than backpropagation and may take advantage of its inherent noise to escape local minima.

It remains to describe how the reward signal is determined for a network with more than one output unit. One way of doing this is to define a sum of square differences error e (just as if we were going to perform a gradient descent), normalize it, and then put $r = 1$ with probability $1 - e$. However, this is not necessary and Gullapalli (1990) provides an interesting example that makes use of a custom-defined reward signal for the control of a robot arm. This work also shows an extension of reward–penalty-style training to nodes that output continuous variables.

For digital nodes, Myers & Aleksander (1988) have developed an algorithm with a reward–penalty "flavour", which they use to train nets of PLNs. However, this is not amenable to analysis and proof of convergence. Gurney, however, showed (Gurney 1989, Gurney 1992a) that the rule of Barto et al. may be adapted with little change to digital nodes, as can the associated proof of learning convergence by Williams. The digital learning rule – assuming a sigmoid output function – is simply

$$\Delta S_\mu = \begin{cases} \alpha[y - \sigma(S_\mu)] & \text{if} \quad r = 1 \\ \lambda\alpha[1 - y - \sigma(S_\mu)] & \text{if} \quad r = 0 \end{cases} \tag{10.11}$$

where μ is the currently addressed site. Notice that the only difference from the rule for semilinear nodes is that there is no input multiplier x_i. Training MCUs with A_{R-P} also follows in a straightforward way and has been implemented in custom VLSI hardware (Hui et al. 1991, Bolouri et al. 1994).

10.5.2 System identification

System identification is a branch of the engineering discipline of control theory that attempts to solve the following problem. Suppose we have an input–output system for which we know the underlying model description but which is not entirely fixed because certain parameters are unknown; how can we go about finding these parameters empirically? Figure 10.17 shows a system with unknown parameters whose internal state description is not directly accessible. Instead, it is corrupted by the addition of noise so that we only have access to imperfect data

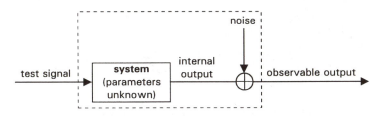

Figure 10.17 System identification.

concerning the system. To obtain an estimate for the internal system parameters we apply a set of test signals, observe the behaviour of the system output and then, by measuring any input–output correlations, we can, in effect, "pin down" the system parameters. How can this be used in training neural nets? Our strategy is to consider the derivatives or slopes required for a gradient descent to be parameters of the network viewed as a system whose model structure is known. In fact, we will consider each node as a separate system, make *estimates* of the gradients locally within each unit, and perform a noisy or stochastic gradient descent.

We start by re-examining the relationship between small changes in function inputs and output. Recall Equation (5.3) for a function y of one variable x, which is rewritten here for convenience (with the small change in x denoted by δx)

$$\delta y \approx \frac{dy}{dx}\delta x \tag{10.12}$$

The multidimensional equivalent of this is that y is now a function of several variables $(x_1, x_2, \ldots, x_n)$ and requires that we sum contributions from each

$$\delta y \approx \sum_i \frac{\partial y}{\partial x_i}\delta x_i \tag{10.13}$$

Returning to the network, we suppose (as with A_{R-P}) that it is stochastic in its behaviour. It is convenient to introduce another notation for the expectation value of the output $\langle y \rangle$ by writing it instead as $\bar{y}$. Then, we define the network error for a single pattern by

$$E = \frac{1}{2}\sum_j (t - \bar{y}_j)^2 \tag{10.14}$$

where the summation is over the output layer and t is a target value (compare (5.15)). Now, although this is an expression for E considered as a function of the output layer variables, it is always possible to imagine that we focus on another layer L by expressing each of the $\bar{y}_j$ in the output layer in terms of the mean outputs in L. Thus, we think of the error E as a function of the form $E = E(\bar{y}_i)$ where the index i refers to nodes in L so that

$$\delta E \approx \sum_i \frac{\partial E}{\partial \bar{y}_i}\delta \bar{y}_i \tag{10.15}$$

189

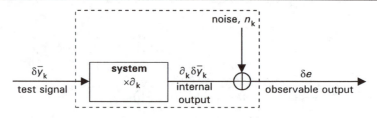

Figure 10.18 System identification for estimating gradients.

We now single out a particular node k, say, and write

$$\delta E \approx \frac{\partial E}{\partial \bar{y}_k} \delta \bar{y}_k + \sum_{i \neq k} \frac{\partial E}{\partial \bar{y}_i} \delta \bar{y}_i \qquad (10.16)$$

The reason for doing this is that we now wish to consider δE as a system output signal in response to test signal $\delta \bar{y}_k$, and to treat the remaining sum as a noise term n_k. That is, we think of k as being responsible for the error and consider the effect of the rest of the layer as noise superimposed on its influence. To clarify this it is convenient to abbreviate $\partial E / \partial \bar{y}_k$ to ∂_k so that we have

$$\delta E \approx \partial_k \delta \bar{y}_k + n_k \qquad (10.17)$$

This does indeed map onto the system identification (SID) paradigm in an almost trivial way as indicated in Figure 10.18. The "system" in this case consists of the operation of multiplication of the input by ∂_k in a single node so that ∂_k is the system's single parameter to be estimated. Of course, there is nothing special about any particular node in the net and we suppose that each one sees things from this subjective perspective in order to find its error gradient. In order to calculate these, it is necessary to provide a series of random signals of the type $\delta \bar{y}_k$. This would be unwieldy if it were not for the fact that this can be made to occur naturally in stochastic units. Details of how this is done, techniques for making the estimates of ∂_k, together with the proof of convergence for SID training, are given in Gurney (1989, 1992a). The effects of noise in the gradient descent and a comparison between nets of digital and semilinear nodes can be found in Gurney (1992b).

It is pertinent here to say a few words about the nature of gradient estimates and noise. The description "noisy" was used for the estimates found under pattern-update mode in backpropagation. However, this use of the term is more in the nature of a paraphrase for a situation that is slightly more complicated. Thus, given a particular input pattern and state of the network, the gradient estimate found in backpropagation is quite deterministic; the "noise" arises in the sense that the estimate may not be in the true direction of a gradient descent (we may sometimes go uphill). The estimates in system identification, on the other hand, are truly noisy; with a given pattern and network state the estimate is entirely dependent on the random pattern of signals produced from a noise source.

It can be shown that, when the gradient estimates are made using the minimum of resources, the SID training rule reduces to something that has the appearance of reward–penalty learning. This is consistent with the fact that both techniques are rooted in the ability of the net to explore possible alternatives, although A_{R-P} uses this to allow the net to discover correct responses, whereas SID uses it to generate test signals in a system identification task.

10.6 Summary

This chapter has broadened the discussion of feedforward nets from semilinear nodes and gradient descent algorithms. A re-evaluation of the function of local synaptic circuits in real neurons leads to the conclusion that the simple linear weighted sum form of the activation may not be fully biologically plausible. One attempt to inject more realism occurs in the sigma–pi node, which uses multilinear terms in its activation.

Another starting point was to note that RAM components can implement arbitrary Boolean functions of their input. These digital nodes were used in the construction of the WISARD pattern discriminators and ADAM associative memories. By using more than two values in each RAM cell (or at each site), it is possible to extend the functionality of digital nodes. This prevents the loss of information in training and opens up the possibility (in the limit of continuous site values) of dealing with digital nodes on a principled mathematical basis. When this is done it transpires that digital nodes and sigma–pi units are intimately related. One problem with digital nodes occurs in their inherent inability to generalize. This may be overcome by promoting clustering of similar site values around trained centres. A further problem arises with the exponential growth of the number of sites with the number of inputs, which may be solved by using multi-cube-type units.

One further node type – the radial basis function – was examined. This implements a Gaussian hump in pattern space and, by linearly combining several such functions, it is possible to approximate any function as closely as we please. RBF nets with fixed centres may be "trained" very quickly by analytically solving a least squares problem for the weights to the output node.

Two new training algorithms were described. The first (reward–penalty) makes use of stochastic nodes to explore the space of possible solutions. It uses a single scalar feedback signal in training, which informs the net whether its current output was "right" or "wrong". A more information-rich technique makes use of ideas from system identification in control theory. This identifies each error gradient (with respect to each node output) as the parameter in a separate system that simply multiplies its input by the gradient. System identification training reduces to reward–penalty in circumstances that minimize the available resources.

10.7 Notes

1. WIlkie Stonham Aleksander Recognition Device, after its inventors.
2. Advanced Distributed Associative Memory.
3. The notation used here is my own and not that used by Myers and Aleksander.

Chapter Eleven

Taxonomies, contexts and hierarchies

Our intention in this chapter is to take a step back and to try and look at neural networks from some high-level perspectives. First, we will attempt to impose some order on the seemingly disparate set of structures, algorithms, etc., that make up the network "zoo". Secondly, we will explore further the consequences of the hierarchical scheme introduced in Chapter 9. Next, we will look at connectionism alongside conventional AI and compare their relative merits in providing an understanding of intelligent systems. Finally, an historical overview helps to complement the structural taxonomy and provides an insight into the nature of the scientific process.

11.1 Classifying neural net structures

On first exposure to the neural net literature it may seem that the whole area is simply a large collection of different architectures, node types, etc., which are somewhat *ad hoc* and not related in any way. It is the intention of this section to try and give a framework for classifying any network that enables it to be viewed as a special instance of, or as a composite of, only a handful of structures. All of the material discussed here has been introduced in previous chapters but is drawn together for a comparative review. We start by looking at the types of task that neural nets can perform and show that their definitions are not always mutually exclusive. Thus, we have seen nets performing classification, associative recall, and cluster template formation. However, these descriptions are in some sense "in the eye of the network designer", and often shade into one another.

11.1.1 Neural net tasks

Consider the first network task we encountered, which was classification with feedforward nets. This has the connotation that a pattern with a large number of inputs is assigned a comparatively small code on the output layer. However, it is perfectly feasible to allow any number of output units and, in particular, there may be equal numbers of inputs and outputs. Then it is possible for the input and output patterns to be the same and the net can be used as an associative memory (Sect. 7.2). Now suppose that the output pattern is still roughly the same size as the input but their contents are quite different. This is still a kind of associative recall but, in order to distinguish it from the previous case, it is referred to as *hetero-associative recall* whereas, if the input and output are the same, we refer to *auto-associative recall*. If there are just a few output nodes is the net performing classification or hetero-association? Clearly there is no hard and fast way of deciding but conventionally we tend to think of the case with few output nodes as classification and that with many nodes as association.

Typically (although not necessarily) classification will make use of Boolean-valued target outputs to make clear the class distinctions. If a net then responds with some nodes failing to reach saturation (i.e. close to Boolean values) we may either interpret its output as an inconclusive result or look for the nearest Boolean class vector.

If, on the other hand, we are using a feedforward net with continuous output, then we may wish to interpret all values of the output in response to arbitrary inputs. This will occur if we are attempting to learn a smooth input–output function in which case we refer to the net as performing *function interpolation*. An example occurred in Section 6.11.2 in which a net was trained to forecast financial market indices whose values were continuous.

Within the context of auto-association in recurrent nets we saw two distinct modes of operation (see Fig. 7.1). In one, the whole pattern was corrupted uniformly by noise and so we think of the recall process as a kind of noise filtering. In the other case, a part of the pattern was known to be intact and represented a key to initiate recall of the remaining part. The network is then behaving as a *content addressable memory* (CAM) since the contents of a pattern are the key to its retrieval. Recurrent nets may also perform hetero-association as shown in Figure 11.1 in which, conceptually, the pattern is divided into two parts and we always clamp one half and recall on the other. By analogy with the feedforward case we may also perform classification if the clamp occupies the bulk of the pattern and the nodes for recall are small in number. Hetero-association is also clearly an example of CAM in operation.

Clamp   Recall

Figure 11.1 Hetero-associative recall in recurrent nets.

Table 11.1 Example of neural network tasks and network types.

Network architecture	Tasks
Principally feedforward	– Classification – Function interpolation

Principally recurrent	– Associative memory
	
	  – Auto-association
	
	    – Noise filtering
	    – CAM
	
	  – Hetero-association (also example of CAM)

Competitive	– Cluster template formation – Analysis of topological relationships

Turning to competitive nets, these can be thought of in two ways. On the one hand they perform a cluster analysis and learn weight vector templates corresponding to the centre of each cluster. Alternatively we can think of the net as a classifier if we interpret winning nodes as signifying pattern classes. As an additional feature, self-organizing feature maps (SOMs) allow us to discover topological relationships (pattern proximities) between input vectors.

The various network tasks and the nets used to perform them are summarized in Table 11.1. The judicious use of the term "principally" in the left hand column emphasizes the fact that the correspondence between task descriptions and nets is not rigid.

11.1.2   A taxonomy of artificial neurons

Many artificial neurons have their functional behaviour defined within the *activation–output* model shown in Figure 11.2. Here, the x_i are a set of n inputs, and q_k a set of N internal parameters. The activation a is a function of the inputs and parameters, $a = a(q_k, x_i)$, and the output y is a function of the activation, $y = y(a)$.

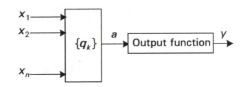

Figure 11.2 Activation–output model of artificial neuron.

Splitting up the node functionality like this can assist the understanding of what "ingredients" have been used in the node make-up. In this model the TLUs and semilinear nodes have as their parameters a set of weights w_k, $k = 1 \ldots n$, and a is just given by the usual weighted sum of inputs. The sigma–pi units have 2^n weights w_k, the radial basis functions have centres given by a set of n vector components w_k, and the digital nodes have their activation defined via a set of 2^n site values S_μ. All of this is summarized in Table 11.2. The point here is that what follows the generation of a – the activation–output function (or, simply, output function) – is wholly independent of the form a takes so that we are, in principle, free to "mix and match" activation forms and output functions.

Examples of output functions are shown in Figure 11.3 where we have chosen to concentrate on their graphical form rather than their mathematical description, many of which have been described previously. The only new member is the "ramp" function, which is given by

$$y = \begin{cases} 0 & \text{if} \quad a < 0 \\ a & \text{if} \quad a \geq 0 \end{cases} \tag{11.1}$$

and has been used by Fukushima (1980) in his neocognitron.

There are two further aspects to node structure. First, the result of the output function may not be used directly but, rather, as a probability in a source of stochastic output that is usually Boolean. Secondly, what we have referred to so

Table 11.2 Forms of activation.

Description	Mathematical form	Used in
Linear weighted sum of inputs	$\mathbf{w} \cdot \mathbf{x}$	TLUs, semilinear nodes
Distance from a centre	$\|\mathbf{w} - \mathbf{x}\|$	RBF units
Multilinear form	$\sum_k w_k \prod_{i \in I_k} x_i$	Sigma–pi units
Site value on hypercube	$S_\mu : \mu = \mathbf{x}$	Digital nodes

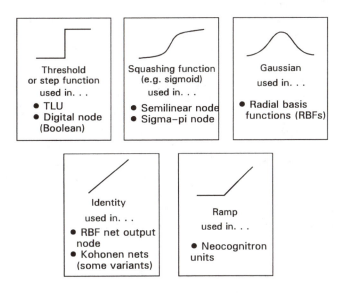

Figure 11.3 Output functions.

far as the "activation" may instead be subject to some kind of temporal integration and decay (recall the leaky integrators). In this case, the quantities in Table 11.2 are acting as an input "driving force" in a more complex relation that determines the final activation. It is possible to modify Figure 11.2 to include these functional additions but this will not be done here.

To summarize: nodes can be specified according to the following criteria:

- Particular choice of activation form (Table 11.2).

- Form of output function (Fig. 11.3).

- Whether the activation is given directly by an expression like those in Table 11.2, or indirectly via leaky-integrator dynamics.

- Stochastic or non-stochastic output.

11.1.3 A taxonomy of network structures and dynamics

The last section dealt with an analysis of the micro-structure of the net at node level; here we deal with the large-scale topology and dynamics.

We have seen three main network architectures: feedforward, recurrent and competitive layers. Within the feedforward genre, the net may or may not be layered, contain hidden units or be fully interconnected from layer to layer. Feedforward nets have trivial dynamics – the input simply initiates a flow of signals that propagate through to the output layer.

197

The main example of a recurrent net we discussed was that due to Hopfield. The nets described in Chapter 7 were fully connected, although this need not be the case; Hopfield-like nets with incomplete connectivity turn out to have a smaller training pattern capacity than their fully connected counterparts. Additionally, there may or may not be symmetric connections or hidden units. The latter have been used in the so-called *Boltzmann machines* (Hinton et al. 1984) where they help form an internal representation of the training environment. Since there is no special distinction between input and output units in a recurrent net, the non-hidden units in the Boltzmann machine are referred to as *visible units* since they may interact directly with the environment. The dynamics of recurrent nets may be synchronous or asynchronous leading to deterministic or probabilistic behaviour respectively.

The final structure – the competitive layer – has a distinct, highly structured architecture and the dynamics are governed by those of its individual, leaky-integrator nodes.

Not all networks are examples of one of these three categories but, if they are not, then it is usually possible to break them down into these architectural building blocks. For example, ART may be thought of as a competitive layer together with a single-layer net whose input is partly derived via the top-down templates. Our summary of network architectures is therefore as follows:

- Is the net one of the three main types (recurrent, feedforward, competitive)? If not, how can it be broken down into components of this form?

- Are there hidden units?

- If feedforward, is the network layered?

- Is the connectivity complete (layer to layer in feedforward nets and node to node in recurrent nets)?

- Are any recurrent, reciprocal connections symmetric?

- If recurrent, are the dynamics synchronous or asynchronous?

11.1.4 A taxonomy of training algorithms

The first kind of training encountered was supervised learning in the guise of the perceptron rule, delta rule and backpropagation. The characteristic of this type of training is that it necessitates a target output vector for each input pattern. Self-organization, on the other hand, requires no such targets and each training pattern is considered a complete whole. Examples of this occurred with the competitive nets and the Kohonen SOMs. Characteristic of self-organization is the use of a Hebb-like rule (possibly with a weight decay term). A further type of "training" took place with the Hopfield nets in which the weights were set by *fiat* according to a prescription formula. However, we saw that this was equivalent to learning incrementally with a Hebb rule and, since there is no separate output with these nets, training in this way is a type of self-organization. The reward–penalty rule and system identification require target vectors of some kind but the signals fed back to the net are less complex than those used in, say, backpropagation. Because of this, some workers choose to think of R–P and the like as belonging to a separate class of learning algorithms although they may also be thought of as part of the supervised family.

Our training taxonomy is then:

- Supervised

    - Complex signal feedback (e.g. backpropagation)
    - Simple signal feedback (e.g. R–P).

- Unsupervised (self-organized).

- Weights given by formulaic prescription.

Another dimension to training concerns the separation of the network operation into distinct training and testing phases. This is the most common state of affairs but is not necessary, as demonstrated by the ART networks, which do not make this distinction.

11.2   Networks and the computational hierarchy

In our description of the ART networks, we found it useful to separate out different strands of the net's function and structure according to a hierarchical system based on that originally propounded by Marr (1982). Here we will apply this scheme to other types of net.

Consider, first, the case of supervised learning using MLPs and backpropagation. There is a training set consisting of input–output vector pairs x_i, y_i that are related by being samples from some underlying mapping or functional relation $f(x) = y$. Let the set of input–output mappings realizable by the network be F; this is restricted by the network connection scheme, number of hidden units, etc. At the computational level we seek a function $\tilde{f}$, a member of F, such that an error measure E (the sum of square differences $(\tilde{f}(x_i) - y_i)^2$) for $\tilde{f}$ is a minimum over F. Depending on the choice available in F, the network function $\tilde{f}$ will approximate more or less to the underlying function f. If it is indeed close to f then we expect there to be good generalization.

At the algorithmic level we perform a steepest descent gradient descent on E with respect to the parameters (the weights) that define $\tilde{f}$. Depending on whether this occurs under serial or batch pattern update, the descent may or may not include noise. In going further, it is useful to differentiate between the

199

forward and backward passes. The former calculates the following function of its hidden unit outputs y_j:

$$y_k = \sigma \left(\sum_j w_{kj} y_j \right) \tag{11.2}$$

where each y_j is, of course, a similar function of the network inputs. This calculation may be thought of as a feature at the system level of implementation. It has, of course, an immediate signal-level implementation in terms of the artificial neurons supporting these functions. Indeed one may argue that the finesse of thinking of the calculation at a higher level than its neural implementation is unwarranted and that we should omit the system level in this case. However, the learning process is quite different. The calculations may be articulated at the system level but the consequent signal-level implementation is not consistent with artificial neuron function. Examples of this are the forming of target–output differences, the summation in the error calculation, and mechanisms to turn on and off the plasticity of the weights between forward and backward passes. Grossberg (1987) has given a graphical description of the signals in backpropagation training and notes that it does not appear neurally inspired; that is, the signal-level implementation does not appear to map well onto the combined function of a set of artificial neurons. The lack of a neural-like signal-level description is sometimes appreciated intuitively when a network is said to be "biologically implausible".

Notice that what is attempted at each level in the description backpropagation is independent of what occurs at the other levels. Thus, at the computational level we are free to define alternative forms for the error E. At the algorithmic level we can then choose to minimize it in any way we please – gradient descent does not have a monopoly here. Other techniques include quasi-random search (Baba 1989) or genetic algorithms (Jones 1993, Nolfi & Parisi 1995). Indeed, even having chosen gradient descent, we are still free to choose the particular technique out of many available, which vary in speed and complexity, and are not bound to use only backpropagation. For example, the so-called conjugate gradient method (Fletcher & Reeves 1964) or second-order techniques (Battiti 1992), which make use of the higher order gradients (rate of change of rate of change). Notice that what we have previously referred to as an algorithm – "backpropagation" – is now viewed as a particular implementation of gradient descent. However, we believe that teasing out the description into the multi-level hierarchy does allow a deeper understanding in terms of what the net is doing, alternatives available, and issues of biological plausibility.

We now turn to self-organization under competitive dynamics. There is still an input set $\{x_i\}$ but no corresponding $\{y_i\}$. Instead there are a fixed number of *templates* w_k, $1 \leq k \leq N$ (we have in mind, of course, the weight vectors in a competitive layer), and a distance measure $d(w_k, x_i)$ that defines how "close" the pattern is to the template. Computationally, we now seek a set $\{w_{ki}\}$ and a mapping $x_i \to w_{ki}$ (patterns to templates) that tends to minimize[1] $\sum_{x_i} d(w_{ki}, x_i)$.

The motivation here is that what constitutes "clustering" is defined via d, for patterns $\mathbf{x}_i$, $\mathbf{x}_j$ that are close together have small values of $d(\mathbf{x}_i, \mathbf{x}_j)$. Finally, we require that the mapping is many to one so that each pattern is assigned only one template. Examples of d that we have seen before are the inner product $\mathbf{x}_i \cdot \mathbf{w}_k$ and the length of the vector difference $\|\mathbf{x}_i - \mathbf{w}_{k^i}\|$.

A typical algorithm then proceeds as follows. Choose a pattern at random, find the current best template match $\mathbf{w}_j$, and then update the template according to some rule like (8.4).

In terms of implementation, it is the search for best template match that highlights the difference in network types. In the Kohonen SOMs this is done using a computer supervised search, which constitutes a system-level implementation. There is then no signal-level detail for these nets. On the other hand, the use of competitive dynamics to find the closest match represents a feature of implementation at the signal level.

It is apparent from the discussion of both types of learning that it is usually the training algorithm proper (rather than the operation of the net in its testing phase) that fails to have a signal-level implementation. Another slant on this observation is the distinction made by Williams (1987) between "on-line" and "off-line" processes in networks. In our language, the former are able to be carried out at the signal level using a network whereas the latter have no obvious network-bound, signal-level description.

11.3 Networks and statistical analysis

On several occasions it has been noted that there were similarities between a net's training algorithm and some technique in statistics or data analysis. For example, we can liken backpropagation to nonlinear regression and competitive learning to some kinds of cluster analysis. Is it the case that all neural nets are simply a reworking of familiar techniques? We claim that, although there are similarities to be drawn out between "classical" methods and networks, the latter do retain a novelty and utility that lies outside of the established methods.

Consider again the MLP defined by (11.2). At the computational level this may be thought of as a model for nonlinear regression that is parametrized by the weights. However, as noted by Cheng & Titterington (1994), this does not correspond to any model of regression previously developed and the form of (11.2) was not given a priori but was based on the network. The network paradigm therefore has the potential to inspire novel computational approaches in a bottom-up way; it is not merely an implementation of given computational strategies and is indeed able to stand on its own merits.

Now suppose we discover a network in a biological setting that appears to have the same architecture as one of those we have studied in its artificial guise. An understanding of the computational and algorithmic aspects of the artificial network promises to provide insight into the nature of these processes in its biological counterpart. There are further benefits if we have a signal-level implementation of the net endowing it with biological plausibility.

11.4 Neural networks and intelligent systems: symbols versus neurons

There are, as pointed out in the first chapter, many ways of viewing connectionist systems depending on which intellectual stance one starts from. Here we wish to focus on networks as one way of building intelligent machines. In attempting this, it is not clear at the outset whether we are obliged to copy the physical structure of the brain, or if it is possible somehow to skim off or extract the essential processes responsible for intelligence and encapsulate them in computer programs. The first approach is fulfilled in the connectionist programme, the latter by conventional symbol-based artificial intelligence or AI. We now explore these issues in more depth.

11.4.1 The search for artificial intelligence

What is artificial intelligence? One definition is that it is intelligent behaviour embodied in human-made machines. In some sense, however, we have simply reposed the question as "what is intelligence?" It appears then that we are in an impasse, for to answer this would pre-empt the whole research programme of artificial intelligence. One way out of this potential "Catch-22" situation is simply to give examples of intelligent behaviour and then to say that achieving machine performance in these tasks, as good as or better than humans, is the goal of artificial intelligence research. Thus, we are typically interested in tasks such as: the perception and understanding of the world from visual input; the generation and understanding of speech; navigation in complex environments while avoiding obstacles; the ability to argue in a common-sense manner about the world; playing games of strategy like chess; doing mathematics; diagnosis of medical conditions; making stock market predictions.

From the early days of computing, in the late 1940s and early 1950s, there have existed two quite different approaches to the problem of developing machines that might embody such behaviour. One of these tries to capture knowledge as a set of irreducible semantic objects or *symbols*, and to manipulate these according to a set of formal rules. The rules, taken together, form a "recipe" or *algorithm* for processing the symbols. The formal articulation of the symbolic–algorithmic paradigm has been made most vigorously by Newell & Simon (1976) and has represented the mainstream of research in artificial intelligence; indeed "Artificial Intelligence" (capital "A" and "I") – or its acronym AI – is usually taken to refer to this school of thought.

Concurrent with this, however, has been another line of research, which has used machines whose architecture is loosely based on that of the animal brain. These artificial neural networks are supposed to learn from examples and their "knowledge" is stored in representations that are distributed across a set of weights. This is in contrast to the AI approach, which requires a computer to be preprogrammed[2] in some computer language and whose representations are localized within a memory store.

In order to appreciate the radical differences between these two approaches, it is necessary to know something about symbolic AI. The following section must serve as the briefest of outlines suitable for our comparison and readers are referred to texts such as those by Winston (1984) and Rich & Knight (1991) for a comprehensive introduction.

11.4.2 The symbolic paradigm

We will illustrate the symbolic approach with the example of playing a game like chess although the details have been chosen for clarity rather than any relation to genuine chess programs. The first ingredient is a method of describing the state of the board at any time. This might easily be represented symbolically by assigning lexical tokens to the pieces and using a grid system for the squares. It then makes sense to say, for example, that "white_pawn(2) is on square(d2)". Next we need to define what the initial state and final (or goal) states of the game are; the system needs to know what constitutes checkmate. It must also have knowledge of what constitutes a valid move. This will consist of a series of rules of the form "If there is a white pawn at square(d2) AND square(d3) is empty THEN the pawn can move to square(d3)". Of course, higher level abstractions of rules like this (which don't require specific square labels, etc.) will almost certainly be used. The use of legal moves should then guarantee that only legal board positions are obtained. Finally we need some controlling strategy that tells the system how to find goal states. This takes the form of a search through the space of board states a given number of moves ahead. At each move a value is assigned to the final board position according to its utility for the chess-playing system. For example, moves that result in loss of pieces will (usually) score poorly. The search may be guided by more rules or heuristics that embody further knowledge of the game: for example, "don't put your queen under direct attack", or "material loss is OK if mate can be forced in two moves".

The main ingredients in such an approach are therefore well-defined rules and their assembly into procedures that often constitute some kind of search strategy. In addition, symbolic descriptions are all pervasive, both in describing the problem explicitly and as tokens in defining the rules. Chess may be thought of as an instantiation of one area of human expert knowledge and, quite generally, AI has sought to articulate these domains in so-called *expert systems* in which each fragment of knowledge is encapsulated in a construction of the form "if *condition 1* and *condition 2* ... then *result*". These have proven very successful in many areas as, for example, in configuring computer systems (McDermott 1982) and giving advice on mineral exploration (Hart et al. 1978).

How are we to implement such systems? The answer lies in the fact that they all represent *computable* procedures. One formal definition of computability is couched directly in terms of a hypothetical machine, the universal Turing machine (Turing 1937). Although all modern, general purpose computers are equivalent to this abstract model they are more normally referenced to another that more closely depicts the way they work. This model – the *von Neumann machine* – also highlights their intimate relation with the symbolic paradigm and is illustrated in Figure 11.4.

The von Neumann machine/computer repeatedly performs the following cycle of events:

1. Fetch an instruction from memory.

2. Fetch any data required by the instruction from memory.

3. Execute the instruction (process the data).

4. Store results in memory.

5. Go back to step 1.

Although the first computers were built to perform numerical calculations, it was apparent to the early workers that the machines they had built were also capable of manipulating symbols, since the machines themselves knew nothing of the semantics of the bit-strings stored in their memories. Thus, Alan Turing, speaking in 1947 about the design for the proposed Automatic Computing Engine (ACE), saw the potential to deal with complex game-playing situations like chess: "Given a position in chess the machine could be made to list all the 'winning combinations' to a depth of about three moves ... " (Hodges 1985).

We can now see how the von Neumann architecture lends itself naturally to instantiating symbolic AI systems. The symbols are represented as bit-patterns in memory locations that are accessed by the CPU. The algorithms (including

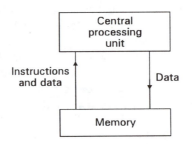

Figure 11.4 The von Neumann machine.

search strategies and rules) are then articulated as computer programs by gradually breaking them down into successively smaller operations until these consist of the instructions that the CPU can directly work on. The machines on which the modern AI fraternity run their algorithms have not changed in any fundamental conceptual way from the pilot ACE, all of these being examples of the classic von Neumann architecture. Granted, there has been a speed increase of several orders of magnitude, and hardware parallelism is sometimes available, but contemporary "AI engines" are still vehicles for the instantiation of the theoretic stance which claims that intelligent behaviour can be described completely as a process of formal, algorithmic symbol manipulation.

Mainstream AI has proved successful in many areas and, indeed, with the advent of expert systems has become big business. For a brief history of its more noteworthy achievements see Raj (1988). However, AI has not fulfilled much of the early promise that was conjectured by the pioneers in the field. Dreyfus, in his book *What computers can't do* (Dreyfus 1979), criticizes the early extravagant claims of the AI practitioners and outlines the assumptions they made. Principal among these is the belief that all knowledge or information can be formalized, and that the mind can be viewed as a device that operates on information according to formal rules. It is precisely in those domains of experience where it has proved extremely difficult to formalize the environment that the "brittle" rule-based procedures of AI have failed. The differentiation of knowledge into that which can be treated formally and that which cannot has been further examined by Smolensky (1988) where he makes the distinction between *cultural* or *public knowledge* and *private* or *intuitive knowledge*. Stereotypical examples of cultural knowledge are found in science and mathematics in which proofs, demonstrations and procedures can be made as clear and as detailed as we wish. Examples of private knowledge include many areas of everyday human activity: the skills of natural language understanding, fine motor control in sport, visual navigation and scene understanding, or even the intuitive knowledge of an expert in some narrow domain such as wine tasting. Public knowledge can be displayed in its entirety in a well-defined way – Newton's laws of motion can be stated unequivocally – and there is no more nor less to them than their symbolic representation. Private or intuitive knowledge can be indicated or pointed to but cannot be made explicit. A tennis professional can indicate how to play a good serve but cannot transfer the required skill directly to the motor areas of your brain – this needs much practice and may never be acquired.

We may draw up a list of the essential characteristics of von Neumann machines (computers) running symbolic AI systems for comparison with those of networks.

- The machine must be told in advance, and in great detail, the exact series of steps required to perform the algorithm. This series of steps is the computer program.

- The types of data it deals with have to be in a precise format – noisy data confuse the machine.

- The hardware is easily degraded – destroy a few key memory locations and the computer will stop functioning or "crash".

- There is a clear correspondence between the semantic objects being dealt with (numbers, words, database entries, etc.) and the computer hardware. Each object can be "pointed to" in a block of memory.

The first point here requires some qualification in the light of the possibility of the machine learning from previous experience (Rich & Knight 1991, Thornton 1992). However, learning in this case can only result in "more of the same" (rules and symbols) and, further, this is constrained to be within the framework provided by the programmer. So, notwithstanding this proviso, the success of the symbolic approach in AI is predicated on the assumption that we can at least find an algorithmic *framework* to describe the solution to the problem. As already noted, it turns out that many everyday task domains we take for granted are difficult to formalize in this way. Further specific examples are: how do we recognize handwritten characters, the particular instances of which we may never have seen before, or someone's face from an angle we have never encountered; how do we recall whole visual scenes, given some obscure verbal cue?

11.4.3   The connectionist paradigm

The neural network or connectionist approach starts from the premise that intuitive knowledge cannot be captured in a set of formalized rules and a completely different strategy must be adopted. It assumes that, by copying more closely the physical architecture of the brain, we may emulate brain function more closely and build machines that can tackle some of these apparently intractable problems. Some features of this approach are as follows:

- Clearly the style of processing is completely different; it is more akin to signal processing than symbol processing. The combining of signals and generation of new ones is to be contrasted with the execution of instructions stored in a memory.

- Information is stored in a set of weights rather than a program. In general, the weights adapt by continually presenting examples from a set of training vectors to the net.

- Processing in a network occurs in a parallel rather than a serial fashion. There is no single CPU and each node can operate independently and simultaneously with other nodes in the net.

- Nets are robust in the presence of noise; small changes in an input signal will not drastically affect a node's output.

- Nets are robust in the presence of hardware failure: a change in a weight may only affect the output for a few of the possible input patterns.

- There is often no simple correspondence between nodes and high-level semantic objects. Rather, the representation of a "concept" or "idea" within the net is via the complete pattern of unit activities, being distributed over the net as a whole. In this way any given node may partake in many semantic representations (however, this is not necessarily the case, a point taken up again in the next section).

- A characteristic feature of their operation is that neural nets work by extracting statistical regularities or *features* from the training set. This allows the net to respond to novel inputs (not seen during training) by classifying them appropriately with one of the previously seen patterns, or by assigning them to new classes. This process of *generalization* is one of the key reasons for using neural nets.

- Nets are good at "perceptual" tasks like pattern classification and associative recall in the presence of noise. These are just the tasks that the symbolic approach can have difficulties with.

11.4.4   Symbols and neurons – a *rapprochement*

We have tried to show that the conventional symbolic paradigm can fail to be effective for tasks where it is difficult to formalize the procedures we use and that an alternative, subsymbolic, network-based paradigm may be more suitable. However, we must be careful not to throw the symbolic "baby" out with its "bath water". AI has been moderately successful in some restricted domains of human expertise and some high-level cognitive skills possessed by humans are most easily formulated in symbolic terms. In particular, the usual applications to which computers are put – mathematics, database retrieval, etc. – are clearly easier to implement on a von Neumann machine than in a neural network.

Further, the connectionist approach has one disadvantage in that, although a solution to the problem may be available, it is usually not clear *why* that particular solution is correct. This is the other edge of the distributed processing sword: patterns of activity across a network are not semantically transparent and, even if we attempt to interpret a node's activity as some kind of micro-feature, these may be difficult to understand and their sheer number may conspire to obscure the reason for a particular network output. Of course, in some sense it might be argued that it is just this insistence on explanation that has hindered previous efforts in AI to develop models of perception and cognition that may have to rely on subsymbolic operation. However, in applications work it is often desirable to have some insight as to how the model is working.

It would appear, therefore, that there may be significant gains to be made by attempting to integrate connectionist and symbolic styles of computing in a hybrid system. In this spirit, the relation between networks and expert systems is reviewed by Caudill (1991) from an applications viewpoint in which several ways of integrating the two approaches are described. First, it may be possible to break a problem down into subtasks, each of which may then be tackled with either an expert system or a network, depending on which is more appropriate. A more tightly bound scenario occurs if the networks are embedded as part of the expert system. For example, the job of finding the appropriate set of rules for any particular input may be likened to one of pattern matching. Thus, the series of conditional clauses ("if" statements) that apply at any time constitute a pattern vector of input statements. In this way, a network may be used to evaluate which rule (or rules) should be used in response to the current state of the system environment. Alternatively, the network may be the mechanism that is activated in response to an "if–then" rule instantiated in the normal way. If a network is clearly superior to a symbol-based system for a particular task but a premium is placed on explanation then it may be possible to run the network in parallel with an expert system, which, although inadequate for solving the problem consistently, may provide some insight as to why the net has chosen the solution it has.

Finally, it is possible, in principle at least, to extract rules from networks. For example, suppose a node in a single-layer net has two large positive weights w_i, w_j, that the node has a threshold-type output function (or very steep sigmoid) and that the inputs and outputs have clear semantic identities (e.g. medical symptoms and diagnosis respectively). Then, if the other weights of the node are sufficiently small it may be possible to write the node's function in the form "If symptom(i) and symptom(j) *then* diagnosis(1)" where the latter is one of the two possible node outputs. This is engendered if both inputs i and j are required to make the node fire and the other inputs cannot contribute significantly to the activation. A full system realization of this form is described by Gallant (1988).

Other workers are not interested so much in providing explanations of the problem-solving process as in providing a connectionist model for high-level, cognitive human skills that have traditionally appeared to be tractable by the symbolic approach. Sun and Bookman provide an introduction to these hybrid cognitive models in a workshop report (Sun & Bookman 1993) and a comprehensive review (Sun & Bookman 1994). The *localist* approach uses the theme (introduced above) of assigning clear conceptual interpretation to individual nodes. This appears to abandon one of the tenets of the connectionist philosophy, namely distributed representations, and Smolensky (1988) has argued for the "proper treatment of connectionism", in which nets can only operate at a *subsymbolic* level and where there are no local high-level semantic representations. Nevertheless it would appear that a useful bridge between symbols and neurons may be built in this way. Other approaches are truly distributed in using whole networks to represent concepts and ideas, and open up the possibility for the combination of local and distributed representations working in concert.

At the very highest level of analysis, Clark (1990) has speculated that we humans may have to emulate a von Neumann architecture within the neural nets that are our brains, in order to perform symbolic-based tasks. That this is a logical possibility was made clear by McCulloch and Pitts in their original paper on the TLU (1943) when they proved that networks of such units could evaluate any Turing computable function.

11.5   A brief history of neural nets

We draw together here some of the key contributions described in previous chapters but in the context of a brief historical narrative that highlights the way ideas in science can, just like hemlines, also be subject to the vagaries of fashion. Many of the most significant papers on neural networks are reprinted in the collection of Anderson & Rosenfeld (1988). Some interesting anecdotes and reminiscences can be found in the article by Rumelhart & Zipser (1985).

11.5.1   The early years

The development of machines that incorporate neural features has always run in parallel with work on their von Neumann-style counterparts. In fact the analogy between computing and the operation of the brain was to the fore in much of the early work on general purpose computing. Thus, in the first draft of a report on the EDVAC, von Neumann (reprinted, 1987) makes several correspondences between the proposed circuit elements and animal neurons.

In 1942 Norbert Weiner (see Heims 1982) and his colleagues were formulating the ideas that were later christened *cybernetics* by Weiner and that dealt with "control and communication in the animal and the machine". Central to this programme, as the description suggests, is the idea that biological mechanisms can be treated from an engineering and mathematical perspective. With the rise of AI and cognitive science, the term "cybernetics" became unfashionable (Aleksander 1980) although it might be argued that, because of its interdisciplinary nature, connectionism should properly be called a branch of cybernetics; certainly many of the early neural net scientists would have described their activities in this way.

In the same year that Weiner was formulating cybernetics, McCulloch and Pitts published the first formal treatment of artificial neural nets and introduced the TLU. Soon after this, Donald Hebb (1949) made his seminal contribution to learning theory with his suggestion that synaptic strengths might change so as to reinforce any simultaneous correspondence of activity levels between the presynaptic and postsynaptic neurons.

The use of the training algorithm in artificial nets was initiated by Rosenblatt (1962) in his book *Principles of neurodynamics*, which gave a proof of convergence of the perceptron rule. The delta rule was developed shortly afterwards by Widrow

& Hoff (1960) and neural nets seemed set for a bright future. However, in 1969 this first flush of enthusiasm for neural nets was dampened by the publication of Minsky and Papert's book *Perceptrons* (Minsky & Papert 1969). Here, the authors show that there is an interesting class of problems (those that are not linearly separable) that single-layer perceptron nets cannot solve, and they held out little hope for the training of multilayer systems that might deal successfully with some of these. Minsky had clearly had a change of heart since 1951, when he had been involved in the construction of one of the earliest connectionist machines in a project that motivated work on learning in his PhD thesis. The fundamental obstacle to be overcome was the credit assignment problem; in a multilayer system, how much does each unit (especially one not in the output layer) contribute to the error the net has made in processing the current training vector?

In spite of *Perceptrons*, much work continued in what was now an unfashionable area, living in the shadow of symbolic AI: Grossberg was laying the foundations for his adaptive resonance theory (ART) (Carpenter & Grossberg 1987b, Grossberg 1987); Fukushima was developing the cognitron (Fukushima 1975); Kohonen (Kohonen 1984) was investigating nets that used topological feature maps; and Aleksander (Aleksander & Stonham 1979) was building hardware implementations of the nets based on the *n*-tuple technique of Bledsoe and Browning (Bledsoe & Browning 1959).

Several developments led to a resurgence of interest in neural networks. Some of these factors are technical and show that Minsky and Papert had not had the last word on the subject, while others are of a more general nature.

11.5.2   The neural net renaissance

In 1982 John Hopfield, then a physicist at Caltech, showed (Hopfield 1982) that a highly interconnected network of threshold logic units could be analyzed by considering it to be a physical dynamic system possessing an "energy". The process of associative recall could then be framed in terms of the system falling into a state of minimal energy.

This novel approach to the treatment of recurrent nets led to the involvement of the physics community, as the mathematics of these systems is very similar to that used in the Ising spin model of magnetic phenomena in materials (Amit & Gutfreund 1985). Something very close to the "Hopfield model" had been introduced previously by Little (1974), but remained comparatively unnoticed because of its heavy technical emphasis.

A similar breakthrough occurred in connection with feedforward nets, when it was shown that the credit assignment problem had an exact solution. The resulting algorithm, "back error propagation" or simply backpropagation also has claim to multiple authorship. Thus it was discovered by Werbos (1974), rediscovered by Parker (1982), and discovered again and made popular by Rumelhart et al. (1986a). In fact it is possible to see the essential concept of backpropagation in Rosenblatt's *Principles of neurodynamics* but the author appears not to have felt able to develop these ideas to a formal conclusion.

Aside from these technical advances in analysis, there is also a sense in which neural networks are just one example of a wider class of systems that the physical sciences started to investigate in the 1980s, which include chaotic phenomena (Cvitanović 1984), fractals (Mandelbrot 1977) and cellular automata (Farmer et al. 1983). These may all be thought of as dynamical systems governed by simple rules but which give rise to complex emergent behaviour. Neural nets also fall into this category and so one view is that they are part of the "new wave" of physical science.

Another factor in the birth of any new thread of scientific investigation is the development of the appropriate tools. In order to investigate the new physical models (including neural nets), it is usually necessary to resort to computer simulation. The availability of this method increased dramatically in the 1980s with the introduction of personal computers and workstations that provided computing power that was previously the province of large, batch-run machines. These new workstations also provided many new graphical tools that facilitated visualization of what was going on inside the numeric simulations they were running. Further, the new computers allowed simple, interactive use and so facilitated experiments that would have been unthinkable 15 years previously by the average worker, given the accessibility and power of the computing resources available.

In summary, therefore, research in connectionism was revived after a setback in the 1970s because of new mathematical insights, a conducive scientific *zeitgeist*, and enormous improvement in the ability to perform simulation.

11.6 Summary

This chapter has looked at some high-level issues. First, we described the various tasks that nets can perform and noted that, although it is convenient to distinguish between them, it is often possible to think of one task as a special case of another. Some order was imposed on the connectionist "menagerie" by introducing taxonomies for artificial neurons, network structures and training algorithms. The computational hierarchy was revisited and applied to MLPs, competitive nets and SOMs. Its application led to the idea that the intuitive understanding of "biological plausibility" may be captured more precisely by an articulation of the network *and* the training algorithm at the signal level of implementation. The similarities and differences between nets and statistical techniques were discussed. Network architectures can lead to new variants of established statistical techniques and may provide insight into the operation of biological networks. Next we looked at neural networks in the context of artificial intelligence and discussed the contrast between the connectionist and symbolic approaches. It was concluded that both have something to offer, depending on the type of problem to be addressed. Finally, we gave a brief history of neural networks, which noted the watershed created by the publication of the book *Perceptrons*. The technical objections raised there have been met in principle but it remains to be seen whether the practice and application can realize the potential offered by the theoretical foundation now being established.

11.7   Notes

1. It may not find the true minimum but should at least act to decrease this sum.
2. This is subject to the proviso that learning has not been implemented in the program. This is discussed again in Section 11.4.2.

Appendix A

The cosine function

The cosine is defined in the context of a right-angled triangle, as shown in Figure A.1. For an angle ϕ (Greek phi) in a right-angled triangle, the cosine of ϕ – written $\cos\phi$ – is the ratio of the side a adjacent to ϕ, and the longest side, or hypotenuse h, so that

$$\cos\phi = \frac{a}{h} \tag{A.1}$$

To explore the properties of this definition, consider the series of triangles shown in Figure A.2. Each panel pertains to one of a series of representative angles ϕ drawn in the range $0 \le \phi \le 180°$, in which all the triangles have the same hypotenuse h. They may be thought of as being obtained by a process of rotating the radius of a circle anti-clockwise around its centre and, at each stage, forming the right-angled triangle whose hypotenuse is the radius and whose base (length a) is along a horizontal diameter. The panels are numbered with increasing ϕ. When $\phi = 0$ (panel 1) the two sides a and h are equal and so $\cos\phi = 1$. As ϕ is gradually increased to small values (panel 2) a is only slightly reduced, and so $\cos\phi \approx 1$ (read $\approx$ as "is approximately equal to"). For larger values of ϕ (panel 3) $\cos\phi$ becomes significantly less than 1. As ϕ approaches 90° (panel 4) a becomes very small and so $\cos\phi$ is almost 0. When $\phi = 90°$ (panel 5) $a = 0$ and so $\cos\phi = 0$.

Now, when ϕ is increased beyond 90° (panel 6), the angle must still be measured with respect to the same horizontal reference but this results in ϕ lying on the opposite side of the hypotenuse to that which it has occupied so far; that is, it lies *outside* the triangle. This is expressed by making a negative so that the

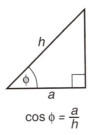

$$\cos\phi = \frac{a}{h}$$

Figure A.1 Cosine relations.

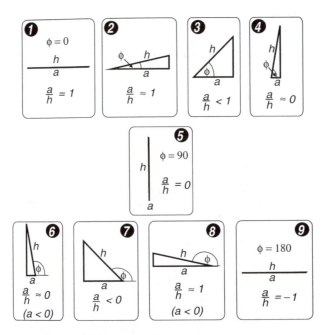

Figure A.2 The cosine function for various angles.

cosines are also negative for the rest of the series. Panels 7–9 show what happens as ϕ increases towards 180°. It can be seen that it is equivalent to a reversal of the sequence in panels 1 through to 3, albeit with the introduction of a negative sign.

By evaluating $\cos \phi$ for all values of ϕ between 0 and 180°, a graph of $\cos \phi$ over this angular range may be obtained, as shown in Figure A.3.

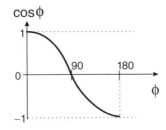

Figure A.3 Graph of cosine function.

References

Aleksander, I. 1965. Fused logic element which learns by example. *Electronics Letters* **1**, 73–4.

Aleksander, I. 1980. Whatever happened to cybernetics? Technical Report N/S/103, Department of Electrical Engineering, Brunel University.

Aleksander, I. & R. C. Albrow 1968. Microcircuit learning nets: some tests with handwritten numerals. *Electronics Letters* **4**, 406–7.

Aleksander, I. & H. Mamdani 1968. Microcircuit learning nets: improved recognition by means of pattern feedback. *Electronics Letters* **4**, 425–6.

Aleksander, I. & T. J. Stonham 1979. Guide to pattern recognition using random-access memories. *Computers and Digital Techniques* **2**, 29–40.

Aleksander, I., W. V. Thomas, P. A. Bowden 1984. WISARD: a radical step forward in image recognition. *Sensor Review* **4**, 120–24.

Amit, D. J. 1989. *Modelling brain function: the world of attractor neural networks*. Cambridge: Cambridge University Press.

Amit, D. J. & H. Gutfreund 1985. Spin-glass models of neural networks. *Physical Review A* **32**, 1007–18.

Anderson, A. & E. Rosenfeld (eds) 1988. *Neurocomputing: foundations of research*. Cambridge, MA: MIT Press.

Anderson, J. A. 1972. A simple neural network generating an interactive memory. *Mathematical Biosciences* **14**, 197–220.

Austin, J. 1987a. ADAM: A distributed associative memory for scene analysis. In *1st IEEE International Conference on Neural Networks*, vol. IV, 285–92, San Diego.

Austin, J. 1987b. *The designs and application of associative memories for scene analysis*. PhD thesis, Department of Electrical Engineering, Brunel University.

Baba, N. 1989. A new approach for finding the global minimum of error function of neural networks. *Neural Networks* **2**, 367–73.

Banquet, J. P. & S. Grossberg 1987. Probing cognitive processes through the structure of event related potentials during learning: an experimental and theoretical analysis. *Applied Optics* **26**, 4931–46.

Barto, A. G. 1985. Learning by statistical cooperation of self-interested neuron-like computing elements. *Human Neurobiology* **4**, 229–56.

Barto, A. G. 1992. Reinforcement learning and adaptive. In *Handbook of intelligent control*, D. A. White & D. A. Sofge (eds), 469–91. New York: Van Nostrand Reinhold.

Barto, A. G. & P. Anandan 1985. Pattern-recognizing stochastic learning automata. *IEEE Transactions on Systems, Man and Cybernetics* **SMC-15**, 360–75.

Barto, A. G. & M. I. Jordan 1987. Gradient following without backpropagation in layered networks. In *1st IEEE International Conference on Neural Networks*, vol. II, San Diego.

Barto, A. G., R. S. Sutton, C. Anderson 1983. Neuronlike adaptive elements that can solve difficult learning control problems. *IEEE Transactions on Systems, Man and Cybernetics* **SMC-13**, 834–6.

Battiti, R. 1992. First- and second-order methods for learning: between steepest descent and Newton's method. *Neural Computation* **4**, 141–66.

Baum, E. & D. Haussler 1989. What size net gives valid generalisation? *Neural Computation* **1**, 151–60.

Bezdek, J. C. & N. R. Pal 1995. A note on self-organizing semantic maps. *IEEE Transactions on Neural Networks* **6**, 1029–36.

Bledsoe, W. W. & C. L. Bisson 1962. Improved memory matrices for the n-tuple pattern recognition method. *IRE Transactions on Electronic Computers* **EC-11**, 414–15.

Bledsoe, W. W. & I. Browning 1959. Pattern recognition and reading by machines. In *Proceedings of the Eastern Joint Computer Conference*, 225–32.

Bolouri, H., P. Morgan, K. Gurney 1994. Design, manufacture and evaluation of a scalable high-performance neural system. *Electronics Letters* **30**, 426.

Bonhoeffer, T. & A. Grinvald 1991. Iso-orientation domains in cat visual cortex are arranged in pinwheel-like patterns. *Nature* **353**, 429–31.

Broomhead, D. S. & D. Lowe 1988. Multivariable functional interpolation and adaptive networks. *Complex Systems* **2**, 321–55.

Bruce, V. & P. Green 1990. *Visual perception: physiology, psychology and ecology*, 2nd edn. Hove: Erlbaum.

Bullock, T. H., R. Orkand, A. Grinnell 1977. *Introduction to nervous systems*. San Francisco: Freeman. (Neural coding – Ch. 6, Sect. B.)

Burke, L. I. 1991. Clustering characterisation of adaptive resonance. *Neural Networks* **4**, 485–91.

Carpenter, G. A. & S. Grossberg 1987a. ART-2: self-organization of stable category recognition codes for analog input patterns. *Applied Optics* **26**, 4919–30.

Carpenter, G. A. & S. Grossberg 1987b. A massively parallel architecture for a self-organizing neural pattern recognition machine. *Computer Vision, Graphics, and Image Processing* **37**, 54–115.

Carpenter, G. A. & S. Grossberg 1988. The ART of adaptive pattern recognition by a self-organizing neural network. *Computer* **21**, 77–90.

Carpenter, G. A. & S. Grossberg 1990. ART 3: hierarchical search using chemical transmitters in self-organizing pattern recognition architectures. *Neural Networks* **3**, 129–52.

Carpenter, G. A. & S. Grossberg 1992. A self-organizing neural network for supervised learning, recognition and prediction. *IEEE Communications Magazine*, 38–49.

Carpenter, G. A., S. Grossberg, C. Mehanian 1989. Invariant recognition of cluttered scenes by a self-organizing ART architecture: CORT-X boundary segmentation. *Neural Networks* **2**, 169–81.

Carpenter, G. A., S. Grossberg, J. H. Reynolds 1991a. ARTMAP: supervised real-time learning and classification of nonstationary data by a self-organising neural network. *Neural Networks* **4**, 565–88.

Carpenter, G. A., S. Grossberg, D. B. Rosen 1991b. ART 2 A: an adaptive resonance algorithm for rapid category learning and recognition. *Neural Networks* **4**, 493–504.

Carpenter, G. A., S. Grossberg, D. B. Rosen 1991c. Fuzzy ART: fast stable learning and categorization of analog patterns by an adaptive resonance system. *Neural Networks* **4**, 759–71.

Carpenter, G. A., S. Grossberg, D. B. Rosen 1991d. A neural network realization of fuzzy ART. Technical Report CAS/CNS-91-021, Boston University.

Caudell, T. P., S. D. G. Smith, R. Escobedo, M. Anderson 1994. NIRS: large scale ART-1 architectures for engineering design retrieval. *Neural Networks* **7**, 1339–50.

Caudill, M. 1991. Expert networks. *Byte*, 108–16.

Cheng, B. & D. M. Titterington 1994. Neural networks: a review from a statistical perspective. *Statistical Science* **9**, 2–54.

Churchland, P. S. & T. J. Sejnowski 1992. *The computational brain*. Cambridge, MA: MIT Press (Bradford Books).

Clark, A. 1990. *Microcognition: philosophy, cognitive science and parallel distributed processing*. Cambridge, MA: MIT Press (Bradford Books).

Conners, B. W. & M. J. Gutnick 1990. Intrinsic firing patterns of diverse neocortical neurons. *Trends in Neuroscience* **13**, 99–104.

Connolly, M. & D. Van Essen 1984. The representation of the visual field in parvocellular and magnocellular layers of the lateral geniculate nucleus in the macaque monkey. *Journal of Comparative Neurology* **226**, 544–64.

Cover, T. M. 1965. Geometrical and statistical properties of systems of linear inequalities with applications on pattern recognition. *IEEE Transactions on Electronic Computers* **EC-14**, 326–34.

Cvitanović, P. 1984. *Universality in chaos*. Bristol: Adam Hilger.

Davis, G. E., W. E. Lowell, G. L. Davis 1993. A neural network that predicts psychiatric length of stay. *MD Computing* **10**, 87–92.

Desimone, R. 1992. Neural circuits for visual attention in the primate brain. In *Neural networks for vision and image processing*, G. A. Carpenter & S. Grossberg (eds), 343–64. Cambridge, MA: MIT Press.

Dreyfus, H. L. 1979. *What computers can't do – the limits of artificial intelligence*. New York: Harper and Row.

Durbin, R. & G. Mitchison 1990. A dimension reduction framework for understanding cortical maps. *Nature* **343**, 644–7.

Fahlman, S. E. & C. Lebiere 1990. The cascade-correlation learning architecture. In *Advances in neural information processing systems*, D. S. Touretzky (ed.), vol. 2, 875–82. San Mateo, CA: Morgan Kaufmann.

Farmer, D., T. Toffoli, S. Wolfram 1983. Cellular automata – proceedings of an interdisciplinary workshop, Los Alamos. In *Physica*, vol. 10D (special volume). Amsterdam: North-Holland.

Fletcher, R. & C. M. Reeves 1964. Function minimisation by conjugate gradients. *Computer Journal* **7**, 149–54.

Fukushima, K. 1975. Cognitron: a self-organizing multilayered neural network. *Biological Cybernetics* **20**, 121–36.

Fukushima, K. 1980. Neocognitron: a self-organizing neural network model for a mechanism of pattern recognition unaffected by shift in position. *Biological Cybernetics* **36**, 193–202.

Fukushima, K. 1988. A neural network for visual pattern recognition. *Computer* **21**, 65–75.

Fukushima, K. 1989. Analysis of the process of visual pattern recognition by the neocognitron. *Neural Networks* **2**, 413–20.

Funahashi, K. 1989. On the approximate realization of continuous mappings by neural networks. *Neural Networks* **2**, 183–92.

Gallant, S. I. 1988. Connectionist expert systems. *Communications of the ACM* **31**, 152–69.

Georgiopoulous, M., G. L. Heileman, J. Huang 1991. Properties of learning related pattern diversity in ART1. *Neural Networks* **4**, 751–7.

Goodhill, G. J. 1993. Topography and ocular dominance – a model exploring positive correlations. *Biological Cybernetics* **69**, 109–18.

Gorse, D. & J. G. Taylor 1989. An analysis of noisy RAM and neural nets. *Physica D* **34**, 90–114.

Graf, H. P., W. Hubbard, L. D. Jackel, P. G. N. deVegvar 1987. A CMOS associative memory chip. In *1st IEEE International Conference on Neural Networks*, vol. III, 469–77, San Diego.

Gray, R. M. 1984. Vector quantization. *IEEE ASSP Magazine* **1**, 4–29.

Grossberg, S. 1973. Contour enhancement, short-term memory, and constancies in reverberating neural networks. *Studies in Applied Mathematics* **52**, 217–57.

Grossberg, S. 1976a. Adaptive pattern classification and universal recoding: I. parallel development and coding of neural feature detectors. *Biological Cybernetics* **23**, 121–34.

Grossberg, S. 1976b. Adaptive pattern classification and universal recoding: II. feedback, expectation, olfaction, illusions. *Biological Cybernetics* **23**, 187–202.

Grossberg, S. 1980. How does a brain build a cognitive code? *Psychological Review* **87**, 1–51.

Grossberg, S. 1987. Competitive learning: from interactive activation to adaptive resonance. *Cognitive Science* **11**, 23–63.

Grossberg, S. 1988. Nonlinear neural networks: principles, mechanisms, and architectures. *Neural Networks* **1**, 17–61.

Gullapalli, V. 1990. A stochastic reinforcement learning algorithm for learning real-valued functions. *Neural Networks* **3**, 671–92.

Gurney, K. N. 1989. *Learning in networks of structured hypercubes*. PhD thesis, Department of Electrical Engineering, Brunel University. Available as Technical Memorandum CN/R/144.

Gurney, K. N. 1992a. Training nets of hardware realisable sigma-pi units. *Neural Networks* **5**, 289–303.

Gurney, K. N. 1992b. Training nets of stochastic units using system identification. *Neural Networks* **6**, 133–45.

Gurney, K. N. 1992c. Training recurrent nets of hardware realisable sigma-pi units. *International Journal of Neural Systems* **3**, 31–42.

Gurney, K. N. 1992d. Weighted nodes and RAM-nets: a unified approach. *Journal of Intelligent Systems* **2**, 155–86.

Gurney, K. N. 1995. Towards a theory of neural-processing complexity. In *Proceedings of IPCAT'95*, Liverpool, UK.

Gurney, K. N. & M. J. Wright 1992a. Digital nets and intelligent systems. *Journal of Intelligent Systems* **2**, 1–10. (Special issue on advances in digital neural networks.)

Gurney, K. N. & M. J. Wright 1992b. A self-organising neural network model of image velocity encoding. *Biological Cybernetics* **68**, 173–81.

Hart, P. E., R. O. Duda, M. T. Einaudi 1978. A computer-based consultation system for mineral exploration. Technical Report, SRI International.

Hartline, H. K. 1934. *Journal of Cell and Comparative Physiology* **5**, 229.

Hartline, H. K. 1940. The nerve messages in the fibers of the visual pathway. *Journal of the Optical Society of America* **30**, 239–47.

Haykin, S. 1994. *Neural networks: a comprehensive foundation*. New York: Macmillan.

Hebb, D. O. 1949. *The organization of behaviour*. New York: John Wiley.

Heims, S. J. 1982. *John von Neumann and Norbert Weiner – from mathematics to the technologies of life and death*. Cambridge, MA: Academic Press.

Heywood, M. & P. Noakes 1995. A framework for improved training of sigma-pi networks. *IEEE Transactions on Neural Networks* **6**, 893–903.

Hinton, G. E. 1987. Connectionist learning principles. Technical Report CMU-CS-87-115, Carnegie–Mellon University. (Reproduced in *Artificial Intelligence* **40**, 185–234, 1989.)

Hinton, G. E., T. J. Sejnowski, D. Ackley 1984. Boltzmann machines: constraint satisfaction networks that learn. Technical Report CMU-CS-84-119, Carnegie–Mellon University.

Hodges, A. 1985. *Alan Turing – the enigma of intelligence*. London: Counterpoint (Unwin).

Hodgkin, A. L. & A. L. Huxley 1952. A quantitative description of membrane current and its application to conduction and excitation in nerve. *Journal of Physiology (London)* **117**, 500–44.

Hopfield, J. J. 1982. Neural networks and physical systems with emergent collective computational properties. *Proceedings of the National Academy of Sciences of the USA* **79**, 2554–88.

Hopfield, J. J. 1984. Neurons with graded response have collective computational properties like those of two-state neurons. *Proceedings of the National Academy of Sciences of the USA* **81**, 3088–92.

Hopfield, J. J. & D. W. Tank 1985. Neural computation of decisions in optimization problems. *Biological Cybernetics* **52**, 141–52.

Hornik, K., M. Stinchcombe, H. White 1989. Multilayer feedforward networks are universal approximators. *Neural Networks* **2**, 359–66.

Huang, Z. & A. Kuh 1992. A combined self-organizing feature map and multilayer perceptron for isolated word recognition. *IEEE Transactions on Signal Processing* **40**, 2651–7.

Hubel, D. & T. N. Wiesel 1962. Receptive fields, binocular interaction and functional architecture in the cat's visual cortex. *Journal of Physiology* **160**, 106–54.

Hubel, D. & T. N. Wiesel 1974. Sequence regularity and geometry of orientation columns in the monkey striate cortex. *Journal of Comparative Neurology* **158**, 267–94.

Hui, T., P. Morgan, K. Gurney, H. Bolouri 1991. A cascadable 2048-neuron VLSI artificial neural network with on-board learning. In *Artificial neural networks 2*, I. Aleksander & J. Taylor (eds), 647–51. Amsterdam: Elsevier.

Hung, C. A. & S. F. Lin 1995. Adaptive Hamming net: a fast-learning ART1 model without searching. *Neural Networks* **8**, 605–18.

Jacobs, R. A. 1988. Increased rates of convergence through learning rate adaptation. *Neural Networks* **1**, 295–307.

Jagota, A. 1995. Approximating maximum clique with a Hopfield net. *IEEE Transactions on Neural Networks* **6**, 724–35.

Jones, A. J. 1993. Genetic algorithms and their applications to the design of neural networks. *Neural Computing and Applications* **1**, 32–45.

Jones, D. S. 1979. *Elementary information theory*. Oxford: Clarendon Press.

Kan, W. K. & I. Aleksander 1987. A probabilistic logic neuron network for associative learning. In *1st IEEE International Conference on Neural Networks*, vol. II, 541–8, San Diego.

Kandel, E. F., J. H. Schwartz, T. J. Jessell 1991. *Principles of neural science*, 3rd edn. Amsterdam: Elsevier.

Karhunan, J. & J. Joutsensalo 1995. Generalization of principal component analysis, optimization problems and neural networks. *Neural Networks* **8**, 549–62.

Kauffman, S. A. 1969. Metabolic stability and epigenesis in randomly constructed genetic nets. *Journal of Theoretical Biology* **22**, 437–67.

Kendall, M. 1975. *Multivariate analysis*. London: Charles Griffin.

Kim, E. J. & Y. Lee 1991. Handwritten Hangul recognition using a modified neocognitron. *Neural Networks* **4**, 743–50.

Kirkpatrick, S., C. D. Gelatt, M. P. Vechi 1983. Optimization by simulated annealing. *Science* **230**, 671–9.

Koch, C. & I. Segev (eds) 1989. *Methods in neuronal modeling*. Cambridge, MA: MIT Press (Bradford Books).

Koch, C., T. Poggio, V. Torre 1982. Retinal ganglion cells: a functional interpretation of dendritic morphology. *Philosophical Transactions of the Royal Society B* **298**, 227–64.

Kohonen, T. 1982. Self-organized formation of topologically correct feature maps. *Biological Cybernetics* **43**, 59–69.

Kohonen, T. 1984. *Self-organization and associative memory*. Berlin: Springer-Verlag.

Kohonen, T. 1988a. Learning vector quantization. *Neural Networks* **1**, suppl. 1, 303.

Kohonen, T. 1988b. The 'neural' phonetic typewriter. *Computer* **21**, 11–22.

Kohonen, T. 1990. The self-organizing map. *Proceedings of the IEEE* **78**, 1464–80.

Kohonen, T., K. Mäkisara, T. Saramäki 1984. Phontopic maps – insightful representation of phonological features for speech recognition. In *Proceedings of Seventh International Conference on Pattern Recognition*, 182–5, Montreal, Canada.

Kosko, B. 1992. *Neural networks and fuzzy systems*. Englewood Cliffs, NJ: Prentice Hall.

Kuffler, S. W., J. G. Nicholls, A. R. Martin 1984. *From neuron to brain: a cellular approach to the function of the nervous system*, 2nd edn. Sunderland, MA: Sinauer Associates.

Lee, Y., S. Oh, M. Kim 1991. The effect of initial weights on premature saturation in back-propagation learning. In *International Joint Conference on Neural Nets*, vol. 1, Seattle.

Linsker, R. 1986. From basic network principles to neural architecture. *Proceedings of the National Academy of Sciences of the USA* **83**, 7508–12, 8390–4, 8779–83. (Series of three articles.)

Linsker, R. 1988. Self-organization in a perceptual network. *Computer* **21**, 105–17.

Lippmann, R. P. 1987. An introduction to computing with neural nets. *IEEE ASSP Magazine*, 4–22.

Little, W. A. 1974. The existence of persistent states in the brain. *Mathematical Biosciences* **19**, 101–20.

Makhoul, J., A. El-Jaroudi, R. Schwartz 1989. Formation of disconnected decision regions with a single hidden layer. In *International Joint Conference on Neural Nets*, vol. 1, 455–60, Seattle.

Mandelbrot, B. B. 1977. *The fractal geometry of nature*. New York: Freeman.

Marr, D. 1982. *Vision*. New York: Freeman.

Martland, D. 1987. Auto-associative pattern storage using synchronous Boolean nets. In *1st IEEE International Conference on Neural Networks*, vol. III, San Diego.

Maxwell, T., C. L. Giles, Y. C. Lee 1987. Generalization in neural networks: the contiguity problem. In *1st IEEE International Conference on Neural Networks*, vol. II, 41–5, San Diego.

McCulloch, W. & W. Pitts 1943. A logical calculus of the ideas immanent in nervous activity. *Bulletin of Mathematical Biophysics* **7**, 115–33.

McDermott, J. 1982. R1: a rule-based configurer of computer systems. *Artificial Intelligence* **19**, 39–88.

McEliece, R. J., E. C. Posner, E. R. Rodemich, S. S. Venkatesh 1987. The capacity of the Hopfield associative memory. *IEEE Transactions on Information Theory* **IT-33**, 461–82.

Milligan, D. K. 1988. Annealing in RAM-based learning networks. Technical Report CN/R/142, Department of Electrical Engineering, Brunel University.

Minsky, M. & S. Papert 1969. *Perceptrons*. Cambridge, MA: MIT Press.

Murre, J. M. J. 1995. Neurosimulators. In *The handbook of brain theory and neural networks*, M. A. Arbib (ed.), 634–9. Cambridge, MA: MIT Press.

Myers, C. E. & I. Aleksander 1988. Learning algorithms for probabilistic neural nets. In *1st INNS Annual Meeting*, Boston.

Nabhan, T. M. & A. Y. Zomaya 1994. Toward generating neural network structures for function approximation. *Neural Networks* **7**, 89–99.

Narendra, K. S. & M. A. L. Thathacar 1974. Learning automata – a survey. *IEEE Transactions on Systems, Man and Cybernetics* **SMC-4**, 323–34.

Newell, A. & H. A. Simon 1976. Computer science as empirical enquiry: symbols and search. *Communications of the ACM* **19**, 113–26.

Nolfi, S. & D. Parisi 1995. 'Genotypes' for neural networks. In *The handbook of brain theory and neural networks*, M. A. Arbib (ed.), 431–4. Cambridge, MA: MIT Press.

Obermayer, K., H. Ritter, K. Schulten 1990. A principle for the formation of the spatial structure of cortical feature maps. *Proceedings of the National Academy of Sciences of the USA* **87**, 8345–9.

Oja, E. 1982. A simplified neuron model as a principal component analyzer. *Journal of Mathematical Biology* **15**, 267–73.

Parker, D. B. 1982. Learning-logic. Technical Report 581-64, Office of Technology Licensing, Stanford University.

Plumbley, M. D. 1993. Efficient information transfer and anti-Hebbian neural networks. *Neural Networks* **6**, 823–33.

Poggio, T. & F. Girosi 1990a. Networks for approximation and learning. *Proceedings of the IEEE* **78**, 1481–97.

Poggio, T. & F. Girosi 1990b. Regularization algorithms for learning that are equivalent to multilayer networks. *Science* **247**, 978–82.

Powell, M. J. D. 1987. Radial basis functions for multivariable interpolation: a review. In *Algorithms for approximation*, J. C. Mason & M. G. Cox (eds). Oxford: Clarendon Press.

Raj, R. 1988. Foundations and grand challenges of artificial intelligence. *AI Magazine* **9**, 9–21.

Rall, W. 1957. Membrane time constant of motoneurons. *Science* **126**, 454.

Rall, W. 1959. Branching dendritic trees and motoneuron membrane resistivity. *Experimental Neurology* **2**, 503–32.

Reed, R. 1993. Pruning algorithms – a survey. *IEEE Transactions on Neural Networks* **4**, 740–7.

Refenes, A. N., A. Zapranis, G. Francis 1994. Stock performance modelling using neural networks: a comparative study with regression models. *Neural Networks* **7**, 375–88.

Rich, E. & K. Knight 1991. *Artificial intelligence.* New York: McGraw-Hill.

Ritter, H. & T. Kohonen 1989. Self-organizing semantic maps. *Biological Cybernetics* **61**, 241–54.

Rosenblatt, F. 1962. *Principles of neurodynamics*. New York: Spartan Books.

Rosin, P. L. & F. Fierens 1995. Improving neural net generalisation. In *International Geoscience and Remote Sensing Symposium*, Florence.

Rumelhart, D. & D. Zipser 1985. Feature discovery by competitive learning. *Cognitive Science* **9**, 75–112.

Rumelhart, D. E., G. E. Hinton, R. J. Williams 1986a. Learning representations by back-propagating errors. *Nature* **323**, 533–6.

Rumelhart, D. E., J. L. McCllelland, The PDP Research Group 1986b. *Parallel distributed processing*, vol. 1, ch. 9. Cambridge, MA: MIT Press (Bradford Books).

Rumelhart, D. E., J. L. McCllelland, The PDP Research Group 1986c. *Parallel distributed processing*, vol. 1, ch. 5. Cambridge, MA: MIT Press (Bradford Books).

Rumelhart, D. E., J. L. McCllelland, The PDP Research Group 1986d. *Parallel distributed processing*, vol. 1, ch. 2. Cambridge, MA: MIT Press (Bradford Books).

Sánchez-Sinencio, E. & R. W. Newcomb 1992a. Guest editorial for special issue on neural network hardware. *IEEE Transactions on Neural Networks* **3**, 345–518.

Sánchez-Sinencio, E. & R. W. Newcomb 1992b. Guest editorial for special issue on neural network hardware. *IEEE Transactions on Neural Networks* **4**, 385–541.

Sanger, T. 1989. Optimal unsupervised learning in a single-layer linear feedforward neural network. *Neural Networks* **2**, 459–73.

Shawe-Taylor, J. 1992. Threshold network learning in the presence of equivalence. In *Advances in neural information processing systems*, J. E. Moody, S. J. Hanson, R. P. Lippmann (eds), vol. 4, 879–86. San Mateo, CA: Morgan Kaufmann.

Shepherd, G. M. 1978. Microcircuits in the nervous system. *Scientific American* **238**, 92–103.

Smolensky, P. 1988. On the proper treatment of connectionism. *Behavioural and Brain Sciences* **11**, 1–74.

Steiger, U. 1967. Über den Feinbau des Neuopils im Corpus Pedunculatum der Waldemeise. *Zeitschrift für Zellforschung* **81**, 511–36. (As reproduced in Bullock, T. H. et al. 1977. *Introduction to nervous systems*. San Francisco: Freeman.)

Stone, M. 1974. Cross-validatory choice and assessment of statistical predictions. *Journal of the Royal Statistical Society* **B36**, 111–33.

Sun, R. & L. Bookman 1993. How do symbols and networks fit together? *AI Magazine*, 20–23. (A report on the workshop on integrating neural and symbolic processes sponsored by the American Association for Artificial Intelligence (AAAI).)

Sun, R. & L. A. Bookman (eds) 1994. *Computational architectures integrating neural and symbolic processes*. The Kluwer International Series in Engineering and Computer Science 292. Norwell, MA: Kluwer Academic.

Tanenbaum, A. S. 1990. *Structured computer organization*. Englewood Cliffs, NJ: Prentice Hall.

Thompson, R. F. 1993. *The brain: a neuroscience primer*. New York: Freeman.

Thorndike, E. L. 1911. *Animal learning*. New York: Macmillan. (For a modern discussion, see Hergenhahn, B. R. 1988. *An introduction to theories of learning*. Englewood Cliffs, NJ: Prentice Hall.)

Thornton, C. J. 1992. *Techniques in computational learning*. London: Chapman and Hall Computing.

Turing, A. M. 1937. On computable numbers with an application to the Entscheidungsproblem. *Proceedings of the London Mathematical Society* **42**, 230–65.

von der Malsburg, C. 1973. Self-organization of orientation sensitive cells in the striate cortex. *Kybernetik* **14**, 85–100.

von Neumann, J. 1987. First draft of a report on the EDVAC. In *Papers of John von Neumann on computing and computer theory*, vol. 12 in the Charles Babbage Institute Reprint Series for the History of Computing, W. Aspray & A. Burks (eds). Cambridge, MA: MIT Press.

Walker, C. C. & W. R. Ashby 1966. On temporal characteristics of behaviour in certain complex systems. *Kybernetik* **3**, 100–8.

Werbos, P. 1974. *Beyond regression: new tools for prediction and analysis in the behavioural sciences*. PhD thesis, Harvard University.

Weymare, N. & J. P. Martens 1994. On the initialization and optimization of multilayer perceptrons. *IEEE Transactions on Neural Networks* **5**, 738–51.

Widrow, B. & M. E. Hoff, Jr 1960. Adaptive switching circuits. In *1960 IRE WESCON convention record*, 96–104. New York: IRE. (Reprinted in Anderson, A. & E. Rosenfeld (eds) 1988. *Neurocomputing – foundations of research*. Cambridge, MA: MIT Press.)

Widrow, B. & S. D. Stearns 1985. *Adaptive signal processing*. Englewood Cliffs, NJ: Prentice-Hall.

Widrow, B., R. G. Winter, R. A. Baxter 1987. Learning phenomena in layered neural networks. In *1st IEEE International Conference on Neural Networks*, vol. II, 411–29, San Diego.

Wieland, A. & R. Leighton 1987. Geometric analysis of neural network capabilities. In *1st IEEE International Conference on Neural Networks*, vol. III, San Diego.

Williams, R. J. 1987. Reinforcement-learning connectionist systems. Technical Report NU-CCS-87-3, Northeastern University, Boston.

Willshaw, D. J., O. P. Buneman, H. C. Longuet-Higgins 1969. Non-holographic associative memory. *Nature* **222**, 960–62.

Willshaw, D. J. & C. von der Malsburg 1976. How patterned neural connections can be set up by self-organization. *Proceedings of the Royal Society B* **194**, 431–45.

Winston, P. H. 1984. *Artificial intelligence*. Reading, MA: Addison-Wesley.

Yu, X. H., G. A. Chen, S. X. Cheng 1995. Dynamic learning rate optimization of the backpropagation algorithm. *IEEE Transactions on Neural Networks* **6**, 669–77.

Zadeh, L. 1965. Fuzzy sets. *Information and Control* **8**, 338–53.

Index